JON PRESS

The Footwear Industry in Ireland 1922-1973

IRISH ACADEMIC PRESS

in association with

C. & J. CLARK LTD

MCMLXXXIX

This book was typeset by
Gilbert Gough Typesetting, Dublin
and is published by
Irish Academic Press Ltd
Kill Lane, Blackrock, Co. Dublin, Ireland
in association with
C. & J. Clark Ltd
Street, Somerset, England.

© C. & J. Clark Ltd 1989

BRITISH LIBRARY CATALOGUING IN PUBLICATION DATA
Press, Jon
The footwear industry
in Ireland, 1922-1973
1. Ireland. (Republic). Footwear industries
Footwear trades. Footwear industries and
trades to 1973
I. Great Britain. Footwear industries &
trades
338.4'76853'09417

ISBN 0-7165-2439-2

Printed by
Betaprint International Ltd, Dublin

JON PRESS

The Footwear Industry in Ireland

CONTENTS

	page
LIST OF ILLUSTRATIONS	7
PREFACE	11
1 Early Years	17
The Early History of the Footwear Industry, 1856-1922	18
The Technological Environment	21
The Footwear Industry and Selective Protection, 1922-32	26
2 Protectionism and Rapid Growth: 1932-36	30
3 Recession in the Footwear Industry: 1936-39	50
4 The Footwear Industry during the Emergency: 1939-45	73
5 Recovery and Crisis: 1945-55	93
6 Economic Planning and Renewed Growth: 1955-61	130
7 The Prosperous Sixties: 1961-70	144
8 Conclusion: Ireland and the EEC	170
APPENDICES	179
NOTES	195
BIBLIOGRAPHY	219
INDEX	223

ILLUSTRATIONS

TABLES

1	The British footwear industry, 1907: output and number employed	19
2	Number of persons employed in the manufacture and sale of footwear in Ireland, 1891-1911	20
3	Size of firms in the Irish footwear industry, October 1935 (classified according to number employed)	32
4	Leather footwear, 1931-33: production and foreign trade	42
5	Imports of shaped soles, heels and uppers (by value), 1930-37	45
6	Manufacturing profit in the Irish footwear industry, 1936-39	62
7	Cost of materials, manufacturing wages and other manufacturing costs, 1936-39	63
8	Pre-tax profit and return on turnover and assets, 1936-39	64
9	Employment in the footwear industry, 1939-45	84
10	Average earnings and hours of work, 1939-45	85
11	Index of prices of sole leather and leather footwear, 1939-45	89
12	Manufacturing costs and manufacturing profit in the footwear industry, 1939-45	89
13	Production costs and pre-tax profits, 1939-45	91
14	Production of heavy leather boots, 1945-55	103
15	Sole leather used and average price per hundredweight, 1945-60	106
16	J.H. Woodington Drogheda (1936) Ltd: ratio of advertising expenditure to turnover, 1952-60	118
17	John Halliday & Son Ltd/Clarks Ireland Ltd: sales breakdown, 1952	122
18	John Halliday & Son Ltd and J.H. Woodington Drogheda (1936) Ltd: share of home production, 1945-56	126

19	Issued capital and assets, 1950-56	127
20	Return on capital, 1945-55	127
21	Clarks Ireland Ltd: destination of sales and share of total Irish footwear exports, 1953-61	140
22	Sales, net profit and return on assets, 1956-61	142
23	Distribution of footwear sales in Ireland and the United Kingdom, 1964	149
24	Retail outlets for footwear in Ireland, 1966-71	149
25	Destination of Irish footwear exports, 1959-70	151
26	Pre-tax profits of Footwear Adaptation Association members, 1962-65	164
27	Profitability of seven Irish footwear companies, 1959-70	166
28	Tariffs on leather footwear, July 1970	167
29	Performance of the Irish footwear industry, 1973-83	172

FIGURES

1	Imports and home production, 1931-36 (footwear wholly/mainly of leather)	44
2	Index of production, boot and shoe factories and total manufacturing industry, 1959-70	148

PHOTOGRAPHS ETC. *following page* 128

1. The closing room at James Winstanley's Dublin factory, 1910
2. James Winstanley's Dublin factory just before the First World War
3. The Blake sole-sewing machine
4. Mr Seán Lemass, Fianna Fáil's spokesman on economic affairs
5. John Halliday & Son's boot factory at Bramley, near Leeds, 1887

6	'Pulling over' ladies shoes
7	John Rawson & Son's factory, in Dundalk in the 1930s
8	'Blacksmith' and 'Stronghold' boots
9	Hallidays' directors in 1938
10	Attaching heels to wood-soled shoes
11	Attaching iron heel pieces and toe bands to wood-soled work boots
12	John Halliday & Son's Quay Street factory, Dundalk, 1948
13	The cutting room in Hallidays' factory, 1948
14	Preparing soles and insoles
15	The lasting department in Hallidays' factory
16	Soles being attached on a multi-station press
17	A direct vulcanising machine
18	Padmore & Barnes' 'Wallabee shoe', a hand-sewn moccasin
19	Wallabee shoes being made on a backpart pre-forming machine

PREFACE

In the nineteenth century Ireland's economic relationship with Britain had essentially been a 'colonial' one. Irish exports consisted largely of foodstuffs for the growing urban markets of mainland Britain, and manufactured goods for the small domestic market were mostly supplied by British industrialists. Employment opportunities were few and the population was steadily depleted by emigration. After the establishment of the Free State in 1922, there was a need to reduce economic dependence on Britain, and the period covered by this book was characterised by growing government involvement in economic affairs to create new jobs and reduce Ireland's balance of payments deficit. Particular attention was paid to consumer goods industries producing items for which a demand already existed in Ireland, and which could be economically produced in small quantities.

The purpose of this book is to examine the experience of the footwear industry since 1922. The footwear industry was an important one in Ireland because in many ways it was well-suited to government needs. Some factories were already in operation, and technical expertise could be acquired without creating undue problems; starting up did not require heavy capital investment; and the industry was labour-intensive and could play a valuable role in creating new employment opportunities. Particular attention will be paid to the ways in which policies of protectionism and self-sufficiency encouraged, or constrained, the growth of the industry. In recent years, Irish industrial development has been undergoing critical analysis, and a number of valuable studies have appeared.* Yet such work has generally rested upon the aggregated data provided by the Central Statistics Office in Dublin, and there is a dearth of detailed case studies relating to individual industries. It is hoped that this book will go some way towards remedying this deficiency.

In Chapter 1, the history of the footwear industry in the nineteenth century is briefly considered and set against the techological background. The chapter

---

*See, for example, K.A. Kennedy and B.R. Dowling, *Economic Growth in Ireland: the Experience since 1947* (Dublin, 1975); M.J. Killeen, *Industrial Development and Full Employment* (Dublin, 1976); P.N. O'Farrell, *Regional Industrial Development Trends in Ireland, 1960-1973* (Dublin, 1975); J.W. O'Hagan (ed), *The Economy of Ireland: Policy and Performance* (Dublin, 1975); J. Lee (ed), *Ireland, 1945-1970* (Dublin, 1979); J.W. O'Hagan, *The Evolution of Manufacturing Industry in Ireland* (Dublin, 1981); M. Daly, 'An Irish Irish for Business? The Control of Manufactures Acts, 1932 and 1934', *Irish Historical Studies* xxiv (1984), 246-272.

concludes with an examination of developments in the 1920s, when the Irish government adopted a rather cautious approach to protection which contributed to a pattern of modest growth within the industry. In Chapter 2, we examine the advent of de Valera's government, and the adoption of a policy of 'self-sufficiency' — a policy which necessitated the introduction of prohibitive tariffs and quota restrictions on imported goods, and which led to a period of very rapid growth in the footwear industry. Particular attention is paid to the relationship between Irish footwear manufacturers and their erstwhile competitors in Britain; British manufacturers played a vital role in the development of the Irish industry by way of royalty agreements which gave Irish producers access to technical expertise, design and management skills, lasts and patterns, and trade marks.

Rapid growth in a protected market did inevitably create new problems for Irish economists and industrialists, and in the later 1930s the Irish footwear industry passed fairly quickly from boom into recession. The problems associated with protection and self-sufficiency are examined in Chapter 3, and serve as an introduction to a more detailed examination of the major characteristics of the footwear industry and its domestic market.

Chapters 4 and 5 consider the experiences of the footwear industries during and after the Second World War. The industry still depended to a considerable extent upon imported machinery and raw materials, and as many essential supplies became unobtainable during the war there was growing concern that some factories would be forced to close or drastically reduce employment levels. The efforts of footwear manufacturers to develop substitute materials is assessed, and particular attention is paid to the use of government controls on wages, prices and profits. These measures were successful in preventing the demise of footwear companies during the war, but, as is shown in Chapter 5, the industry was not in a strong position to benefit from the post-war boom in consumer demand. Between 1945 and 1955 recovery was interrupted by frequent recessions which created an atmosphere of crisis within the industry, and the evidence suggests that manufacturers were slow to respond to changes in demand trends — in particular, the move towards lighter footwear. Nevertheless, the early 1950s did see significant innovations in technology, quality control techniques and marketing, and some manufacturers at least were taking action to improve efficiency and generate new business.

Chapter 6 examines the events of the later 1950s, when the footwear industry began to experience more favourable trading conditions. Growth rates accelerated in the late 1950s and early 1960s, and the publication of the government's *Programme for Economic Expansion* in 1958 inaugurated what was to prove the longest period of prosperity in the industry's history. Chapter 7 assesses the industry's performance during the 1960s. An im-

Preface

portant theme is the move towards free trade, for Ireland's growing interest in closer trading links with Europe necessitated a relaxation of import restrictions.

The footwear industry had to prepare for increasing competition in the home market and make serious efforts to develop export business. Because confidential information is not available for recent years, my original brief was to end the story in 1973, when Ireland joined the EEC. However, it now seems essential to conclude with a brief description of the industry in the 1970s and 1980s, to determine whether it was successful in meeting the challenge of free trade.

I have tried to present a balanced and critical account of the Irish footwear industry's development. The demands of a relatively small home market have inevitably had an effect upon the efficiency of the industry, and it is necessary to examine its weaknesses as well as applauding its successes. The role of economic planning also requires critical assessment; although government planners have played a major part in stimulating growth, some measures have not had the intended result, and, in the short term at least, have imposed additional limitations upon the footwear industry.

There are inevitably some topics which require more detailed examination than is possible here. In particular, one would like to know more about business organisation, recruitment patterns and the role of key executives. Information on these topics is, however, scarce. It will also be noted that this book is primarily concerned with footwear made wholly or mainly of leather (or, more accurately since the 1950s, footwear with uppers wholly or mainly of leather). Most Irish footwear produced during the period under discussion was made of leather, and information on this category tends to be the most complete and the most detailed. Nevertheless, footwear of other materials cannot be entirely ignored, and in particular one would like to be able to say more about the growth of rubber footwear production; the increasing popularity of the wellington led to the demise of the heavy leather boot and resulted in a major reshaping of the Irish footwear industry. Unfortunately, rubber footwear production was not accorded a separate category in official statistics; the Irish Dunlop Co. Ltd was the only producer of rubber footwear in Ireland, and it was necessary to preserve confidentiality. However, Irish Dunlop has been very willing to help, and in particular I must thank Mr Donal Duggan for finding the time to answer my questions.

The major groups of records relating to the footwear industry requires some description. The official publications of the Dublin Stationery Office include a number of useful series which are listed in the bibliography. Particularly valuable are the *Census of Industrial Production, Trade and Shipping Statistics* and the *Irish Trade Journal* (later the *Irish Statistical Bulletin*), although some of the series did not start until the mid-1920s and records for the war years are incomplete. It should also be noted that while official statistics of footwear production are available from 1926 information relating to sales is scarce. It is usually necessary to refer to the quantity or value of production for the Irish market rather than to retail sales, and this is not entirely satisfactory; on occasion there was quite a wide discrepancy between the quantity of footwear produced and the actual quantity sold to consumers.

The records of individual companies are also an important source of information. In addition to the records required by company law it has been possible to examine the confidential records of quite a few companies. The most comprehensive collection of records are those relating to John Halliday & Son Ltd. They include confidential accounts, internal memoranda and copies of correspondence with government departments and other manufacturers, and they provide invaluable evidence about the company's gradual emergence as a market leader. These records are now held by the Museum and Archives Department of C. & J. Clark Ltd.

The records of other Irish footwear companies are generally less complete; it must be remembered that most of them were small, and it was often unnecessary to communicate decisions by written memoranda. Moreover, serious interest in Irish business history is a fairly recent development, and businessmen have often been unaware of the type of evidence required by the historian. It is encouraging to note that the Business History Department of the Irish Public Records Office is now developing close ties with Irish companies in order to remedy this situation. Nevertheless, the following companies were able to provide a considerable amount of valuable information: J.H. Woodington, Drogheda (1936) Ltd; James Winstanley Ltd; Dubarry Shoemakers Ltd; Padmore & Barnes Ltd; and the Edenderry Shoe Company Ltd.

I have also been able to interview a number of individuals who have played a key role in the development of the Irish footwear industry, and these personal contacts have greatly facilitated the task of assessing the available evidence as well as rectifying some major omissions. In the United Kingdom, Arthur Halliday and Bancroft Clark have given me the benefit of their long experience of the Irish footwear industry, and have also found the time to read and comment on the manuscript. I should also like to express my gratitude to Mr Stephen Lowry, formerly Managing Director of J.H. Woodington; Mr Philip Purcell, formerly Company Secretary, Padmore & Barnes; Mr F.J. Scott, formerly Managing Director, Dubarry; Mr Philip McLoughlin, Mr Lowry's predecessor at Woodington; Mr Denis O'Neill, formerly Managing Director of James Winstanley; and Messrs E.J. and K. Connolly, respectively Chairman and Managing Director of Blackthorn Shoes Ltd, Dundalk.

Preface

This project has been financed by the Museum and Archives Department of C. & J. Clark Ltd, and I should like to thank successive Managers of the Department for their assistance. Patrick Keith, James Boswell and Neil MacDonald have spent a good deal of time answering my many queries, and Judith Dempster has coped admirably with much of the typing. I should also like to record my appreciation of the help I received from John Vosper (Intelligence Office, C. & J. Clark Ltd) and from Eileen Finnegan of Clarks Ireland Ltd.

I should also like to express my gratitude to Bernard Alford, Professor of Economic and Social History at the University of Bristol, who has been associated with the project from its inception, and has been able to offer many helpful comments and criticisms. Finally, I must thank Nikki, my wife, for reading the finished manuscript and pointing out the worst excesses of my literary style. As always, any faults which remain are my own.

Jon Press
Bristol, August 1988

1
EARLY YEARS

Under the terms of the Anglo-Irish Treaty of 1922 the twenty-six counties of Southern Ireland achieved dominion status; as Meenan has noted, this 'implied full autonomy, partly qualified by vestiges of imperial supremacy'.[1] The Treaty was a compromise, which was represented by the Irish negotiators as the best that could be achieved without further violence, but it was opposed by many Irishmen who believed that it would ultimately weaken the demand for full independence. Ratification was followed by a period of civil war, which lasted until the Irregulars called off the fight in May 1923. Cosgrave's Provisional Goverment had therefore to establish a constitution and construct the machinery of government at a time when its authority largely rested upon opposition to the rule of violence, and possible concessions to the Republican element were limited by the need to retain the goodwill of the British government.

Economically, Ireland was heavily dependent upon Britain. The British market for agricultural produce was very important to Irish farmers, and the principal Irish industries were those which produced goods for which there was a ready market in Britain: brewing, distilling, malting, jute manufacturing, and various industries associated with agriculture, like bacon-curing and butter-making.[2] Many Irish industries, however, were confined to their domestic market, where they found it very difficult to compete with British rivals. These included flour-milling, tobacco manufacturing, clothing, boots and shoes, papermaking and fertilizers.[3]

In the domestic-orientated sector, industry was widely dispersed and largely comprised of small firms producing for a limited local market. The level of home demand for manufactured goods was low, for Ireland's population was small and a primarily agrarian economy made for a low population density and low per capita incomes. The population had been steadily depleted by emigration, and although demographic change had made a repetition of the mass exodus of the 1840s and 1850s impossible[4] the population continued to fall until 1931.[5] In 1901 the population of Ireland was 4,390,219, of whom 3,154,366 lived in the twenty-six counties which were to be included in the Free State;[6] in 1926, the total population of the Free State was approximately 2,970,000.[7]

The Early History of the Footwear Industry, 1856-1922

In the nineteenth century, the demand for footwear in Ireland was largely met by craftsmen shoemakers, who were to be found in even the smallest communities. Most enterprises employed only one or two workers, and the bulk of their output consisted of heavy farm boots, made by hand by traditional methods. The larger-scale production of ready-made footwear was confined to a few small factories located in the major centres of population. The earliest factory was established in Back Lane, Dublin — an area with a tradition of shoemaking — by James Winstanley.[8] Most sources state that factory production started in 1856, although there is some evidence that the firm was trading as Winstanley & Jepson in 1852.[9] Initially production probably consisted largely of clogs, but a full range of boots and shoes was being produced by 1881.[10] In 1870 the Killarney firm of R. Hilliard & Sons opened a factory for the production of heavy boots,[11] and a third factory commenced production in Cork some ten years later; this was the Lee Boot Manufacturing Company, which was established by the Dwyer family as an extension of its existing wholesale drapery business.[12] Shortly thereafter, two more factories commenced production, one in Clonmel[13] and another in Belfast.[14] Winstanleys, however, was by far the largest of those early factories; according to the available evidence production increased from about 3,000 pairs per week in 1881 to 4,800 pairs per week in 1887-88, by which time about 300 men and boys and 100 women and girls were employed. The company had an interest in retailing from the earliest days, and by 1881 had five shops in Dublin.[15]

During the last quarter of the nineteenth century Irish footwear producers were experiencing increasing competition from factories in mainland Britain. Between 1850 and 1900 the output of the British footwear industry rose rapidly with the introduction of machinery and the consequent extension of factory production. At the same time, export markets were contracting because of American competitors and the erection of tariff barriers,[16] and consequently British manufacturers were becoming increasingly interested in the Irish market. British competition was already a serious problem for Irish footwear producers by the early 1880s. According to a letter from James Winstanley to Thomas Sexton in 1885, Irish manufacturers supplied no more than 25 per cent of home demand, and exports were virtually nil.[17] Winstanley claimed that the Irish market was being ruined by cheap and shoddy footwear from Britain, and that British manufacturers offered low prices and extravagant discounts to attract Irish custom.[18] This criticism of the quality of British shoes may have been unjustified, and certainly the larger drapers, who were the major customers for footwear in Ireland, preferred to buy these imported goods; demand for home-produced footwear fell steadily until the end of the century.

There may have been some improvement in the fortunes of the Irish industry in the early years of the twentieth century — Cullen has suggested that there was little increase in the value of footwear imports between 1904 and 1914[19] — and a number of new factories also appeared. The firm of Hearne & Cahill was established in Waterford in the late 1890s, and Michael Governey of Carlow and Thomas Murphy of Dundalk commenced factory production around 1900.[20] Nevertheless, footwear manufacture in Ireland was still being conducted on a small scale compared with the rest of the United Kingdom.

TABLE 1

The British footwear industry, 1907: output and number employed

	Ireland	Scotland	England/Wales	Total
Boots, shoes & slippers;				
Pairs	542,000	3,030,000	94,412,000	97,984,000
Value (£)	192,000	987,000	18,897,000	20,066,000
Wage-earners & salaried persons (excluding outworkers)	2,026	8,028	116,772	126,826
Average ex-factory price per pair (£ p)	0.35	0.33	0.20	0.20
Per capita output;				
Pairs	268	377	809	773
Value (£)	95	123	162	158

Source: *Final Report of the First Census of Production, 1907*, Cd. 6320 (1912), pp. 419-20.

The data provided by Table 1 are not particularly accurate, especially in the case of small concerns, but the general pattern is clear. Irish footwear production was not only small-scale; per capita output was also significantly lower and average ex-factory price significantly higher than in England, Wales and Scotland. The Irish *Census of Population* suggests that the total number of persons earning a living from the manufacture and sale of footwear was steadily declining (Table 2). Again, the figures are not particularly accurate as the *Census* at this date was classified according to occupation rather than industry, and made no attempt to distinguish between factory operatives, handicraft workers, repairers and retailers, but the total number of persons entered as 'boot and shoe makers and dealers (excluding clogs)' fell by about 36 per cent between 1891 and 1911.

TABLE 2

Number of persons employed in the manufacture and sale of footwear in Ireland, 1891-1911

	1891	1901	1911
Males	20,218	15,378	12,971
Females	1,190	942	659
	21,408	16,320	13,630

Source: *Census of Ireland, General Reports*, 1891 part II, pp. 119, 126; 1901, pp. 122, 129; 1911, pp. 13-4, 19-20.

Faced by competition from the cheaper footwear of British manufacturers, the Irish factories were unable to secure a significant share of the home market. The handicraft trade suffered a steady decline and although rural shoemakers continued to supply country people with heavy farm boots until the 1920s and there remained a small market for high-class hand-sewn footwear in the larger towns, an increasing proportion of the craftsman shoemaker's time was spent in repairing mass-produced footwear from British manufacturers.[21]

The First World War gave the Irish footwear industry something of a respite; many British companies were kept busy by government contracts and increased prosperity amongst Irish agricultural workers boosted home demand.[22] The end of the war, however, brought a renewed onslaught upon the Irish market by British manufacturers. In the post-war period British factories lost export sales as a result of high tariffs and fluctuating exchange rates in Continental markets, while foreign producers were encroaching upon the British domestic market. British manufacturers therefore paid increased attention to the Irish market, which already accounted for more than one-third of their 'overseas' sales. British goods were highly competitive, and sales were not affected by the growth of nationalist sentiment in Ireland. By 1926 the Twenty-six Counties were importing almost four million pairs of boots and shoes per year, nearly all of which came from Britain.[23] Irish production at that time was only some 300,000 pairs per year; by British standards this represented the output of one medium-sized factory.

The Technological Environment

The success of British manufacturers in the Irish market was due to their lead in the techniques of mass-production; Irish producers could not compete in terms of price or quality and had lagged behind their British counterparts in a rapidly changing technological environment.

The adoption of factory methods of production was a relatively late development in shoemaking, for progress was impeded by the nature of the raw materials and the production processes involved. Leather has a number of characteristics which make it particularly suitable for footwear. It is flexible enough to be shaped to fit the foot yet sufficiently durable to be stitched or tacked without tearing; it can be tanned to acquire a degree of weatherproofing while permitting the foot to 'breathe'; and it is available in a wide range of thicknesses and finishes. But, being a natural product, it does not possess uniform characteristics. Quality and substance (thickness) vary from hide to hide according to the diet, age and sex of the animal, the incidence of parasite holes and other blemishes, and the skills of the flayer and tanner. Similarly there are variations in different parts of an individual hide. The best-quality leather comes from either side of the backbone (the butt), while leather from the belly, flanks and neck is thinner and more flexible to accommodate the animal's movements, and, especially in fully-grown animals, may be lined with growth marks.

For this reason, cutting out the types for a pair of shoes — or 'clicking', as it is traditionally termed — was (and still is) a highly skilled operation. The objective was to make the most economic use of each hide or skin, whilst ensuring a good appearance in the finished shoe. The best leather was mainly used in the vamp (forepart) as it is the most noticeable part of the shoe and is subject to the most flexing. Lower quality leather could be cut into the quarters as they were normally reinforced with stiffeners or other backing material. Quarters were matched at the heel seam and to the adjoining vamp, and to achieve a good match adjacent parts of the shoe were therefore best cut from adjacent parts of the hide. The lightest leathers were suitable for linings, tongues and trimmings, which might also be made from hides split into two or more thin layers. All this meant that careful planning was essential before the clicker began cutting out, and there was no substitute for experience.

Natural variations in the raw materials had also to be allowed for in the various and intricate tasks involved in stitching and shaping the upper and attaching the sole. Once the parts had been cut out to prepared patterns, the uppers were marked for stitching and sewn together with needle, awl and waxed thread; a high degree of accuracy was needed to ensure that the completed upper did not wrinkle when pulled into shape over the last.[24] Once fitted over the last, the upper was secured to the insole by stitching or tacking, and the sole, already roughly cut to shape, was attached.

For most types of footwear, the traditional welted construction was preferred. The upper was pulled over the last and temporarily tacked to a recess around the lower edge of the insole. A narrow strip of leather — the welt — was then sewn to the edge of the insole, the stitches passing through the upper to hold it in place. Finally the sole was stitched to the welt, which then acted as a hinge around the foot. The welted technique produced a very strong and durable shoe, and was suitable for a wide range of footwear, from high-quality men's shoes to walking shoes and work boots. Welted footwear could be repaired easily; a valuable attribute, as leather soles were not particularly long-lasting, and, especially in the best quality work, the thickness of the sole was limited by considerations of appearance and weight of the shoe.

Welted footwear, however, was not very flexible, and lightweight shoes were usually made by the turnshoe method. An insole was not used, and the upper was stitched directly on to the edge of the sole, which was feathered to reduce its bulk. The characteristic feature of this construction was that the shoe was made inside out, and was later turned so that the seam lay inside the shoe. After the sole had been attached, the heel and trimmings were added, and the shoe would then be left on the last for several days to ensure that it would retain its shape. Finally, there were a number of finishing operations; these included burnishing edges (or ironing after treating them with matching inks), fitting socks or linings to cover inside seams and heel-fixing nails, and cleaning and polishing uppers.

The techniques of shoemaking were therefore labour-intensive, and the nature of the basic material and the production processes meant that the early factories continued to use traditional handicraft methods. Factories began to appear in Britain in the early decades of the nineteenth century, although many processes were still carried out by outworkers. Soles and uppers would be cut out in the factory, but 'closing' (stitching) the uppers and 'making' (the term applied to the process of pulling the upper over the last and insole and attaching the sole and heel) was done at home. By mid-century, however, these processes were beginning to move into the factory, and production was being concentrated in a few major centres — notably Northampton, Stafford, Leeds and Leicester.[25]

Factory production in these areas expanded rapidly with the acceleration of technological innovation in the 1850s. The key technological developments took place in Britain and the United States, and the Irish footwear industry was to remain heavily dependent upon British technology and technical assistance throughout the period covered by this book. William Stephens Clark of Street invented the first simple machinery for building and attaching heels in the early 1850s, and Singer, Howe and Thomas sewing machines were adapted for stitching uppers with waxed thread.[26] American treadle machines for cutting sole leather were introduced in Street and Leicester around 1859, and in the following year the most important invention of the mid-nineteenth century appeared — the American McKay sole sewing machine, which was known in Britain as the Blake sewer. The Blake machine chain-stitched the sole through the upper and insole with a single waxed thread, and enabled the operative to sew approximately 300 stitches per minute, compared with the 10-20 of the hand sewer.[27] With the appearance of an improved model in 1864 the Blake sewer was widely adopted and remained the principal method of attachment for middle to low grade footwear until it was replaced by the cemented method from the 1920s. The Blake machine was not used for better quality footwear, however, since increased output was achieved at the expense of quality; Blake-sewn shoes lacked the flexibility and durability of hand-sewn welted footwear. The machine was also unsuitable for lightweight footwear, which continued to be handmade by the turnshoe method.[28]

The deficiencies of the Blake sewer led to the appearance of a number of machines which imitated the principles of the hand-sewn welted construction, but skilled hand labour was still needed for some operations until the introduction of Charles Goodyear's welt sewing machine in 1872. The first Goodyear machines made a backstitch, and were reputed to have been 54 times as fast as hand-stitching with needle and awl. Further improvements were made to the machine in the 1880s and 1890s.[29] The manufacture of cheap heavy footwear by the riveting process was also mechanised in the third quarter of the nineteenth century.[30] Crick's sole-piercing and riveting machine was patented in 1853, and required less skilled labour than other sole-attaching machinery.[31] From the 1870s the range of machinery available steadily broadened. Cutting presses and heeling machinery appeared, and lasting was speeded up by the development of pulling-over machinery and a magnetic machine tacker. Many of the finishing processes, including edge-paring, burnishing, sole-levelling and polishing, were also mechanised.[32]

Despite these advances, there were still some limitations to the economies which could be effected by mechanisation. Technical innovation was primarily directed at improving the speed of production rather than at improving quality and appearance; the traditional methods of construction were the product of long experience and were not easily improved upon by machine methods. With the exception of the Blake machine, which offered a simpler alternative to the hand-sewn welted process, the machinery available did not offer new methods of shoemaking, but instead imitated hand work as closely as possible, and the use of these early machines usually meant a decline in quality. Where quality was the main requirement, and provided that skilled labour was readily available, it was still preferable to retain hand processes. Furthermore, technical development was uneven, and the fact that some processes remained unmechanised created production bottlenecks.

Although technical development was uneven, the concentration of the production processes did lead to increased productivity, especially after the introduction of an American innovation which became known as the 'team' system; each operation, whether manual or mechanised, was sub-divided into a number of simple and repetitive tasks, and the number of operatives in each department was carefully balanced to ensure that work flowed smoothly from clicking to finishing.[33] Justifiably, perhaps, the National Union of Boot and Shoe Operatives was afraid that the team system would debase the status of their members and permit the employment of a greater number of juveniles, and its policy was 'designed to nullify the economic advantages of machinery for the employers'.[34] In the 1850s manufacturers had been able to overcome opposition to mechanisation fairly easily, but the Union was growing rapidly in strength and influence during the 1880s and 1890s. The conflict of interests culminated in the major lock-out of 1895, when the Union's funds were exhausted and it was forced to abandon its opposition to mechanisation and factory production. Henceforth, manufacturers in Britain were able to re-organise their factories and improve efficiency in both manual and mechanised processes without further opposition.

Another significant development was the appearance of a more concentrated shoe machinery industry. The number of machine-making companies in Britain proliferated in the late decades of the nineteenth century, but growing American dominance in machine production meant that the most successful companies were those which were able to produce American-designed equipment under royalty agreements. The English & American Machine Company, for example, controlled the British rights to the Goodyear machine. In 1899 English & American's parent company, the Goodyear Shoe Machine Company, joined forces with two other major American manufacturers to form the United Shoe Machinery Company. Their British subsidiaries were amalgamated as the British United Shoe Machinery Company (BUSMC) and assumed a dominant position in the British shoe machinery industry. BUSMC followed the American trend by making its machinery available on lease. The exact nature of the lease depended upon the type of machine involved; where the number of revolutions could be counted, payment was usually on a royalty basis with an agreed minimum figure, while other leases specified a fixed annual rental. In neither case were there 'quantity discounts' for large customers.

The general consensus of opinion is that the availability of machinery on lease had a major effect upon the development of the footwear industry. In particular, it has been argued that new companies and small existing companies were not put at a disadvantage compared with their larger rivals, and that the possibility of leasing rather than investing capital in equipment meant that it was relatively easy to enter the industry.[35] The leasing system did not meet with universal approval, however, since BUSMC initially favoured 'tied' leases; if a customer required a machine which was manufactured under a BUSMC patent he had to sign a contract which prevented him from using machinery from other manufacturers anywhere in his factory. This tied lease policy led to litigation with the independent machinery manufacturers and with the Federation of Boot and Shoe Manufacturers of Great Britain and Ireland and was eventually made illegal in 1907, but the propaganda campaign mounted by BUSMC's opponents could not obscure the fact that the company was able to offer a very valuable service to footwear manufacturers. Regardless of the possible benefits accruing from the leasing system — and a conclusion on this subject would require detailed examination of the terms on which leases were held — it is clear that the development of a strong centralised shoe machinery supplier had a significant effect upon the growth of the footwear industry. BUSMC was able to draw upon the resources of its American parent and took the lead in invention and innovation, thus freeing the British footwear manufacturers from the need to invest heavily in research and development. It provided a full range of up-to-date machinery with balanced outputs to minimise production bottlenecks and a highly efficient back-up service; leased machinery was usually serviced free of charge.

By the beginning of the twentieth century, therefore, the British footwear industry had been transformed by mechanisation and the consequent extension of factory production. Its concentration in several major centres encouraged specialisation and some degree of cooperation between firms, tended to reduce overheads and transport costs, and made available a pool of skilled labour. It was supported by a strong shoe machinery industry and after 1895 it had a relatively free hand in such matters as the adoption of new machinery, the employment of labour and the establishment of quality control procedures. It also possessed a powerful trade association which offered a valuable market intelligence service.

Irish manufacturers could of course benefit from these developments to some extent, but their distance from the major centres of production and the main British market placed them at a disadvantage. They relied on British suppliers for much of their leather and for essential items like lasts, tools, tacks and rivets, which made for higher transport costs. They also found it difficult to attract skilled labour and managerial talent, and there tended to be a time lag before they adopted new techniques. In 1922, it seemed likely that the Irish Free State would continue to be economically dependent upon Britain, and the future of the Irish footwear industry did not look very bright unless the government could introduce measures to reduce the competitiveness of British goods.

The Footwear Industry and Selective Protection, 1922-32

The creation of the Irish Free State in 1922 initially did little to reduce imports from Britain. The Provisional Government was preoccupied with the establishment of the various organs of state. Economic expertise was lacking, and Irish politicians were wary of any measures which might alienate the British government. Economic policy, insofar as it existed, was dominated by the need for retrenchment and rigid control of expenditure. The Fiscal Inquiry Committee, which was appointed in 1923 to examine the fiscal system and recommend changes which might be made to aid industrial and agricultural development, set the tone for economic policy for the rest of the decade. Its Report recommended a cautious approach to protection, reflecting the widely-held belief that measures to reduce British imports might lead to political repercussions as well as retaliatory duties. It was also felt that the interests of some existing industries would be best-served by the maintenance of free trading conditions; major industries like brewing and foodstuffs were dependent upon exporting.[36]

Moderate tariffs were however imposed upon a number of commodities which were being produced for the home market, and which were considered suitable for encouragement. These included clothing, soap, confectionery, furniture, and boots and shoes; a 15 per cent *ad valorem* duty was imposed on all imported boots, shoes and slippers in April 1924. This policy of 'selective protection' was continued until Cumann na nGaedhael was defeated in the 1932 General Election, and it was a response to the emergence of an increasingly vocal protectionist lobby in the Free State. For example, the Dublin Industrial Development Association was initially opposed to tariffs, but by the mid-1920s there were increasingly frequent complaints that old-established Irish firms were being driven out of existence by imports from Britain. In February 1924, the Association resolved that

> This Association ... hereby calls on the Government to proceed without delay to promote legislation designed to safeguard, protect and encourage such industries as the national interest demands, and which at present are in a depressed and critical condition and liable to extinction if the existing system of Free Imports be further continued.[37]

In the later 1920s the Association — which represented business interests throughout the Free State, not just the Dublin manufacturers — made strenuous attempts to encourage protectionist measures, and promoted a series of 'Buy Irish' campaigns.

In the footwear industry, 1924-32 was a period of moderate but encouraging expansion. In May 1924 five footwear companies were in operation in the Irish Free State: Hearne & Cahill, Waterford; Michael Governey & Co, Carlow; the Lee Boot Manufacturing Co. Ltd, Cork; R. Hilliard & Sons, Killarney; and James Winstanley, Dublin. The total output of the five factories was about 300,000 pairs per year, which represented 7 per cent of home demand. Output consisted largely of heavy agricultural footwear, although a wide variety of other types were produced in small quantities.[38] Between 1924 and 1929 the existing factories were expanded and a number of new businesses appeared: Fitzpatrick & Co, Athlone; Freer & Co, Cork; the Hanover Shoe Co. Ltd, Cork; the Celt Boot Co. Dundalk; Mullen Mills Ltd, Emyvale, Monaghan; John Halliday & Son Ltd, Dundalk, Louth; and S.A. Wiltshire, Dublin. Not all these companies made the grade, however; the Celt Boot Co. commenced production of men's welted boots and shoes early in 1926, but it lacked capital and was liquidated some eighteen months later.[39] Two others, Fitzpatricks and Freers, had also ceased production by 1928.[40]

The Irish Free State's first *Census of Industrial Production* in 1926 showed that footwear production had risen to approximately 500,000 pairs, with an ex-factory value of about £318,000. Much of this was in the heavy boot sector, which possessed two important advantages for Irish producers. Firstly, the technical skill required was of a lower order than for other types of footwear; durability rather than fine workmanship or appearance was of prime importance. Secondly, this was one area where manufacturers could realise economies of specialisation. Manufacturers in other sectors of the footwear market had to produce a wide range to meet their customers' needs, but producers of agricultural footwear could concentrate upon a few 'bread and butter' lines. The bulk of Hallidays' output, for instance, consisted of just two types. This was important because the length of production runs was a major determinant of a footwear factory's efficiency. In 1926, heavy boots made up about 63 per cent of total production in the Irish Free State, while the remaining 38 per cent consisted of a variety of light boots and shoes. The industry continued to expand in the later 1920s, and by 1929 output had reached 521,340 pairs, worth £339,197. Total employment in footwear factories had risen steadily, from about 500-600 in 1922 to about 1,000 in 1926 and 1,056 in 1929.[41]

It would of course be unwise to assume that the 1924 tariff was the sole cause of this period of modest growth in the footwear industry; it can be argued that there was a general improvement in trading conditions during the middle 1920s which made for greater opportunities for expansion.[42] Nevertheless, the footwear industry had, on the whole, benefited from the policy of selective protection followed by Cosgrave's government. By the end of the decade, however, it was becoming apparent that the Irish footwear manufacturers had not succeeded in wresting more than a fraction of the market from their British competitors. Although they were doing well in heavy boots, agricultural footwear made up less than half the total volume of sales in Ireland. In other sectors of the market imports retained their dominant position. In October 1928, a Department of Industry and Commerce minute noted that in the boot and shoe industry

> the margin of protection is comparatively small and the outside firms have been able to maintain their market even though the figures of employment for the domestic forms seem to indicate moderate but steady expansion.[43]

Even with the addition of the 15 per cent duty British manufacturers were able to offer good quality footwear at prices which Irish factories could not match. When the Dublin Industrial Development Association made repeated efforts to persuade Dublin shops to stock Irish-made shoes, the retailers generally replied that Irish boots were saleable, but that in lighter shoes — especially ladies' fashion shoes — the public preferred to buy imports.[44] Although total imports declined from a peak of 4.5 million pairs in 1925 the figure remained above 4 million pairs for the rest of the decade, and still accounted for 89 per cent of total consumption in Ireland in 1929.[45]

By the end of the 1920s, therefore, the indications were that the Irish footwear industry had expanded as far as the moderate protection of the 1924 tariff would allow. If there were to be further growth, the competitiveness of British goods would have to be reduced. However, it was becoming apparent that high tariffs by themselves would not be sufficient to ensure the prosperity of Irish industry. Initially, there had been a tendency in a number of industries for manufacturers to regard protection as a panacea for their difficulties. In the leather industry, for instance, the number of tanneries had fallen from eighteen in 1900 to five in 1923, and the Tanners' Federation called for protection on several occasions. One witness before the Fiscal Inquiry Committee in 1923 claimed that the industry would supply the whole of Ireland's needs if granted protection.[46]

This view was not shared by the government. In 1926, it decided to set up a Tariff Commission to make detailed reports on applications for protection, but its chairman, Mr J.J. McElligott, was opposed to tariffs and under his leadership the Commission showed a marked reluctance to recommend the imposition of tariffs.[47] The government's caution was justified by the experience of those industries which had been granted a measure of protection; as Daly had remarked, the imposition of selective tariffs proved a double-edged sword. In some industries, including footwear, the duty was too low to blunt the edge of British competition, and imports continued to flow in. In other industries where tariffs were higher large British companies responded to the legislation by setting up factories in the Free State or taking over well-known Irish firms.[48] By 1928 Lever Brothers dominated the Irish soap industry, whilst more than half the output of the confectionery industry was accounted for by firms like Rowntree, Clarnico Murray and Mackintosh.[49]

Instead of reducing foreign competition, raising the duty on footwear imports seemed likely to hasten the demise of native industry.[50] There were signs that economic penetration of the Irish footwear industry by British firms was already beginning. John Halliday and S.A. Wiltshire, both British manufacturers which sent a large part of their output to Ireland, had already found it expedient to commence operations in Ireland. The modest duty of 1924 had not prevented them from selling their products in the Free State, but the growing support for Eamon de Valera's Fianna Fáil Party had given them cause for concern. Fianna Fáil had been accepted as the legitimate opposition to Cosgrave's ruling Cumann na nGaedheal Party from 1927, and was increasingly identified with demands for prohibitive tariffs. To tackle the problem of economic penetration, Fianna Fáil also proposed to introduce measures designed to ensure that industrial development took place under Irish control. Policies such as these had been impracticable during the 1920s, but changes in the general political and economic climate after 1929 made them increasingly attractive and acceptable.

2
PROTECTIONISM AND RAPID GROWTH
1932-36

During the Great Depression, the Irish Free State participated in the world-wide trend towards protectionism. Cumann na nGaedheal's cautious and selective protectionism policy, which had achieved a measure of success in the 1920s, was now subjected to growing criticism, and in February 1932 Eamon de Valera's Fianna Fáil Party took office for the first time. Fianna Fáil was committed to protection and self-sufficiency, and during the 1930's tariffs and quota restrictions were imposed upon a wide range of items. By the beginning of 1938, it was calculated that 1,947 different articles were subject to import controls.[1]

A policy of protection and self-sufficiency was possible in 1932 because of the decline of international trade; Ireland's export-orientated industries, which favoured free trade, were badly hit, and their interests were no longer of paramount importance. Another consideration was the growing problem of long-term unemployment in Ireland; traditionally, unemployment had been alleviated by emigration,[2] but in the Depression emigration opportunities were greatly reduced. Protection was attractive to the Irish because it promised to reduce economic dependence on the United Kingdom, stimulate Irish agriculture and industry, and thus deal with the pressing problem of unemployment. It not only harked back to the ideas of Arthur Griffith and 'traditional' Irish nationalism,[3] it now had the blessing of contemporary economists,[4] and, when de Valera's dispute with the British over land annuities led to economic sanctions, it had the advantage of making a virtue out of a necessity.[5]

Under government supervision, Ireland was to industrialise on the basis of consumer goods industries for which a domestic market already existed and which could be produced on a small scale without excessive cost. Seán Lemass, who was Fianna Fáil's leading spokesman on economic affairs, was appointed Minister for Industry and Commerce,[6] and under his leadership the government assumed a much wider responsibility for industrial development than had hitherto been the case.

Increased duties on footwear came into effect in April 1932. Leather footwear became subject to a 37.5 per cent (25 per cent preferential) *ad valorem* rate, whilst the rate for non-leather and children's footwear was set at 22.5 per cent (15 per cent preferential).[7] Shoes for infants and young children (sizes 0-6) were exempted from duty. Footwear from Britain — which made up about 90 per cent of all imports — were initially subjected to the preferential rates but this ended as a consequence of the 'Economic War'; when de Valera refused to continue the land annuities which had been paid by the Cosgrave government under the Anglo-Irish financial agreements of 1922-6, the British government terminated Ireland's exemption from the general 10 per cent duty imposed by the 1932 Import Duties Act,[8] and introduced substantial duties upon imports of Irish livestock, dairy produce and meat.[9] The Irish government in turn imposed retaliatory duties under the 1932 Emergency Imposition of Duties Act.[10] In the case of footwear, tariff rates were modified by the Emergency Imposition of Duties (No. 5) Order, which came into force on 24 December 1932.[11] Imports from Britain, but not from the Commonwealth, became liable to the full rate, which was reduced to 30 per cent for leather footwear and 20 per cent for non-leather and children's footwear.[12]

Further alterations were made in 1933 and 1934. From 30 September 1933 the tariff on children's footwear (sizes 7-1) was increased to 30 per cent and finally, by a resolution of the Committee of Finance of Dáil Éireann dated 9 May 1934, the preferential rate was abolished, making all imported footwear liable to a 30 per cent *ad valorem* duty.[13]

This tariff remained in force with only minor adjustments for the rest of the decade, but in 1934 additional restrictions were imposed by the Control of Imports Act. Under this Act, orders were made on 18 September 1934 prohibiting the importation of virtually all types of footwear except under licence,[14] and quota restrictions were introduced. Although the quantities permitted fluctuated considerably (Appendix IV), the intention was gradually to exclude foreign companies from the leather footwear market and to restrict their share of the less important non-leather market.

The imposition of duties in 1932 led immediately to a period of intense activity in the Irish footwear industry. New plant was laid down in existing factories and a number of new companies were established. By June 1933, five new firms had appeared: the Limerick Shoe and Slipper Co. Ltd; Toone & Son Ltd, Kells; Edward Donaghy & Sons Ltd, Drogheda; John Rawson & Son (Ireland) Ltd, Dundalk; and J.H. Woodington (Drogheda) Ltd. The total number of factories in operation had risen to 14. Early in 1934, they were joined by another when Padmore & Barnes (Ireland) Ltd commenced production in a purpose-built factory at Kilkenny. The introduction of quotas provided a further stimulus. By 1935, 23 establishments for the manufacture of footwear were included in the *Census of Industrial Production* (excluding clog makers and manufacturers of boot and shoe components). It should be noted, however, that quite a few of them were very small, even by Irish standards.

TABLE 3

The size of firms in the Irish footwear industry, October 1935 (classified according to number employed)

Less than 20	2
20 - 49	3
50 - 99	2
100 - 249	9
250 - 499	5
500 and over	2
	23

Source: *Census of Industrial Production, 1932-6*, Table VII, p. 20.

Nevertheless, some of the firms established between 1934 and 1936 were of considerable importance in the light of the subsequent development of the footwear industry. In particular, one might mention Stedfast Shoes Ltd, Carrickmacross, Co. Monaghan, which was founded in 1935 and commenced production of medium-grade ladies' sandals and slippers in April 1936; Traly Footwear Ltd, Tralee, Co. Kerry, and Leslie Cunnington Ltd, Clonmel, Co. Tipperary which were also established in 1935; Dubarry Shoemakers Ltd, which was established in 1936 by local interests at Ballinasloe, Co. Galway to provide employment in the area; Connolly Shoes, Dundalk; and the Edenderry Shoe Company, Edenderry, Co. Offaly. Most of them were family concerns, with the bulk of the issued shares — particularly the shares with voting rights — being held by the owner or his immediate relatives. When a local development committee had been involved in the establishment of a footwear factory, as in the case of Dubarry Shoemakers, its investment might be represented by shares. On a few occasions, too, a company's shares were offered in small quantities to important customers. But of the companies operating in Ireland in the early 1930s, only Padmore & Barnes was established as a public company, although Woodingtons also went public in 1936.

In view of the policies of the new Fianna Fáil government, it is interesting to note that British companies became heavily involved in the expansion of the Irish footwear industry. As noted earlier, a few British companies had already established factories in the Free State by 1932. These were mostly heavy boot manufacturers which had come to depend upon the Irish agricultural market and were worried by the popular support for Fianna Fáil's protectionist plans. The first British company to start operations in Ireland was John Halliday & Son Ltd. This company had been established in

Bramley, near Leeds, in 1868, and like the other manufacturers in Leeds, it specialised in the production of heavy hob-nailed boots. In 1927 the managing director, Fred Halliday, determined to commence production in the Free State.[15] Premises at Quay Street, Dundalk were purchased from the liquidated Celt Boot Co., and between 30 and 40 key operatives moved from Bramley to Dundalk. John Halliday & Son Ltd was registered in Ireland as a private limited company in August 1928 with an issued capital of £14,000. The Bramley company was to provide plant, trade marks and goodwill but in fact it did not long survive the establishment of the Dundalk factory; production ceased in March 1930 and the company was wound up two years later.

With the tightening up of import restrictions in 1932, a number of other British companies followed Hallidays' lead. Edward Donaghy & Son Ltd had commenced production of heavy boots in Ulster in the early 1920s, and after partition it was cut off from its major customers in the rural South. In 1932 it moved lock, stock and barrel to Drogheda. Another British heavy heavy boot manufacturer which began producing footwear in Ireland was J.H. Woodington of Kingswood, Bristol. A disused meat packing plant on the quayside at Drogheda was acquired and production initially consisted largely of heavy agricultural boots marketed under Woodingtons' 'Bone-Dry' brand. Women's lace-up boots and men's and boys' shoes were also made. Woodingtons was also involved in the establishment of the Gorey Leather Co. Ltd at Gorey, Co. Wexford, which supplied much of the leather used in the Drogheda factory.

Irish factories were also established by British manufacturers of good quality light shoes — especially ladies' fashion shoes — which believed that their expertise would enable them to do well in the Irish market. Early in 1932, an Irish subsidiary was set up by John Rawson & Sons Ltd, a company which specialised in ladies' shoes and which had three factories in Leicester, employing about 800 workers. Benjamin Rawson, the managing director, arranged with the Ministry of Defence to lease part of the army barracks in Dundalk[16] and the company quickly became the biggest footwear manufacturer in Ireland, producing about 13,000 pairs per week and employing more than 500 workers.[17] As well as its high quality ladies' shoes, the company soon began to produce men's shoes and a range of children's footwear.[18]

Another manufacturer of good quality shoes was Padmore & Barnes Ltd of Northampton. This company was incorporated in 1895 and originally specialised in the manufacture of men's welted boots and shoes. It was one of the first manufacturers to introduce footwear in different widths for broad or narrow feet and also claimed to be the originator of the 'in-stock' system.[19] After the First World War, Padmore & Barnes commenced production of lighter machine-sewn women's shoes by way of an arrangement with Mason & Marson Ltd of Stafford, which later became a wholly-owned subsidiary.[20] Early in 1933, Padmore & Barnes took the decision to establish an Irish subsidiary and began the search for a suitable site. Initially a location near Dublin was favoured but the local industrial development committee in Kilkenny had for some time been striving to devise ways of relieving unemployment in the city and was very eager to persuade Padmore & Barnes to come to Kilkenny. Everything possible was done to encourage the company; the locational advantages of Kilkenny were stressed and the local authority was persuaded to offer incentives in the form of rent rebates. To help bring the negotiations to a successful conclusion, the development committee raised about £4,000 from 50-60 local subscribers, and commenced construction of a 35,000 square foot factory; building work commenced before Padmore & Barnes' directors had made any firm commitment to come to Kilkenny.[21] Padmore & Barnes (Ireland) Ltd was incorporated as a public company on 10 January 1934 with an issued capital of £20,000. S.J. Davis, who owned a controlling interest in the parent company, was appointed chairman, and J.P. Hawe, the Borough Treasurer at Kilkenny, was elected to the board to represent local interests. The Northampton company undertook to make all patterns, trade marks and patent rights available to the Irish company.

The extent of British involvement in the development of the Irish footwear industry seems somewhat surprising in view of Fianna Fáil's emphasis on protection and self-sufficiency. In fact there was something of a conflict of interests here. Fianna Fáil was certainly very worried about the activities of British concerns because they threatened to perpetuate the old 'colonial' relationship which de Valera was trying to destroy. The events of the 1920s had clearly demonstrated the dangers of allowing foreign firms to commence operations behind the tariff wall. Yet, on the other hand, the fundamental objective of Fianna Fáil policy was to tackle the chronic unemployment problem by stimulating industrial development, and foreign capital, entrepreneurial skill and technical expertise were badly needed. An examination of the government records which have survived reveals that politicians and civil servants devoted a great deal of thought to this issue. Political and ideological considerations did not lead them to reject British assistance out of hand; foreign involvement was to be permitted, but would be subject to close supervision by the Department of Industry and Commerce. In June 1932, the new Minister for Industry and Commerce, Sean Lemass told the Dáil that

> We have no objection to foreign capital in Irish industry if it does not mean foreign control. We do not object to foreign companies estab-

lishing branch factories here where there is obviously room for them, where it is to our advantage that they should come here, and where we are in a position to institute such regulations and safeguards as in our opinion are necessary to protect our own interests.[22]

The regulations and safeguards to which Lemass referred were embodied in the Control of Manufactures Acts of 1932 and 1934.[23] Briefly, the 1932 Act laid down that any company established after 1 June 1932 which did not have a majority of Irish shareholders had to obtain a New Manufacture Licence, which was to be issued at the sole discretion of the Minister for Industry and Commerce. In practice, licences could usually be obtained by companies proposing to manufacture commodities not already being made in Ireland, but would only be issued if the Minister was satisfied that the foreign company would not jeopardise the interests of native industry. The 1934 Act introduced further controls to close loopholes in the legislation. Some foreign companies had discovered that the intentions of the 1932 Act could be evaded by selling non-voting shares to Irish investors, and it was laid down that in future a company would only be exempt from government regulations if two-thirds of the shares with voting rights were in the hands of Irish nationals. A majority of directors (excluding full-time managing directors) were also to be citizens of the Free State.

The conditions under which foreign owners operated footwear factories in Ireland varied from firm to firm. John Halliday & Son was owned by British interests, and because it was set up before the Control of Manufactures Acts came into operation the new regulations did not apply and it was able to act as if it were an Irish company. Padmore & Barnes (Ireland) Ltd was also able to obtain exemption because of the loophole in the 1932 Act. Its initial capital of £20,000 was divided into 15,000 £1 cumulative preference shares and 5,000 £1 ordinary shares. 6,000 of the preference shares were allotted to the local subscribers in Kilkenny and the remainder offered to Padmore & Barnes' Irish agents, but the ordinary shares were held by the English parent company. More than 50 per cent of the issued capital was therefore held by Irishmen as the 1932 Act required; but the limited rights attached to preference shares meant that effective control was retained in English hands.

Quite a number of British companies drew on local capital when setting up footwear factories in Ireland; but as far as one can tell relatively few were prepared to allow control to pass to Irish business interests. Instead, most British-owned firms applied for New Manufacture Licences and operated under the close supervision of the Department of Industry and Commerce. Numerous restrictions were imposed on companies operating under a New Manufacture Licence. Foreign nationals were not to be employed in any post unless the Minister was satisfied that it could not be filled by an Irish citizen; in practice, the Minister usually permitted footwear firms to bring a small number of 'keymen' — technical experts and foremen — to Ireland during the starting-up period. Irish materials were also to be used as far as possible; this became an important consideration when the Irish leather industry began to expand under government encouragement.[24] Some New Manufacture Licences also stated the locality in which the factory had to be built, although this was not common in the case of footwear firms. The licence could also impose conditions on the type of footwear which a company could produce. A company like John Rawson & Son was able to obtain a New Manufacture Licence because it was primarily a producer of light ladies' shoes, and therefore was not in direct competition with native producers; it will be recalled that most of the older footwear firms in Ireland were manufacturers of heavy boots. The Licence granted to J.H. Woodington in May 1933 laid down that children's shoes were to make up at least three-quarters of total output.[25]

The legal constraints upon the activities of foreign nationals in the Irish footwear industry therefore appear to have been considerable. The *Irish Times,* for instance, claimed that the controls made the Minister of Industry and Commerce 'a virtual dictator of the country's economic life'.[26] Theoretically a exempt company like John Halliday possessed a substantial advantage over Rawsons or Woodingtons. In practice, however the Control of Manufactures Acts were not quite so onerous a burden as one might assume; government officials and footwear manufacturers soon came to a *modus vivendi*, and, in general, relations were amicable. The Department of Industry and Commerce held frequent meetings with the manufacturers and showed some flexibility in its operations of the controls. For instance, the Minister was usually prepared to allow newly-formed companies to import pre-fabricated components — particularly uppers — under duty-free licences.[27] This helped factories to commence production quickly. On occasion, too, it seems that government officials were prepared to waive the regulations in order to create new jobs. J.H. Woodington, for instance, was primarily manufacturing heavy boots at this date, and thus did not comply with the terms of its licence. Meenan has noted that such understandings between department officials and manufacturers were quite common; and when the legislation was eventually modified in 1958 it was reported that no prosecution had ever been initiated for breach or evasion of the regulations.[28]

In general, the legislation appears to have been intelligently applied; the Fianna Fáil ideal of 'Irish industries controlled by Irishmen and operated through the instrumentality of Irish Capital'[29] was not achievable, but an acceptable compromise had been reached. If Irish economic growth did not always take place under Irish ownership, it did at least take place under Irish supervision. And, although the Acts were an irritation, they did not deter British companies from setting up factories in the Irish Free State.

Another potential drawback to British ownership was the legacy of anti-British sentiment left by the 1916 Rising, the troubles of 1919-21 and partition. Since the 1890s Irish nationalism had been expressed in economic as well as in political terms; there were a number of appeals to 'buy Irish' and boycott British goods. The Economic War and the call for self-sufficiency tended to perpetuate this tradition. But this did not prove to be a major problem for the British manufacturers who set up footwear factories in Ireland in the 1930s. Local development committees often proved very eager to attract British footwear firms. Even in Dundalk, where the proximity of the border tended to increase tensions, Fred Halliday was able to maintain good relations with his Irish employees. A good deal of tact and understanding was required, however; unlike Halliday, Benjamin Rawson tended to be somewhat intransigent in his dealings with local interests, and experienced considerable opposition when he tried to expand his Irish business. One accusation which received attention in the local press was that his company preferred to employ cheap juvenile labour from country districts rather than family men.[30] This was perhaps rather unfair since all footwear factories employed juvenile labour to a considerable extent and it is probably indicative of personal animosity rather than a general dislike of British involvement in Irish industry.

British ownership, therefore, did not impose very severe constraints upon footwear manufacturers. And in some key areas — notably the training of operatives, the acquisition of managerial expertise, and the provision of working capital — it conferred quite significant advantages.

The absence of a pool of skilled labour, such as existed in the British centres of production, meant that it was necessary to train large numbers of 'green' operatives. Admittedly, technological developments had eased the problem somewhat. The only major innovation of the first three decades of the twentieth century had been the introduction of the cemented process,[31] but there was a steady improvement in the efficiency of existing machinery and production techniques; in particular there was a continuing trend towards the subdivision of the production sequence into a large number of relatively simple tasks. This reduced the degree of skill required and made it easier to train workers in areas which lacked a tradition of shoemaking. A number of factors facilitated the training process. In a few towns, notably Dundalk, factories were able to take advantage of training schemes set up under the auspices of local vocational training committees. A particularly significant development was the 1933 agreement between the footwear manufacturers and the National Union of Boot and Shoe Operatives (NUBSO) which provided for the introduction of a special 'green labour' pay scale. This lasted for up to four years from a firm's inception and helped to keep wage bills down while trainees were learning to operate the machines. Government assistance was also of some importance; particularly noteworthy were the steps taken to permit newly-formed companies to import shaped components — especially ready-made uppers — under duty-free licence. This enabled a company to get into production quickly and avoid the bottlenecks which, especially in the closing department, were likely to result from the inex- perience of operatives and supervisory personnel.

But, whilst these developments helped to *speed up* the training period, the problem remained a substantial one. In the 1930s — and indeed until relatively recently — factory production of ready-made footwear retained a significant 'craft' element in many of its processes. This was particularly true of tasks like leather grading and clicking but nowhere in the production sequence had the operatives descended to the level of mere machine-minders. British companies like John Rawson, Padmore & Barnes and J.H. Woodington possessed a significant advantage because they were able to bring executives and a nucleus of trained workers over from the United Kingdom to help them get into full production.[32] Supervisors and operatives could also be sent to the parent factory on training courses. Furthermore, a very wide range of services could be made available; technical and design information could be supplied and some firms also used lasts, patterns and components which had been produced in Britain. At Padmore & Barnes, for example, the intention was to reproduce the 'Northampton touch'; Northampton's reputation for high quality footwear was second to none, and this policy meant that Padmore & Barnes was to produce footwear to a standard hitherto unknown in Ireland. This required considerable assistance from the parent company, since the Kilkenny workforce was almost totally lacking in the necessary skills. A number of operatives were sent to Northampton for training, and the parent company's executive staff, designers and pattern cutters had to put in a tremendous amount of overtime over a period of about two years to bring the Kilkenny factory to a state of efficiency.[33] A particularly vital role was played by W.H. Irons, who came to Kilkenny in 1934, and had been widely regarded as one of the best shoemakers in Britain.[34] As at John Rawson & Son, the task of getting the factory into production was facilitated by the Minister of Industry and Commerce's readiness to permit the importation of made-up uppers from the parent company, thus minimising the production bottlenecks which might result from the complexity and variety of the tasks performed in the closing department.[35]

As far as capital requirements were concerned, it has usually been assumed that entry into the footwear industry was relatively easy. In the 1930s there was little evidence to suggest that large companies neccessarily possessed a significant advantage over their smaller rivals. Economies of scale and specialisation were not entirely absent but it was quite possible to run a small factory reasonably economically. The owner could retain a large measure of control over a small company, and this kind of personal involvement was valuable in view of the shortage of managerial talent. The possibility of leasing equipment rather than buying it may have helped, particularly in the case of royalty-type leases which did not penalise the smaller company. Furthermore, heavy investment in buildings was not necessary. In most Irish towns there were vacant premises which could be adapted for footwear manufacture, and in a number of instances local development committees were willing to offer them on favourable terms to attract employers to the area. It was therefore possible to commence operations on the basis of a fairly small investment. In 1934, for example Hallidays' issued capital stood at £20,000 while Stedfast Shoes and the Edenderry Shoe Co. started operations with an issued capital of £12,000 and £6,000 respectively.

But while starting capital requirements were fairly low, this was not always the case with working capital. There were a number of reasons why footwear production tied up considerable sums of money. Materials, which represented roughly two-thirds of manufacturing costs, had to be ordered in advance of sales. Orders from wholesalers and retailers were subject to seasonal fluctuations, and manufacturers had to build up stocks of finished goods against peak periods of demand. Suppliers in Ireland were unable, and importers unwilling, to give generous credit terms to footwear manufacturers, but their retail and wholesale customers had come to expect them and in many cases were notoriously dilatory in settling their accounts. These considerations will require more detailed attention at a later stage, but at this point it is simply necessary to note that in every footwear company current assets were considerably larger than fixed assets. At John Halliday & Son, for example, the proportion of total assets held in the form of stocks and current debt rose from 64 per cent (1930) to 77 per cent (1936). In addition, it is apparent that as output grew the working capital needed to run the business rose faster than investment in fixed assets.

The imbalance between share capital and working capital requirements meant that more Irish footwear firms were faced by periodic cash flow crises, which on occasion — as in the case of the Celt Boot Company — could be sufficiently serious as to lead to the demise of the company. Banks therefore played a significant role in the growth of the footwear industry by providing short-term loans and overdraft facilities. The major creditor of a footwear firm was nearly always its bank.

British-owned companies, however, were able to borrow working capital from their parent company. Padmore & Barnes regularly received loans from Northampton to finance stock purchases at peak buying periods, and also received such items as lasts and patterns at less than the market price. A similar comment could be made about Rawsons and Woodingtons. Hallidays, of course, was no longer associated with a British company but Fred Halliday was still able to make use of his contacts in the British footwear industry to obtain favourable credit terms from suppliers. The fact that payment of bills could be deferred until revenue from sales had begun to come in helped to keep working capital requirements to a minimum. This advantage, however, disappeared with Fred Halliday's death in February 1936, and with the Irish government's insistence that the company should buy an increasing share of its raw materials from Irish suppliers — who were not in a position to give extended credit.[36] Fred Halliday's nephew Arthur Halliday took control of the business, and one of his first tasks was to find the additional capital needed to keep the business running. This was to lead in 1937 to the issue of 30,000 £1 cumulative preference shares.

Thus, financing a footwear company and training operatives, supervisors and management could present considerable difficulties. They were not insurmountable, but it was quite apparent that firms operating under British ownership possessed a considerable advantage. This, together with the obvious superiority of British manufacturers in production and marketing expertise, meant that a number of Irish-owned companies were now eager to enter into association with their former competitors.

Agreements between British and Irish manufacturers displayed a number of basic similarities. They gave the Irish company access to much needed design and technical expertise, and usually permitted it to produce footwear bearing the British company's brands for the Irish market against a royalty payment.[37] In most instances, lasts, patterns and knives were supplied from the United Kingdom, operatives and managers could be sent to Britain to gain experience, and the British company sent technicians to Ireland to ensure that production was brought up to the required standard.[38] Agreements were particularly important if a manufacturer was interested in entering a different sector of the footwear market; production and marketing techniques varied, and experience gained in one type of footwear was not necessarily applicable in other sectors. Thus, in 1934, R. Hilliard & Son of Killarney — primarily a heavy boot manufacturer — entered into association with Palmers of Leicester and built a new factory for the production of women's shoes. In this context, it is interesting to note that Padmore & Barnes (Ireland) Ltd took steps to come to an arrangement with C. & J. Clark Ltd of Street. Initially, production at the Kilkenny factory consisted largely of men's shoes, as this was the type of footwear in which its Northampton parent was most experienced. The decision to commence production of high-quality ladies' shoes towards the end of 1934, however, created the need for additional expertise. Padmore & Barnes' Stafford subsidiary, Mason & Marson Ltd, did manufacture women's and children's shoes, but Clarks was widely recognised as the market leader in this sector. Its reputation was largely based upon its expertise in design and last manufacture and upon the strength of its branding.

S.J. Davis, Padmore & Barnes' managing director, approached Hugh B. Clark, then in charge of sales. Preliminary investigations revealed that the Kilkenny factory was currently producing about 3,000 pairs per week with a potential capacity of 5,000 pairs per week and that the women's shoes which Padmore & Barnes had recently begun to produce were of a consistently lower standard than Clarks'.[39] It was agreed that Bancroft Clark should visit Kilkenny and that the proposal should be carefully investigated,[40] but Clarks was wary of a move into the Irish market. Firstly, it lacked the managerial strength for an expansion of this nature and, secondly, its directors felt it might be unwise to tie up capital in Ireland at a time when they were contemplating an extension of their experiments in retail trading.[41] On the other hand, Clarks' brand reputation in Ireland was dwindling rapidly as the tariffs and quotas took effect and some members of the board had misgivings about giving up a possible opening for profitable business.[42] Sidney Lowry, Clarks' sales chief for the whole of Ireland, also visited Kilkenny and reported favourably.[43] Discussions continued into 1935, but Clarks' board remained divided on the advisability of a tie-up with the Irish company, and eventually negotiations were broken off. One stumbling-block was the fact that Padmore & Barnes were already making women's shoes in Ireland to a lower standard than C. & J. Clark. Bancroft Clark's view was that bad habits would already have been acquired which would entail retraining of operatives and management.[44] Probably of more significance was the fear that Clarks' design and technical expertise would eventually get back to Padmore & Barnes in Northampton.[45]

Although this proposal did not come to fruition, it was indicative of a general belief in the footwear industry that considerable advantage accrued from a British connection. Such agreements were particularly valuable to help an Irish factory to get into full production rapidly, but the advantages were by no means confined to the starting up period, and close relationships between British and Irish manufacturers remained a feature of the footwear industry throughout the period covered by this book.

After 1932, protection led to a rapid increase in footwear production. As can be seen from Appendix I, leather footwear production roughly trebled between 1931 and 1934, from 660,000 pairs to 1,965,000 pairs. Employment in the industry followed a similar pattern, increasing from 1,125 to 2,977.[46] It is interesting to note that there were significant variations in the growth rate in different sectors of the footwear industry. Table 4 shows that, as was to be expected, Irish manufacturers had strengthened their position in the heavy boot market between 1931 and 1933 and by the latter date accounted for nearly three-quarters of total production of this type of footwear. But it is also clear that this sector had experienced a relative and absolute decline.

TABLE 4

Leather footwear, 1931/33: production and foreign trade

(000 pairs)

	1931			1933		
	Heavy boots	Other types of leather footwear	Total	Heavy boots	Other types of leather footwear	Total
Home production	280	380	660	511	1,079	1,589
Imports	635	3,269	3,904	200	2,570	2,770
Less exports	5	—	5	1	—	1
Total production for the Irish market	911	3,649	4,560	709	3,649	4,358
Home production as % total production for the Irish market	31%	10%	14%	72%	30%	36%

Source: *Census of Industrial Production.*

The market for better types of leather footwear — lighter adults' shoes and children's footwear — was much larger. It had hitherto been dominated by foreign manufacturers, and imports still made up about two-thirds of total production in 1933 but this was an area in which Irish output was expanding rapidly as the tariffs took effect. Irish manufacturers who had previously confined their activities to the heavy boot sector now began to produce other types of leather footwear and, in addition, a number of new companies were set up between 1932 and 1934 which from the onset began to concentrate upon the lighter types of leather footwear. As we have seen, this development was particularly associated with companies which were linked by ownership or association with British manufacturers. John Rawson, for example, was best-known for its ladies' fashion and walking shoes and also produced men's welted boots and shoes and children's veldtshoen sandals with crepe rubber soles. Padmore & Barnes never made heavy boots, although it did make lighter, softer boots[47] while Stedfast Shoes concentrated upon the production of light shoes and slippers.

The Irish footwear companies did not, however, display any interest in the production of non-leather footwear and the Irish government did not feel justified in subjecting this type of footwear to the high rate of duty payable on leather boots and shoes. Non-leather footwear, as defined by the *Census of Industrial Production*, included both rubber boots and a variety of footwear made of other materials, such as house shoes and slippers and crepe-soled sandals and shoes with uppers of canvas or other fabrics. This was an important growth area in the early 1930s, largely because non-leather footwear tended to be very cheap; although non-leather footwear made up 29 per cent of the total pairage on sale in Ireland in 1933, it represented just 8 per cent of the total value. A major development in the non-leather sector was the growing importance of the rubber wellington, which lacked the durability and comfort of a leather boot but which was appreciably cheaper and completely waterproof. Irish manufacturers were unable to produce wellingtons because the technology was quite different from that of leather footwear, and in any case, was protected by patents held by the inventors. Imports of rubber footwear rose from 897,156 pairs (£90,679) in 1930 to 1,126,716 pairs (£85,582) in 1933, and by the latter date they represented about one-fifth of total imports. In addition, it will be noted that there was a significant reduction in the average price per pair. Imports of footwear of other materials were growing very rapidly indeed; in the same period they increased from 241,476 pairs (£30,956) to 1,448,040 pairs (£104,022). Irish manufacturers lacked any expertise in the mass production of cheap shoes and in 1933 home production of this type of footwear amounted to less than 30,000 pairs, worth just £3,756.[48]

In short, while Irish manufacturers were able to increase their share of the market for leather footwear they made little progress in the production of non-leather footwear, and virtually all Ireland's requirements in this sector were still supplied by foreign manufacturers. Although this did not constitute *direct* competition for the Irish footwear industry, there was nonetheless a possibility that the Depression would encourage the public to buy cheap non-leather imports in preference to the better-quality (and more expensive) leather footwear produced by the home manufacturers.

Even more worrying to Irish manufacturers was the fact that the average price of imported footwear was steadily falling in all sectors of the market. As can be seen from Appendix II, the average ex-factory price of Irish-produced footwear was also falling between 1930 and 1934, but imported boots and shoes were still appreciably cheaper and it was feared that foreign manufacturers would retain a large share of the Irish market despite the higher tariffs imposed by Fianna Fáil. In May 1934, for example, there was a call from the Dundalk branch of NUBSO for a total prohibition of imports, especially in the case of very cheap footwear from Britain and Japan.[49]

Not surprisingly, the government did not comply with this request, for it was doubtful whether the Irish factories possessed the capacity or experience to cope with the rapid expansion of output which it would entail, but such demands undoubtedly influenced the decision to regulate imports by quota restrictions rather than tariffs.

The introduction of quotas led to an increase in the rate of growth of the Irish footwear industry. Between 1934 and 1936, output grew by about two and a half times, and by the latter date it had reached 4,857,576 pairs — a figure which would not be surpassed until 1946. Light footwear continued to be the major growth area; whereas the output of heavy boots increased by about 50 per cent between 1934 and 1936, total production of men's and boys' shoes nearly doubled and women's and girls' shoes nearly trebled. Although leather footwear continued to represent more than 90 per cent of Irish production, some progress was also made in the *other materials* sector by firms like the Limerick Shoe & Slipper Co. and in 1936 production in this category had reached 403,740 pairs.

By 1936, total imports had fallen to 159,644 pairs. The composition of imports had also changed. As quotas were fixed on the basis of quantity rather than value, retailers were now preferring to import their more expensive lines. A significant consideration was that Irish manufacturers were concentrating

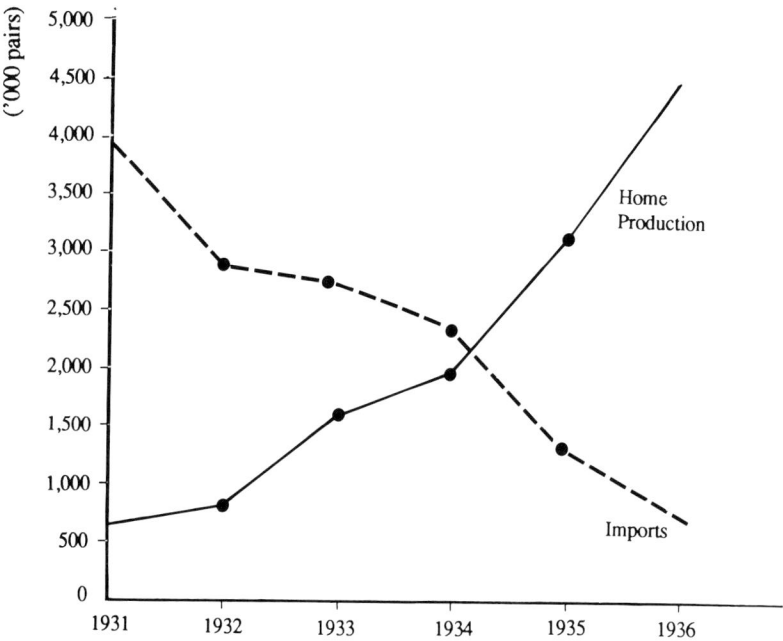

FIGURE 1: Imports and home production, 1931-36 (footwear wholly/mainly of leather)

Sources: *Census of Industrial Production; Trade and Shipping Statistics.*

upon mid-price lines and the similarity between the styles offered by competing manufacturers restricted the choice available to the consumer. Expensive foreign-made shoes found a ready market because of their reputation. Reputation is of considerable importance in the marketing of footwear, especially in the more expensive categories, and there was a widespread belief that imports offered a wider choice, better quality and superior styling. An element of monopoly pricing was therefore possible and after 1935 the average price of leather footwear imports rose quite sharply.[50]

While imports of footwear were declining rapidly, the growth of home production led to increased demand for imported raw materials and components. Many of the necessary materials, such as tacks, thread, solutions, cements and inks, could not be competitively produced in Ireland because the level of demand was too low, and were usually supplied by specialist concerns located in the British centres of production. Similarly, shoemaking machinery was not made in Ireland and most factories operated BUSMC machines under leasing agreements.[51] Lasts and press knives were also usually of British origin. There was also a demand for partly-finished components to alleviate delays and production bottlenecks during the starting up period.

TABLE 5

Imports of shaped soles, heels and uppers (by value), 1930-37

£

1930	1931	1932	1933	1934	1935	1936	1937
11,134	8,432	30,052	65,861	56,032	68,032	77,613	10,700

Source: *Trade and Shipping Statistics.*

As can be seen, imports of components rose fastest during 1932 and 1933 and 'buying-in' continued to play an important part in the development of the Irish footwear industry until duties were increased in 1936-7.[52]

Demand for leather was also rising rapidly and an increase in leather imports was inevitable in the short term; the Irish tanning industry had been in recession and lacked the capital to finance an expansion programme to meet the sudden upswing in demand, Moreover, none of the Irish tanneries produced chrome-tanned upper leather in 1932. While imports of undressed sole and insole leather rose by about a half between 1932 and 1936, imports of dressed leather for uppers more than trebled. [53] But the government's intention was that the development of the footwear industry should stimulate the domestic leather producers, and the footwear factories were obliged to use a steadily increasing proportion of Irish leather. In 1933, duties were imposed on imported sole and insole leather at a rate of 37.5 per cent *ad valorem* (25 per cent preferential)[54] and in October 1935 a similar rate was applied to dressed upper leathers.[55] After 1934 the Irish leather industry grew rapidly, and a number of new tanneries were established. Irish Tanners Ltd was set up in 1934 and, in the following year, opened a large sole leather tannery at Portlaw, Co. Waterford. A small subsidiary tannery (also for sole leather) was opened at New Ross, Co. Waterford, in the same year. In 1936, two tanneries producing side and upper leather were established at Dungarvan, Co. Waterford and Gorey, Co. Wexford. Upper leather had not previously been manufactured in Ireland.[56] The Gorey Leather Company supplied most of the leather used in J.H. Woodington's heavy boot production.[57] In 1938, another large upper leather tannery was opened at Carrick-on-Suir by Plunder & Pollak (Ireland) Ltd, bringing the total number of tanneries to eight.[58] In that year, Irish output of leather exceeded the quantity imported for the first time.

During this period of rapid expansion the National Union of Boot and Shoe Operatives was doing its best to bring about the unionisation of the Irish footwear industry.[59] NUBSO had organised its first Irish operatives in Cork in 1885,[60] but had received very meagre support. In the early 1930s, there was considerable hostility to British-based unions and matters were complicated by sectarian rivalries between de Valera's supporters and those who had accepted the treaty. Len Smith, the Union President, and Fred Gould, who was appointed National Organiser for Ireland in October 1931, had to work hard to win the operatives' confidence. Branches were established in each town or city as new factories came into operation.[61] The Irish membership, which stood at 378 in 1932, rose to nearly 3,000 by the end of 1935 and 4,224 by the end of 1937 — by which date roughly 80 per cent of the labour force had been enrolled.[62]

By the end of 1934, terms and conditions virtually equivalent to the British National Agreement had been applied to considerable sections of the industry and agreement had been reached with the manufacturers on the establishment of a National Arbitration Board.[63] As in Britain, negotiations were to be conducted on a national level by a biennial joint conference of NUBSO and the Boot Manufacturers' Federation, and by 1936 about 75 per cent of Irish footwear production was being conducted under the National Agreement.[64] The wage structure of the industry was closely modelled upon the British pattern and was based upon agreed minimum daywork payments and piecework payments.[65] The main method of payment in the footwear industry was originally the piece rate, but by the last quarter of the nineteenth century mechanization had made existing piecework statements obsolete. The manufacturers wanted to adopt daywork so as to prevent wages rising in proportion to output, and this led to the major dispute of 1895. The eventual settlement was a victory for the manufacturers, who were able to use the method of payment they preferred.[66] In practice, this meant that piece-rate working was largely confined to a few of the more skilled operations.

National wage settlements date from the First World War when flat-rate bonuses were given to all workers to meet the rapid increase in the cost of living. In the 1930s, minimum daywork rates for adult workers were settled at the biennial joint conferences and juveniles' minimum rates were graded according to age. Automatic adjustments were made to these rates in accordance with changes in the cost of living index and there were also some negotiated increases to reduce the gap between the earnings of male and female operatives. It should also be noted that most workers did not receive the minimum rate; instead, the minimum rate was used as a basis for calculating 'contract day rates' which were negotiated on a local basis and took the nature of the work being performed into account. Contract rates included bonuses for any work done in excess of the agreed quantity. Where piecework statements were in use, they were set at a rate which gave the average worker an earning capacity of not less than 25 per cent above the equivalent minimum daywork rate.

The major advantage of this system was its flexibility. The nationally-agreed minimum provided a framework within a large number of piecework statements and contract time rates could be negotiated to cater for the great variety of operations performed and for variations in the labour input of different factories and different types of footwear. Consequently, it is hardly surprising that wage agreements in Ireland assumed the same characteristics as the agreements which the NUBSO negotiated with the British footwear manufacturers' federation. Apart from the 'green labour' agreement which was applicable to newly established factories, Irish minimum rates and employment conditions corresponded quite closely to those operating in the United Kingdom.

Much had been achieved within a fairly short time and the unionisation of the Irish footwear industry had proceeded rapidly despite the problems which faced the Union leadership. Apart from the hostility which a British union faced in Ireland, it must be remembered that many of the towns in which footwear factories were located lacked an industrial tradition, and it was not easy to persuade workers that it was in their interest to join the Union. Moreover, the labour force included large numbers of women and juveniles who were considered hard to organise. Steady jobs were at a premium in Ireland and it might appear unwise to antagonise an employer who had indicated his dislike of trade unionism. On the other hand, some workers — notably those at Hallidays', Donaghys', and Woodingtons' factories — felt that wages and conditions were so good as to make membership of a trade union unnecessary. In fact, it was noted in April 1934 that conditions of employment at Hallidays' factory were already equal or superior to those which the Union was trying to establish at other factories.[67] Hallidays however, proved sympathetic to the Union's objectives and insisted that all the operatives joined the Union. Union membership was later made a condition of employment in the factory.

The key-note to Union policy, therefore, was co-operation with the manufacturers in order to establish a framework within which negotiations on wages and conditions could take place on both a national and a local level. And while the Union had been successful in organising the industry and establishing minimum wage rates, its influence was still limited in some respects. For example, the only real control over a manufacturer's powers of hiring and firing operatives was the restriction placed upon the use of juvenile labour, which was not to exceed 25 per cent of the total labour force or 33 per cent of any department. Limited Union power helped to ensure that it would depend upon negotiation and conciliation rather than militancy and confrontation in its dealings with the employers.

By 1936, government officials could look upon the progress of the footwear industry with some satisfaction. In the short term at least, their policies had proved remarkably successful and the footwear industry's growth rate had been far above the national average. Between 1931 and 1936 the gross output of Irish manufacturing industry rose by an average of 10.5 per cent per annum.[68] In the footwear industry, pairage rose by an average of 145.8 per cent per annum in the same period; value of output increased by 90.2 per cent per annum; and average employment increased by 106.2 per cent per annum.[69] These spectacular growth rates were of course achieved upon a very small base; nearly two-thirds of the factories covered by the 1936 *Census of Industrial Production* were new concerns which had commenced operations since 1929.[70] Nevertheless, many of the starting up difficulties had been overcome. Padmore & Barnes, for example, had been able to get its shoes up to an acceptable standard and no longer relied upon imported components to keep the factory running smoothly. The company made a pre-tax profit of £7,616 in the year ending January 1936; although this was quite small in absolute terms, it represented a very good return on capital of about 24 per cent, and in view of this satisfactory state of affairs the board was able to recommend an ordinary dividend of 25 per cent.[71] Woodingtons' profits also increased rapidly to around £16,000 in 1935 and 1936 which represented a return on assets of about 24 per cent.

The growth of the Irish footwear industry was particularly remarkable when compared with the experience of British manufacturers at this time. In the United Kingdom, the growth of mechanisation had permitted output to expand to well beyond the level of demand in the home market, and the industry had come to rely upon export business to a considerable extent. The Depression revealed the vulnerability of export-orientated industries and the footwear industry had to be content with a very modest growth rate; between 1924 and 1935 output rose by just over one per cent per annum.[72] Moreover, there was a steady fall in the value of sales from £46.9 million to £37.6 million.[73] This was partly due to falling raw materials prices and to increased efficiency, but it was also due to the need to hold prices down at a time of high unemployment. Consequently, profit margins were being squeezed and the British factories were faced with the prospect of over-production. In contrast, Irish firms were reaping the benefits of reliance upon the home market, and had been able to expand at a rate which compared favourably with their British counterparts and with Irish manufacturing industry generally. However, the boom years of the early 1930s were followed by recession which was to reveal some of the weaknesses of the Irish footwear industry and demonstrate that a policy of protection and self-sufficiency presented its own peculiar problems.

3

RECESSION IN THE FOOTWEAR INDUSTRY 1936-39

Between 1932 and 1936 the footwear industry had experienced a very rapid growth in output which was largely attributable to government assistance and encouragement. This steady tightening-up of import restrictions was particularly significant; as British competition was progressively excluded by tariffs and quotas, the domestic industry was able to acquire a much larger share of the home market. This process of import substitution proceeded rapidly; Irish factories accounted for 81 per cent of the home market in 1936 and 91 per cent in 1937. This was undoubtedly an impressive achievement, but in the late 1930s the strong upward trend was interrupted, and the footwear industry went into recession.

Many of the problems facing the footwear industry in the late 1930s were essentially due to the nature of the Irish market. Industrialists in Ireland have always had to come to terms with the constraints imposed by the low level of domestic demand. The total population of the Twenty-six Counties was still falling slowly from 2,971,992 in 1926 to 2,965,854 in 1936.[1] Total footwear sales in Ireland were around five million pairs per year;[2] and although this might seem an impressive number, it should be noted that in 1935 just over 100 million pairs were sold in the United Kingdom.[3] Once import substitution had taken place, therefore, the upward trend would quickly be brought to a halt unless the public could be persuaded to buy more shoes. Unfortunately, this was not possible during the 1930s. Per capita consumption was held down by the generally low level of real incomes in Ireland, and by the difficulties caused by the Depression and the Economic War. Moreover, the experience of the footwear industry has usually been that per capita consumption does not change rapidly. Changes in real incomes, fashion trends and the use of branding and advertising have not had much success in persuading the public to buy more pairs of shoes, although they undoubtedly help determine which *quality* and *make* they buy. In Ireland there was little change in the pairage sold per capita until the 1960s. Nor would the Irish manufacturers be able to develop export business as a basis for future growth; the industry was not competitive with foreign rivals, and in any case opportunities for overseas trade were limited in the 1930s by the worldwide move towards protectionism. Between 1936 and 1939 footwear exports totalled just 468 pairs,[4] and exports continued to represent an insignificant proportion of total production until the 1950s.

Protection and self-sufficiency therefore implied stagnation once the existing demand had been met, and this occurred between 1936 and 1938. The establishment of many new factories between 1932 and 1936 meant that the industry could now produce more boots and shoes than it could sell. As manufacturers' stocks of finished goods built up, production cutbacks became inevitable. Total production declined from 4,810,764 pairs in 1936 to 4,610,700 pairs in 1937 and 4,442,592 pairs in 1938.[5]

The consequence for the labour force was redundancy or short time working. In January 1937, for example, Arthur Halliday noted that John Halliday & Son had produced 236,000 pairs of boots and shoes in 1936 and sold 205,000 pairs. Sales for 1937 were unlikely to exceed 200,000 pairs because of growing competition from more recently established manufacturers,[6] and with 31,000 pairs already in hand it was necessary to reduce the factory's output from 5,000 pairs per week to about 3,500.[7] A total of 93 employees — nearly one-third of the labour force — were dismissed in order to keep the rest fully employed.[8] In the industry as a whole, total employment fell by 8 per cent, from 5,974 (October 1936) to 5,508 (October 1938),[9] and the reduction would have been much more drastic if most manufacturers had not opted for short time working instead of redundancy. (Generally speaking, manufacturers were reluctant to make trained workers redundant because they might not be able to get them back if trading conditions improved.) The usual procedure was to work one week on, one week off rather than, say, a three day week, because workers could not claim unemployment benefit for very short lay-offs.[10] Short time working as a consequence of unfilled order books had first begun to occupy the attention of Union officials in June 1936,[11] and by February 1937 there were widespread reports of factories working below capacity.[12] In this month the Cork branch of NUBSO called for a total ban on imports.[13] Kilkenny reported its worst-ever month in November 1937[14] and by the following January the Dundalk branch was asking the other branches to consider closing their membership books because of the number of trained Union members who were out of work.[15]

The market for footwear in Ireland was not only relatively small; it was further sub-divided into a number of distinct sectors. An obvious distinction was between men's, women's and children's shoes, but the market could also be divided according to the type of construction used and the style of footwear involved. In other words, the market tended to become *compartmentalised*, and a company's customers tended to identify it with a certain type of footwear and a certain price bracket. In Britain, this compartmentalisation had progressed to the point where the footwear market could be considered as a number of distinct markets rather than a single entity, and this worked to the manufacturer's advantage. A manufacturer could concentrate upon producing a limited range of footwear, thus reaping the economies associated with specialisation.

In Ireland, however, this sort of concentration was not possible because of the low level of demand. Admittedly, companies tended to be identified with certain types of footwear, and wholesale and retail buyers had no doubts as to where a company's strength lay; John Rawson, for example, was particularly noted for its ladies' fashion shoes, James Winstanley for a wide range of welted and Blake-sewn shoes and John Halliday for welted hobnailed boots. But in Ireland the market was too small to enable manufacturers to specialise in just one type of footwear. Most of the companies which were established before 1934 were primarily heavy boot manufacturers and, as we have seen, this sector was attractive not because it was particularly large, but because the public's needs could be met by a fairly limited range of boots. If the Irish market had been sufficiently large to keep heavy boot manufacturers fully occupied they would have been in a strong position compared with manufacturers of lighter shoes, because the latter usually had to make a much wider variety of different styles in fairly small quantities. Unfortunately, this was not the case because the market for heavy boots was beginning to contract in the 1930s. Rubber boots were beginning to take a significant share of the market for agricultural footwear because they possessed a number of significant advantages. They were cheap but durable, they were waterproof and they were lightweight and flexible. The only company producing rubber boots in Ireland was the Irish Dunlop Company Ltd, which commenced operations in 1936. Output quickly reached 300,000 pairs per year; in comparison leather boot manufacturers produced about 750,000 pairs per annum at this time. In addition, there were growing signs of a general trend towards lighter shoes, particularly in the case of women's and children's footwear. Demand for women's and girls' lace-up boots was declining rapidly and by 1937 they represented only 6 per cent of total women's footwear production.[16] This trend was partcularly associated with the more sophisticated urban markets of the eastern towns where a demand for fashion footwear was beginning to appear before the war.

Heavy boot manufacturers were therefore obliged to produce a variety of other types of lighter footwear — an area in which they lacked production and marketing expertise, and in which they had to compete with a number of companies which already had experience in lighter footwear. The manufacturers of lighter footwear, in turn, were affected by growing competition for sales. The general pattern, then, was that all the Irish manufacturers were facing a shortage of orders, and were casting around for new business to fill their factories. Given that the level of demand was fairly static, manufacturers could only expand at the expense of their rivals, and there was fierce competition for sales. This, inevitably, weakened the footwear manufacturers' position *vis-à-vis* their wholesale and retail customers.

Wholesaling was quite well developed in Ireland in the 1930s, and was especially strong in Cork and Limerick. A number of wholesalers had built up their business via a connection with English exporters; for a variety of reasons, British companies were never particularly successful in mounting their own sales operations in Ireland, and usually appointed an Irish agent to handle sales. The Dublin firm of Mavitty & Nesbitt was probably the best-known agent in Ireland at this time, and had handled Hallidays' and Rawsons' Irish sales before these companies moved to the Free State. With the progressive exclusion of imports from the Irish market, wholesalers were obliged to place an increasing share of their custom with Irish manufacturers. About half of Woodingtons' sales were to wholesalers in 1936/37, major customers including the Dublin firms of Hannan & Co. and Gannon Brothers, and Woods of Sligo.[17] Mavitty & Nesbitt continued to distribute Hallidays' boots and shoes after 1928, and their importance can be gauged by the fact that Thomas Mavitty became Hallidays' first chairman. Similarly, Matthew Connolly continued to handle Wiltshires' accounts after the Bristol company established its Dublin factory in 1934, although he set up a factory of his own in 1936.[18]

The main advantage of dealing with these wholesalers was of course that they were very substantial customers by Irish standards. But there were also a number of drawbacks. The introduction of a middle man meant narrower profit margins for the manufacturers. In addition it was a buyer's market, and wholesalers were in a position to 'shop around'. Buyers would usually view all the competing manufacturers' lines before placing their orders, and could demand quantity discounts and favourable credit terms. In March 1938, when the recession was at its worst and most manufacturers were holding abnormally large stocks, there were reports that wholesalers were wanting to buy at low prices.[19] A decision to increase ex-factory prices required careful consideration, because goodwill counted for little in the wholesale trade, and price was all-important. A matter of a few pence per pair could mean the loss of an order, and this could have serious effects upon a manufacturer who relied upon a few large customers. Consequently, the wholesale footwear market was the sector most prone to price cutting. In view of these considerations, a number of manufacturers began to concentrate upon selling direct to retailers.

Ireland lacked the large department stores and multiple footwear chains which were coming into prominence in the United Kingdom. There were a few multiples — notably Denson Ltd and Tylers Ltd[20] — but by Irish standards any concern with more than five shops was a large multiple, and their activities were largely confined to Dublin and the east coast towns. Apart from these, retailing was in the hands of a large number of small independent concerns. In fact, many of the Irish factories' retail customers were primarily drapers who sold a small quantity of boots and shoes as an extension of their other business, and outside Dublin and the east specialist footwear shops were probably in the minority. Consequently, turnover per retail account was relatively low, and the difficulties of supplying large numbers of small accounts tended to push up the manufacturers' administration and distribution costs. In addition, the cash reserves of many of these small independents were very limited, and this influenced their buying habits. Firstly, they were reluctant to place large advance orders until they saw how a season's lines were selling, and this meant that the flow of orders to the manufacturer tended to be bunched around peak periods of demand. In other words, the retailer did not share the risk with the manufacturer, who was obliged to build up stocks in advance of sales to avoid being swamped by a rush of mid-season orders. Secondly, retailers demanded long credit. The usual terms were 6.25 per cent for seven days and 5 per cent for one month, but small independents were notoriously dilatory in settling their accounts, and still deducted the maximum discount before settling up. The manufacturer, in fact, was obliged to finance his own business because he was not able to obtain similar credit terms from his suppliers; the Irish tanneries' usual terms were 3.5 per cent for seven days or 2.5 per cent for one month, and materials from overseas manufacturers were usually on a cash-with-order basis. Thirdly, the fact that retailers carried very small stocks made the adoption of an 'in-stock' system particularly useful, but the small size of individual accounts increased the expense of maintaining such a scheme.

The nature of the Irish retail market also tended to increase manufacturing costs. Small independent retailers wanted a wide range of styles in small quantities, and the weakness of the footwear market meant that manufacturers had to humour their customers' whims at the expense of production efficiency. Arthur Halliday, for example, felt that it was desirable to provide a full range of footwear lest customers should switch to a rival manufacturer who could meet all their requirements. [21] Opportunities for standardisation were extremely limited, and 'mixed bag' production was the rule. Production of this nature was not very profitable, because it involved short production runs and often led to production bottlenecks as the management and workforce struggled to cope with unfamiliar designs and processes. Flexibility rather than efficiency had to be the key-note in factory organisation, and the lay-out of the machinery had to be capable of frequent adjustment for the production of different lines. Similarly, the need for flexibility placed a premium upon skilled operatives who could quickly adapt to perform a number of different operations. Some workers, although skilled in their own particular speciality, were quite unable to move to a different operation without a substantial drop in their output. This not only complicated the task of balancing the flow of production; it could also lead to a worsening in labour relations if reallocated workers were not compensated for the reduction in their earnings while adapting to a different task. Of course, the problem of combining flexibility with efficiency was hardly new to the footwear industry; indeed the team system had been developed with this in mind. However, if the manufacturer was obliged to accept a series of small and diverse orders, much of the benefit of the team system was lost because of the need to re-balance the team structure whenever a different line was introduced to the production sequence.

Thus the small size of the home market and the structure of wholesaling and retailing in Ireland created serious difficulties for footwear manufacturers in the later 1930s. Fierce competition for sales created a buyer's market, and manufacturers had to accept any orders they could get to fill their factories regardless of their suitability or profitability.

The footwear industry was very much the product of government intervention; and in view of the difficulties which boot and shoe manufacturers faced in the late 1930s, the wisdom of government policy has been questioned in a number of ways. Whilst it is generally accepted that a move towards economic nationalism was inevitable and indeed desirable in the 1930s, it has also been argued that the *type* of encouragement offered had a number of unfortunate effects upon Irish economic development. Keynes, for example, cautioned against a hasty imposition of tariffs and quotas,[22] and Johnson has noted that the warning was not heeded; government officials were often overoptimistic about the possibilities for industrial expansion, and duties and quotas were often levied in an arbitrary fashion. Protection did not rest upon a reasoned assessment of the best types of stimuli to apply but instead owed much to the emotional atmosphere engendered by the Economic War.[23] Three more specific criticisms have also been made: firstly, that the government encouraged the establishment of an excessive number of small weak firms; secondly, that the government failed to make the most of its opportunities to influence the location of factories; and thirdly, that government officials created problems by their attempts to encourage intermediate industries as well as consumer goods industries. How justified are these criticisms?

The footwear industry does provide some evidence to support the assertion that the Irish economy was characterised by an excessive number of small firms of below-average productivity.[24] In the mid-1930s, the number of footwear factories in Ireland continued to grow rapidly. The total number of footwear establishments listed in the *Census of Industrial Production* — excluding clog makers and manufacturers of shoe components — rose from

23 in 1935 to 31 in 1936 and 35 in 1937. It is also clear that this was typically an industry of small concerns; only seven companies employed more than 250 workers, and only two more than 500 (see Table 3, Chapter 2).

In the 1930s at least, smallness did not neccessarily mean inefficiency. In the British footwear industry at this time, Hillman found that buying departments functioned most efficiently in firms employing 120-450 workers, but that factories employing 40-60 workers were able 'to reap all possible technical efficiencies'.[25] This was largely due to the ability of small firms to lease sophisticated, up-to-date machinery. Similar conditions applied in Ireland, and meant that a small footwear factory was a practical proposition; this, after all, was one of the reasons why the industry was deemed suitable for encouragement by the Fianna Fáil government. But if the economies of scale were relatively limited, this was not true of the economies of specialisation; long production runs were the key to efficiency, and small firms should ideally produce a fairly limited range of shoes. In Ireland in the later 1930s, however, this was not possible; as we have seen, footwear manufacturers were obliged to produce a 'mixed bag' in small quantities for the limited home market. Fierce competition for sales, surplus production capacity and the prevalence of short time working also suggested that too many footwear factories had been established.

From the mid-1930s, there were growing complaints from footwear manufacturers and trade union officials, who were quick to blame government officials for their difficulties. The industry demanded an end to the encouragement of new firms by the Department of Industry and Commerce, and, if possible, the introduction of measures designed to prevent new producers from entering the industry.[26] The government, however, was not willing to meet these demands. It must be remembered that the creation of new jobs was a major part of Fianna Fáil policy. The establishment of new factories might not be to the advantage of existing footwear manufacturers, but it might well confer more general economic and social advantages. In addition, it may be questioned whether the Department of Industry and Commerce really had the power to determine the number of footwear factories in operation. The Department could prevent foreign-owned firms from setting up in overcrowded sections of the industry, but it was not in a position to prevent the establishment of Irish-owned firms which did not need a licence. Although the Department was well aware of the problem of overcapacity, it could do little to dissuade Irish businessmen from entering the industry. Moreover, it would have been politically very damaging to have been seen to be trying to prevent the establishment of Irish firms in an industry which already had a substantial British presence. It is clear, therefore, that the government was in a difficult position, its powers being limited by both legal and political constraints. Although Fianna Fáil took a much wider responsibility for economic development than its predecessors had done, this was still far from a totally planned economy. One should not make too much of the criticisms of interested parties like established manufacturers or trade union officials. Nevertheless, there is no doubt that the existence of surplus production capacity was to cause long-lasting problems for the Irish footwear industry.

The second criticism which has been made of government policy in the 1930s is that more could have been done to influence the location of footwear factories.[27] In footwear manufacturing, as in many other industries, the locational advantages of Dublin were overwhelming. It was by far the biggest market, and was the major centre for a number of important ancillary services, including BUSMC's Irish headquarters and service depot. It also possessed good road, rail and sea communications. However, the government wanted to ensure the economic development of the whole of the Free State not just the Dublin region, and further concentration of industry in Dublin was discouraged whenever possible. Of the newer footwear factories, none were located in Dublin, and the choice of a relatively under-developed location was a virtual guarantee of whole-hearted support from the Minister of Industry and Commerce.[28] Such a policy made a good deal of sense in political and social terms but it has been argued that the government did not make the most of its opportunity to influence the location of footwear industries because it did not make any attempt to encourage concentration of the industry into a few suitable areas. Instead, the 1962 Report of the Committee on Industrial Organisation argued that the policy of decentralisation followed after 1932 tended to mean location as far as possible from Dublin without any significant effort at centralisation or concentration elsewhere.[29] There was some evidence of concentration in Louth, with three factories in Dundalk and two at Drogheda, but most of the other factories were spread throughout the eastern half of the country, and there were also a few manufacturers in the west such as Dubarry Shoemakers at Ballinasloe and R. Hilliard & Sons at Killarney. In its survey of the Irish footwear industry, the Committee on Industrial Organisation therefore concluded that

> analysis of the various locations does not suggest that the factors which, in location theory, are regarded as the most important were generally uppermost in the minds of those selecting locations for footwear factories here.[30]

Such statements require close examination. It must be noted that the Department of Industry and Commerce's ability to determine the location of footwear factories was in fact limited; in many cases locations were determined by local businessmen or local development associations. The

Department, in short, could encourage but not dictate the choice of a suitable location.

It should also be emphasised that the advantages of centralisation were not so clear-cut in Ireland as they were in Britain. Firstly, a high coefficient of localisation is particularly desirable in industries which display producer interdependence to a marked degree. In Britain the shoemaking industry had reached a point where there were advantages in specialisation; many manufacturers relied upon specialists for a wide variety of ancillary services, and there was also some evidence of co-operation between manufacturers in the interests of efficiency. This was not the case in Ireland; competition for sales made the manufacturers fiercely independent. Secondly, the location of footwear factories in areas outside the heavily populated Dublin conurbation was not necessarily disadvantageous from the point of view of the supply of labour; other important variables were the level of demand from other local industries and the age structure and quality of the labour supply.[31] In Ireland, of course, competition for labour was hardly a problem; a considerable number of the workers taken on by the footwear factories had been previously unemployed. Ireland's demographic structure meant that juvenile labour was particularly abundant, and in most footwear factories considerable numbers of juveniles were employed on less skilled tasks. As for the quality of the labour force, the lack of established centres of footwear production with a pool of trained labour meant that one location was pretty much as good — or as bad — as another. Most manufacturers agreed that the biggest headache was not the actual training of operatives but the more fundamental problem of accustoming their employees to the discipline of factory production. The concept of working steadily from eight to six was alien to them, and it took some time to accustom them to the routine of factory production. This problem affected manufacturers in the larger eastern towns as well as those in more rural areas. For example, Dundalk was considered to be an attractive location for footwear manufacture because it already possessed something of an industrial tradition[32] but many of the town's footwear operatives had not been employed in industry before.

The lack of centralisation in the Irish footwear industry, therefore, was not as serious as one might have supposed. However, a dispersed location pattern did have some drawbacks which tended to worsen over time. In particular, it prevented the establishment of any centralised training facilities and tended to emphasise the insularity of individual companies — a characteristic which, according to the Committee on Industrial Progress, tended to mitigate against innovation and rationalisation in the industry.[33]

The third criticism of government policy in the 1930s is that it tended to increase raw materials costs. Despite the emphasis on protectionism and self-sufficiency, the footwear industry, like many of the industries encouraged by de Valera's government, was obliged to import most of its raw materials. Many items could not be made economically in the small quantities Irish manufacturers required, and were therefore obtained from British suppliers. These included lasts, knives, patterns, tacks, thread, inks and dyes. It was inevitable that imports of these materials should rise as the output of the Irish footwear factories grew, and it was of course preferable to import raw materials rather than finished goods. But there was a conflict of interests when Irish raw materials were available. The supply of leather to the footwear industry is a case of point. The government wanted to revitalise the Irish leather industry, which had been in decline in recent years because of British competition.[34] Duties were placed on imported leather,[35] and the government insisted that Irish footwear manufacturers should use an increasing proportion of home-produced leather. As a result, new tanneries were opened and output rose rapidly.[36] But this development did not in general work to the advantage of the footwear manufacturers. Foreign leather was cheap and available in a wide range of grades, finishes and colours. Irish leather was much less desirable. The choice was limited, and the quality distinctly variable — Irish hides were often blemished by fly holes, and Irish flaying and tanning was held to be inferior to foreign work.[37] Home-produced leathers were also relatively expensive. In 1936, for example, the average cost of imported sole and insole leather was £5.95 per hundredweight; the average cost of similar leathers from Irish tanners was £7.20 per hundredweight.[38]

This demonstrated one of the drawbacks of a policy of autarky; it is always very difficult to deal effectively with 'intermediate' commodities which are the finished product of one industry and the raw material of another. Footwear manufacturers would undoubtedly have preferred to continue importing their leather, and argued that they should be encouraged at the expense of the tanners because their industry was the bigger employer.[39] But this argument was not acceptable to the government; it was considered that the interests of the economy as a whole dictated that protection should be extended to both the footwear industry and the leather industry.

How, then, are we to assess the economic policies of the Fianna Fáil government in the 1930s? Clearly, the government faced a very difficult task. Political and social considerations, as well as purely economic considerations, had to be taken into account; and the experience of the footwear industry indicated the problems, as well as the benefits, associated with protectionist policies. But we must be careful not to make too much of the criticisms which have been levelled at Fianna Fáil's economic policies. Such criticisms are easily made with the advantage of hindsight and it must be remembered that techniques of economic planning have progressed considerably in recent decades. As Dr Garret Fitzgerald has commented,

It was probably better that a somewhat haphazard and patchy industrial structure should spring up behind these rather ill-considered protective walls than that the industrial development should be impeded by over-caution.[40]

This survey of the economic climate in which the footwear industry was operating gives rise to two important questions. Firstly, it has been argued that, for a variety of reasons, production costs were rising significantly in the later 1930s, and that profitability was consequently low. To determine whether this is correct, we need to examine the statistical evidence relating to the industry as a whole and to individual firms. Secondly, we need to examine the *response* of individual companies to the production and marketing problems which they experienced in this period.

To begin with, Appendix I suggests that the total pairage produced by the Irish footwear factories between 1936 and 1938 dropped by about 7.7 per cent. But the value of sales dropped by only 2 per cent, and it is therefore evident that manufacturers were able to make some price increases. After falling from 61.0p to 37.5p per pair between 1930 and 1936, the average ex-factory price of Irish-produced leather footwear then began to rise, reaching 43.4p by 1939. A more detailed examination of the *Census of Industrial Production* data also reveals that this trend was common to all sectors of the market, and suggests that a general increase in prices was needed because all the Irish manufacturers were faced by increased manufacturing costs. The manufacturers agreed, however, that rising ex-factory prices were insufficient to offset the increase in manufacturing costs, and that the intense competition for sales had obliged them to absorb part of the increase.

There is some evidence to support this contention. There was certainly a marked increase in the cost of raw materials during the latter half of the decade, and it seems clear that this was primarily caused by the switch to Irish-made leather. The effect of protection was to push up leather prices above world levels, and between 1936 and 1938 the average price per hundredweight of undressed sole and insole leather used by the footwear industry rose by about 24 per cent, from £4.90 to £6.10. Dressed upper leather exhibited a similar trend.

Labour costs also rose in the late 1930s, and this requires some explanation; if Ireland had a serious unemployment problem, why was the footwear industry unable to benefit from cheap labour? A number of observers have stated that minimum wage rates in Ireland at this time were rather higher than their British equivalents.[41] Ireland shared a common labour market with Britain, and it may be that manufacturers had to set wage rates at a level sufficient to prevent trained workers from migrating towards better employment opportunities in Britain. This argument needs to be stated with caution because of the assumptions it makes about the mobility of labour at this time, but it was probably significant in the case of clickers and the other more skilled operatives.

The unionisation of the footwear industry also had an influence upon wage rates. In some respects union influence was fairly limited; it could not prevent redundancies and short time working in 1937-38, and nor could it arrest the wildcat strikes which sometimes resulted.[42] But it had been able to obtain a National Agreement which in some respects was actually superior to its British counterpart. By September 1939, the minimum day work rate stood at £3.20 for men and £2.10 for women, compared with the British minima of £2.90 and £1.90 respectively.[43] In addition, the working week was cut from 48 to 44 hours at the beginning of June 1936, and there was an across-the-board wage rise of 7.5 per cent to make up for the loss of earnings.[44] In Britain the working week fell from 48 hours in 1936 to 46 hours in 1938 and 45 hours in 1939.[45]

It might seem strange, in view of the difficulties which the industry was facing, that manufacturers did not attempt to reduce minimum wage rates. The explanation may be that wage bargaining in the Irish footwear industry was based upon National Agreements made between the Union and the Boot Manufacturers' Federation; as individual manufacturers could not obtain an advantage over their competitors, and as the industry as a whole did not have to be competitive with foreign producers, perhaps the Federation was not quite as wage rate conscious as might have been expected. Minimum day work rates, of course, do not tell the whole story. Average earnings tended to be rather nearer the minimum wage in Ireland than they were in Britain; the workers were less experienced, and opportunities to earn bonuses were very limited.

Nevertheless, it seems clear that labour *costs* were higher than in Britain because productivity was relatively low; short-time working and mixed-bag production were inefficient. Pairage per operative had risen fairly quickly between 1932 and 1936 as the new Irish factories got into full production, but the 1936 figure was still only 80 per cent of the average per capita output of the British footwear industry, and the gap widened again as the trade recession of 1937-38 took effect.[46] Another reason why labour costs were rising in this period was that most Irish operatives were not on piece work. Increases in day work rates were made according to changes in the cost of living rather than changes in labour productivity, and the extension of protection to many domestic consumer goods industries pushed up the cost of living in the later 1930s.[47] In view of this, it may be asked why the Irish manufacturers did not switch to piece rate working. According to Arthur Halliday, the reason was that the original piece work statement, which was made by the Cork manufacturers and the local trade union branch, and which was later embodied in the National Agreement, was set too high, and hence piece work was not attractive to the manufacturers. On the other hand, it may be that the manufacturers did not want to adopt piece work because it would have significantly reduced operatives' earnings at a time of falling output, causing industrial unrest and the loss of trained workers.

It seems clear that increases in ex-factory prices were insufficient to offset the combined effect of increased raw materials prices and labour costs. Table 6 provides a summary of the aggregate data provided by the *Census of Industrial Production*. In the *Census*, the cost of materials, fuel and packaging is deducted from 'gross output' (net selling value) to give a 'net output' figure; wages and salaries are then deducted to given 'remainder of net output' (manufacturing profit). It does not give a full account of manufacturing costs, therefore, but is probably as complete as can be expected, given the diversity of accounting methods in use and the need to retain confidentiality.

The data shows that the ratio between manufacturing profit and net selling

TABLE 6

Manufacturing profit in the Irish footwear industry, 1936-9

	Gross output £	Remainder of net output £	Remainder of net output as % gross output £
1936	1,822,102	350,921	19.3
1937	1,793,454	299,893	16.7
1938	1,743,206	284,953	16.3
1939	2,024,145	350,368	17.3

Source: *Census of Industrial Production.*

value fell significantly between 1936 and 1938, and then began to recover. Unfortunately, the information provided by the *Census of Industrial Production* is insufficiently detailed to permit an examination of pre-tax net profits and returns on assets. In particular, no information is given on administration and distribution costs; although they were fairly low in comparison with materials costs and manufacturing wages, they tended to rise as output fell below full capacity. The general impression is that the industry's net profit was falling and that the return on capital was unsatisfactory, but to evaluate this proposition it is necessary to consider the performance of individual companies.

Not surprisingly, detailed information on profitability in the 1930s is hard to come by. Printed reports and accounts are of course available for the two public companies, Padmore & Barnes and J.H. Woodington, and the latter company has also made available a considerable quantity of unpublished material. Most of Hallidays' records have also survived, but the other private companies have been unable or unwilling to supply any information.

The evidence which has been obtained via individual companies confirms that in relative terms there was a significant increase in manufacturing costs. A brief summary of the figures for Hallidays and Woodingtons is given in the following table, although the use of differing accounting methods means that they are not directly comparable either with each other or with the *Census of Industrial Production* figures for the industry as a whole.

TABLE 7

Cost of materials, manufacturing wages and other manufacturing costs, 1936-39

	Materials as % net selling value	Manufacturing wages as % N.S.V.	Other manufacturing costs as % N.S.V.	Manufacturing profit as % N.S.V.
John Halliday & Son Ltd				
1936	n.a.	n.a.	n.a.	n.a.
1937	55.4	19.3	6.4	18.9
1938	58.8	23.8	8.4	9.0
1939	48.0	19.9	7.4	24.7
J.H. Woodington Drogheda (1936) Ltd				
1936	44.9	21.7	3.2	30.2
1937	47.2	26.4	4.6	21.8
1938	62.1	22.6	3.3	12.0
1939	37.8	27.9	3.1	31.2

Source: company accounts.

These figures confirm that there was an increase in the cost of materials, especially in the case of J.H.Woodington. This was largely due to increased leather prices, but wages and other manufacturing costs also increased, and in both cases there was a marked reduction in manufacturing profits. Warehouse, sales and administration costs cannot be given for Hallidays because of the way the accounts were compiled, but at Woodingtons they increased steadily from 13.8 per cent of net selling value in 1934 to 17.0 per cent in 1938.

Table 8 provides information on the pre-tax profits and return on capital of Hallidays, Woodingtons and (where available) Padmore & Barnes. Clearly, profits were very small, and represented a very unsatisfactory return on turnover and assets. Moreover, by Irish standards these were fairly substantial companies which possessed the advantage of British ownership, and it is hard to believe that smaller, Irish-owned companies fared any better.

TABLE 8

Pre-tax net profit and return on turnover and assets, 1936-39

	Turnover £000	Net profit £000	Net profit as % turnover	Net profit as % total assets
John Halliday & Son Ltd				
1936	125	9	7.2	14.1
1937	114	3	2.6	4.3
1938	120	(loss 3)	—	—
1939	153	9	5.9	11.5
J.H. Woodington Drogheda (1936) Ltd				
1936	106	16	15.1	13.9
1937	86	6	7.0	5.2
1938	80	3	3.8	2.8
1939	97	7	7.2	6.1
Padmore & Barnes (Ireland) Ltd				
1936	n.a.	11	n.a.	16.7
1937	n.a.	8	n.a.	13.9
1938	n.a.	6	n.a.	10.9
1939	n.a.	8	n.a.	20.0

Source: Company accounts.

Incidentally, Woodingtons' profit/assets ratio was particularly poor because, unlike any other Irish footwear company, it was overcapitalised. The company went public in 1936, and a new company, J.H. Woodington Drogheda (1936) Ltd, was formed with a capital of £100,000. J.H. Woodington picked a very opportune moment, for the company's performance at this time seemed very satisfactory, and goodwill was valued at £30,000. This was nearly double the starting capital of the firm just four years earlier. In the light of the company's subsequent experience, however, this was clearly excessive, and over-capitalisation was to prove a continuing problem.

In general, it appears that the heavy boot manufacturers were worst hit by the recession. Their profits were badly hit by the declining demand for their products and the consequent need for 'mixed bag' production. Hallidays' and

Woodingtons' return on assets was appreciably worse than that of Padmore & Barnes, and it is noticeable that the two Irish companies which were least affected by short time working were Traly Footwear Ltd and Leslie Cunnington Ltd of Munster,[48] neither of which made heavy boots.

Manufacturers of light footwear appear to have fared somewhat better, although their profits were also affected by the fierce competition for sales. There is some evidence to suggest that these companies' costs were lower because they were usually more recently established than the heavy boot manufacturers, and hence employed a greater proportion of green and juvenile labour.[49] Although this was partially offset by the lower productivity of inexperienced workers and the extra costs associated with the starting-up period, it must be remembered that during the recession the minimisation of costs rather than the maximisation of output was of prime importance. With the trend towards lighter shoes it was becoming apparent that this sector offered a more secure basis for future growth, and although firms like Padmore & Barnes and John Rawson undoubtedly had their own problems they could afford to be somewhat less pessimistic than heavy boot manufacturers like Edward Donaghy or J.H. Woodington.

This examination of profitability confirms that the recession was indeed a serious one. This poses two interrelated questions. Did the recession lead to an abnormally large number of failures among footwear firms? And did the industry become increasingly oligopolistic as weaker companies went to the wall?

The *Census of Industrial Production* shows that there was indeed a reduction in the number of footwear producers in Ireland. After reaching a peak of 45 in 1937 the number of establishments included in the *Census* fell to 43 in 1938 and 37 in 1939. But it seems clear that only the very weakest concerns went out of business; the largest to do so was probably Messrs Edwards' Dublin factory which closed in January 1939 with the loss of 50 jobs.[50] Generally speaking, footwear manufacturers preferred to soldier on, only closing if losses reached alarming proportions. Two factors helped to explain why they chose this course of action. Firstly, most of a company's capital was tied up in stocks and current debts, and could not be easily realised if it was liquidated. In addition, the other manufacturers were unlikely to want to take over an unsuccessful factory as a going concern at a time when they were having difficulties in keeping their own factories busy. Secondly, most footwear producers were privately-owned firms, and there was a natural reluctance to close down or sell out. Owners were often prepared to continue devoting their time to an unremunerative business in the hope that trading conditions would improve.

These considerations presented an obstacle to oligopoly. Generally speaking, an oligopolistic structure is usually associated with industries in which the economies of scale are considerable and where there is a marked lack of differentiation between the products of competing manufacturers. Under these circumstances, the wealthier and more dynamic companies can reap these economies and develop strong branding policies to persuade the public that their products, although apparently similar to the competition, actually possess qualities which made them particularly desirable. The Irish footwear industry was indeed characterised by a lack of product differentiation; shoes from different manufacturers were often very similar and did not possess distinctive features based on superior design or different construction. An obvious point is that nearly all the Irish manufacturers used BUSMC machinery, and no company possessed a technological advantage. A lack of differentiation was probably inevitable in the heavy boot sector, but it also applied to the light footwear manufacturers. Most Irish companies concentrated upon the middle-price tickets; competition for imports was still significant in the high-price sector, and in any case demand was very limited. Similarly, the lack of a quantity market meant that the mass production of cheap footwear was unattractive.

But in Ireland this did not lead to strong branding policies, and in general brands were mere distinguishing names rather than the pivot of a strong marketing policy. Most companies lacked marketing expertise, and tended to sell on the basis of price rather than brand reputation.

Nor was there any evidence of a move towards oligopoly. Apart from the reluctance of many owners to become involved in take-overs, it must be remembered that mixed bag production predominated, and opportunities for specialisation were very limited. Moreover, there was nothing to suggest that large footwear companies were necessarily more efficient, either in Ireland or the United Kingdom.[51] According to Silverman, the optimum size of a footwear factory was as low as 5,000 pairs per week.[52] This was the approximate size of Hallidays, Padmore & Barnes and Woodingtons at this time, although Rawsons was considerably larger, producing perhaps 10,000 pair per week in the late 1930s. Finally, it may be asked which Irish firms, if any, could reasonably be expected to dominate the Irish market.

They would have to be companies primarily interested in light shoes rather than heavy boots,[53] with sufficient capital to wear down the competition by dropping prices and offering good credit terms. A British connection and strong management would also be a major advantage. The two companies which come to mind are Rawsons and Woodingtons. The former was already the largest footwear producer in Ireland, while the latter was unique in possessing capital reserves which exceeded its current requirements. As we shall see, the possibility of a merger between John Rawson and John Halliday & Son was briefly considered, but neither Rawsons nor Woodingtons was able to take over weaker rivals and thus increase its market share during the recession. This was partly due to the fact that they operated under British ownership; the Irish government was unlikely to respond favourably to the domination of the Irish market by a British company. It was also due, however, to a number of problems which faced these particular companies. In the case of Rawsons, the company was beset by labour difficulties which, as we have seen, were due both to sectarian disputes and the attitude of management. Labour troubles at Rawsons came to a head in April 1937, when the management resorted to drastic measures. After a three-day unofficial strike, the factory manager, F.J. Scott, closed the factory and sacked all 652 employees. The factory remained closed for a fortnight, and the labour force was then re-employed department by department. Eventually 592 operatives were taken back, but the remainder, whom the company considered the hardcore of militants who had instigated the trouble, were not re-hired.[54] Although Rawsons' actions met with widespread opposition, the Union was not able to secure their reinstatement, nor stop the subsequent employment of green labour to replace the trouble-makers.[55]

Another reason why the company was unable to dominate the industry was that Benjamin Rawson retained close personal control, and even relatively minor decisions had to be referred to Leicester for his consideration. As the Irish executives were deprived of responsibility it was very difficult for them to operate successfully at a time when flexibility and adaptability were of vital importance. A similar point could also be made about Woodingtons. In comparison with other Irish footwear companies, Woodingtons was fairly sophisticated in its use of accounting and budgeting methods; six-monthly budgets and balance sheets were prepared and quite detailed monthly figures could be abstracted from its accounts. But it seems clear that this information was prepared for the benefit of Mr. J.H. Woodington himself, who retained a controlling interest in the company and who still lived in the West of England. His Irish directors, who were responsible for day-to-day decision making, often found it very difficult to get the information they needed to run the business efficiently.[56]

In short, the characteristics of the Irish footwear market, coupled with the fact that no Irish company really possessed a significant advantage over its competitors, meant that the industry did not move towards oligopoly as the recession took effect. Instead, it continued to consist of a fairly large number of small companies, which continued operating despite profit records which represented a very unsatisfactory return on assets.

It remains to consider what remedies were adopted by individual companies. The most usual reaction to the problem of falling sales was, as we have seen, to switch to short time working and cast around for new lines to fill the factory. In many cases it was a question of taking any orders that were going, but some manufacturers attempted to introduce new ranges to complement their existing products.[57] There was also evidence of a general tightening-up of production costs; although not much could be done to reduce labour costs, most companies tried to use their materials as efficiently as possible and keep rejects to a minimum.[58] In addition, there was a tendency to return unnecessary machinery to BUSMC, although manufacturers had to keep some spare machines in reserve in case of breakdowns or an upswing in demand. A number of companies also began to move towards direct selling to retailers, thus avoiding the very cut-throat wholesale sector. In 1938, for example, Woodingtons actually increased its prices to wholesalers in order to encourage retailers to buy direct from the factory.[59]

The most significant development, however, was Hallidays' decision to commence production of good quality women's and children's footwear — a decision which eventually enabled the company to leave the declining heavy boot sector altogether. There were, however, two problems which had to be overcome. Firstly, there was a shortage of working capital for the new venture; and secondly, Hallidays lacked technical expertise outside the heavy boot sector. Its initial range of women's shoes was not successful and it quickly became apparent that outside assistance was needed.

One suggestion which was considered by Hallidays' board, was the possibility of an amalgamation with Rawsons — a much larger company with greater resources and an established reputation for women's footwear. Benjamin Rawson had indicated his willingness to amalgamate,[60] and a joint office arrangement, whereby Hallidays undertook much of Rawsons' administration work, was already in existence. Unfortunately, a merger would imply a virtual take-over by Rawsons, which would supply approximately four-fifths of the total assets of an amalgamated company.[61] There were also personal objections to Benjamin Rawson's autocratic style, and relations between the two companies were not improved by Hallidays' decision to enter into direct competition with Rawsons in the women's sector.

This proposal, therefore, did not receive any further attention and Hallidays' board had to examine other means of solving the company's financial and technical problems. Arthur Halliday had already taken the decision to approach C. & J. Clark Ltd of Street for the assistance which the company needed.[62] The approach to Clarks marks the turning-point in Hallidays' fortunes. Until then, the company was merely an average-sized concern of undistinguished profitability — in short, a typical representative of the Irish footwear industry. The agreement with Clarks was not exactly a panacea for the shortcomings of the Irish company, but thereafter — and especially after 1945 when conditions returned to some semblance of normality — Hallidays was able to acquire a steadily increasing share of the Irish market.

The choice of Clarks was an obvious one; Arthur Halliday already knew the Clark family, and he was also aware of their unrivalled reputation for women's and children's shoes. Of the British manufacturers, Clarks alone had been able to expand during the recession in the early 1930s. Above all, Clarks led in the vital field of last design and the company's chief lastmaker, Teddy Mackay, was highly regarded in the British industry. Arthur Halliday wanted Clarks' lasts for his women's shoes, and he wanted Sidney Lowry, Clarks' sales chief in Ireland, to sell them for him.[63]

Clarks was also favourably disposed towards the idea of production under licence for the Irish market, because, as we have seen, it lacked managerial strength and was unwilling to tie up capital in an Irish venture. Given a suitable opportunity, Clarks was prepared to come to an agreement, because its sales in the Free State were rapidly dwindling. In the 1920s the company had had a very good business in Ireland, for Sidney Lowry was a very successful salesman, and shoes manufactured under the Clarks brand were well received by retailers. After the introduction of quotas by de Valera's government, Lowry was forced to concentrate upon Ulster, and his sales in the Twenty-six Counties fell from £20,000 in 1930 to £4,000 in 1938.[64] Although Arthur Halliday was not aware of it, the negotiations between Padmore & Barnes and C. & J. Clark had not yet been finally broken off. Two other approaches by Irish companies had also been evaluated and rejected by Clarks' board.[65] John Halliday & Son possessed a substantial advantage over Padmore & Barnes in that it was no longer associated with an English parent company, and after visits to Bancroft Clark and Sidney Lowry in July 1937,[66] Clarks' solicitors, Arthur Cox & Co. of Dublin, began the preparation of an agreement between the two companies.[67]

After much negotiation, a five-year contract was signed in February 1938, and came into effect on 1 April of that year.[68] Clarks was to provide lasts, patterns, and designs, together with all the technical advice and assistance needed to bring Hallidays' products up to the standard associated with the Clarks brand. John Halliday & Son was to remain in control of manufacturing and was to pay a royalty of 2.5p per pair[69] with a minimum payment of £2,000 per annum.[70] Clarks wanted to retain control of sales and of its trade marks, and so a subsidiary, Clarks Ireland Ltd, was set up.[71] Clarks Ireland Ltd actually owned the trade marks, designs and lasts and retained sole selling rights for Clarks shoes in Ireland. Sidney Lowry was to be employed by Clarks Ireland to sell the shoes which Halliday made under the Clarks brand, a vital position from which he could offer Hallidays' management the benefit of his experience with Clarks shoes whilst keeping Street informed as to the progress of the new venture.

In theory, therefore, John Halliday & Son and Clarks Ireland remained separate companies, one responsible for manufacturing, the other for sales and technical support. But in practice, the division between the companies was not at all clear-cut, for Hallidays handled Clarks Ireland's administrative work and they possessed an identical board of directors. The relationship between the two companies was seriously questioned by the Department for Industry and Commerce on the grounds that it was merely a device to circumvent the legislation and establish a degree of foreign control over a protected industry — which of course it was — but thanks to Cox's careful work it could not be challenged, and remained in force until the coming of free trade in the 1970s.[72]

For Clarks, the big advantage of this agreement was that it could use John Halliday & Son to gain access to the Irish market, instead of relying on its own resources. The initial outlay was quite small in view of the potential returns; nevertheless, Clarks did begin to acquire a steadily growing interest in Hallidays to bind the companies closer together,[73] and a considerable amount of effort was invested in the project. Hallidays got good value for the fees it paid. It was able to send operatives and supervisory staff to Street for training, and received expert advice; for example, James Hill, Clarks' chief chemist, made frequent visits to Dundalk.[74] Particularly important was the ability of Sidney Lowry to overcome the prejudice against Irish-made footwear, and convince the trade that his lines were saleable at Clarks' current prices. He was able to suggest a number of ways in which the quality of the product could be improved,[75] and he quickly established Clarks as the best brand for women's and children's footwear in Ireland.

Starting-up costs led to a small loss, but Clarks Ireland's sales rose rapidly from £16,000 in 1938 to £51,000 in 1939.[76] Although the move into women's and children's shoes did not enable Hallidays to drop its existing lines, sales of Clarks brand shoes via Clarks Ireland Ltd represented 33 per cent of Hallidays' turnover in 1939, and made a substantial contribution to the improvement in the company's trading record. In addition, the company was largely able to avoid the short time working which bedevilled the other heavy boot manufacturers.[77]

Clearly, Hallidays' response to the problems facing footwear manufacturers (and especially heavy boot manufacturers) during the recession was exceptional, and it was to prove exceptionally successful; during the next two decades, the company moved steadily towards a position of market leadership, and the growing reputation of Clarks brand shoes enabled it to introduce an element of monopoly pricing. As far as the other manufacturers were concerned, however, it is hard to avoid the conclusion that they simply concentrated on soldiering on with their existing lines, making the most of such opportunities as became available and hoping that the market would improve.

By the beginning of 1939, there were signs that the worst of the recession was over. Total output for 1939 was nearly as high as the 1936 peak, at 4,801,392 pairs, and most manufacturers reported a considerable improvement in turnover and profits.[78] NUBSO reported a decrease in short time working,[79] and the total number employed in the industry showed a slight rise in 1938.[80] This was partly due to a general improvement in the state of the economy. Wage rises and reduced unemployment led to an increased demand for consumer goods, in which the footwear industry shared. This general improvement was in turn partly due to the normalisation of relations with the United Kingdom under the Anglo-Irish Free Trade agreement of April 1938. Briefly, the agreement brought the Economic War to an end. It permitted free entry into Britain for most Irish exports, whilst allowing Ireland to continue to protect her new industries.

Footwear manufacturers, however complained that government activity continued to have an adverse effect upon their sales. The real damage was done by the uncertainty over the future of quotas; although the Irish government reserved the right to use quotas to protect its industries, it was agreed that they would be reviewed by the Eire Prices Commission with a view to replacing them by a duty which would take into account the relative costs of production in the two countries.[81] This proposal was resisted by the Irish footwear manufacturers, who believed that the industry relied upon the *exclusion* of British competition, and that this could be achieved by quotas but not by tariffs. The manufacturers' fears seemed justified by a drop in orders when the terms of the agreement became known. Many retailers and wholesalers anticipated a flood of imports, and held off the market until the future of quotas was decided.[82] In fact, the Boot Manufacturers' Federation and NUBSO were able to present a strong case for the retention of quotas when the Price Commission finally began its review towards the end of 1938,[83] and a decision was never made,[84] but the effect of the uncertainty was to prolong the recession. It was not until early in 1939 that the normalisation of trading conditions began to have a beneficial effect upon the footwear industry.

It also seems clear that the ending of the recession was not due to the solution of the fundamental problems which had faced the footwear manufacturers. Only John Halliday & Son had taken decisive action to solve its difficulties, and despite the low level of profit margins, most companies paid little attention before the Second World War to the problems of co-ordinating sales and design policy and organising labour and machinery for maximum output efficiency. The general improvement was largely due to the fact that the manufacturers, by dint of short time working and production cut-backs, had adjusted their output in accordance with the level of demand. Once demand had been cut, the manufacturers were able gradually to dispose of their accumulated stocks through their retail and wholesale customers; and as further orders came in they were able to reduce short time working, although most companies continued to operate below their potential capacity. The basic problem of an excessive number of footwear manufacturers operating in a small and highly competitive home market, therefore, had not been solved. Although it eased during the Second World War, when the manufacturers were preoccupied with shortages of raw materials rather than inadequate demand, it was to cause renewed difficulties as the footwear industry adjusted to post-war conditions.

4

THE FOOTWEAR INDUSTRY DURING THE EMERGENCY
1939-45

Although Ireland remained neutral, the Second World War inevitably had a profound effect upon her economy. In the 1930s, factors operating on the demand side had been the principal determinant of industrial performance; during the Emergency, industrialists and government officials were to be preoccupied by problems of supply. Despite the emphasis on self-sufficiency, the Irish economy still depended upon imports for a wide range of raw materials and producer goods, together with those consumer goods which could not be competitively produced on a small scale. Britain was by far the most important supplier, and her wartime needs, coupled with the effect of the U-boat blockade, meant that she could no longer meet Ireland's requirements; imports from Britain fell sharply, especially in 1942-43. Irish exports fell more slowly because of the demand for foodstuffs in Britain, and in 1943-44 Ireland's external trade balance showed a small surplus for the first time since the establishment of the Free State.[1] Ireland's dollar reserves were also growing because remittances continued to come in from Irish emigrants to the United States. Nevertheless, Irish manufacturers found it difficult to use these reserves to develop alternative sources of essential supplies because of the British embargo on the supply of a wide range of 'strategic goods' to neutral countries. And in November 1939 the American government prohibited its merchant ships from entering the war zone; consequently, all American cargoes had to be transhipped at Lisbon, which was costly and time-consuming.[2]

The supply of essential materials in the event of a major war had long been recognized as a threat to the Irish economy and a number of government departments had been involved in contingency planning since 1935.[3] In September 1939, the government established a new Department of Supplies, which was to play a key role during the Emergency by directing the supply and distribution of agricultural and industrial products. Lemass moved over from Industry and Commerce with his Secretary, John Leydon, and was replaced by Seán MacEntee.[4] A large number of regulating orders was made under the Emergency Powers Acts and the Department of Supplies was also involved in the creation of Irish Shipping Ltd. This company, which was set up in March 1941 under the chairmanship of John Leydon, proved to be a notable success; it played a vital (if fairly small-scale) role during the course of the war, bringing in urgently needed supplies for many industries.[5]

During the course of the war, government controls were steadily extended and tightened up. In the agricultural sector, farmers were encouraged to increase their arable acreage in order to reduce dependence upon imported grain and free cargo space for industrial materials. In industry, controls were considered necessary to safeguard employment. Early in 1941, for example, MacEntee made a very pessimistic appraisal of the state of the economy. He concluded that industrial unemployment was likely to rise sharply as overseas supplies were cut off, for native raw materials could only be substituted for imports to a very limited degree, and a review of alternative uses for factories and equipment had produced depressing results.[6] The government's policy was therefore to encourage manufacturers to maintain employment wherever possible by sharing the work available amongst the existing labour force.

Implicit in this policy was a wide range of controls on industrial activity, and a Reference Tribunal was established under the Emergency Powers legislation to regulate such matters as wage rates and trade union bargaining, directors' remuneration and proposed increases in nominal capital.[7] In May 1941, the Trade Union Act was introduced to institute arbitration machinery and eliminate unnecessary strikes and competition between unions. Direct bargaining with employers ceased and negotiations were only to be conducted by bodies which represented an industry as a whole. Such bodies, whether they represented management or employees, were to obtain a licence before becoming the legal negotiators for an industry; they were required to deposit a substantial sum with the government to establish their bona fides;[8] and they also had to have a registered office in Ireland and compile a comprehensive register of membership. Once both parties to a dispute had obtained a licence, the dispute could then be referred to an Arbitration Board for settlement. Cost of living-linked wage increases were brought to an end and wage rates were frozen by 'Standard Wage Orders'. Negotiations on bonus awards had to be submitted for the approval of the appropriate government department.[9]

The controls were accepted by the unions because it was recognised that the maintenance of employment levels was of paramount importance. A wage freeze and restrictions on negotiating rights was the price that had to be paid if manufacturers were to be deterred from cutting their labour forces at a time when supply problems were causing a drop in output. If the unions were to continue to support these measures, however, it would be necessary to regulate profits and prices in order to prevent the price of raw materials and finished goods from rising sharply under market pressures. Price fixing was introduced by the Department of Industry and Commerce in July 1941.

Manufacturers were to submit proposed price increases for the Department's approval and were to supply copies of their current price lists.[10] During 1942, a large number of commodities became subject to rationing to check the imbalance between supply and demand, and in October of that year the Reference Tribunal's powers were widened to include the regulation of profits. By this date, virtually every aspect of industrial activity was subject to government supervision, although the Department of Supplies did not become actively involved in the determination of production priorities until towards the end of 1943.

Government control could not prevent a significant drop in industrial output during the Emergency; its efficacy was of course limited by the fact that Ireland did not control materials supplies. Over the period from 1938 to 1943, the total output of manufacturing industry averaged about three-quarters of the figure for the previous quinquennium,[11] and in most industries there was a fairly steady decline to a low point in 1942 or 1943. Nevertheless, it seems clear that government policy was successful in its prime objectives; the structure of Irish industry was safeguarded, and a sharp increase in unemployment was avoided. Yet it is undeniable that the plethora of government regulations exacerbated the difficulties of running a business during the Emergency, and the many restrictions were to have a significant effect upon the ability of Irish industrialists to prepare for post-war conditions.

The footwear industry was ill-prepared for wartime conditions. It had depended upon Britain and America for a wide variety of items, from machinery to hob-nails, polishes and cardboard boxes, and the manufacturers were doubtless aware that they would be in difficulties if they were cut off from their suppliers. Yet the available evidence suggests that in the late 1930s most manufacturers were too preoccupied with their immediate problems to devote much attention to the consideration of contingency plans. It may be that records relating to this topic have not survived, but even Hallidays' records, which are relatively complete, make only one reference to it; in September 1939, it was decided to draw up a weekly list of the supplies used so that items could be re-ordered promptly to avoid the expected transport delays.[12]

There was, however, some evidence of a build-up of materials stocks in anticipation of shortages and price rises, although it is only possible to be specific in the case of John Halliday and of the two public companies, Padmore & Barnes and J.H.Woodington. Hallidays' stock levels at the end of the financial year (November) rose from £18,420 in 1938 to £31,165 in 1939 and £37,632 in 1940. Woodingtons was also buying heavily at this time and stocks nearly doubled between 1938 and 1940, from £30,527 to £56,440. Admittedly this trend may have been partly due to price increases. Padmore

& Barnes, however, did not stockpile; stock levels at the Kilkenny factory remained stable between 1938 and 1940 at around £26,000 to £28,000.[13] It seems likely that other Irish footwear factories were also unable to follow Hallidays' example. Some lacked the capital to engage in heavy buying while others possessed insufficient warehouse space. Dubarry Shoemakers certainly did not stockpile materials[14] and a report from Waterford implies that the same was true elsewhere.[15]

The first reports of shortages came from Drogheda in October 1939[16] and by the following August most centres were reporting hold-ups due to a scarcity of materials and irregular deliveries.[17] As far as leather was concerned, the real problem at this time was irregular supply rather than an actual shortage. Import duties were suspended[18] and the Department of Supplies intervened to safeguard supplies of leather in June 1940 when an order was made under the Emergency Powers Legislation prohibiting the export of cattle hides, calf skins and leathers, except under licence.[19] Indeed, it seemed for a time as if the companies which had bought large stocks had made a mistake, for the war did not take its expected course and leather prices actually fell in mid-1940.[20]

Much more serious was the shortage of metallic grindery and other items which were not made in Ireland because they could not be competitively produced in small quantities. There was, for example, only one manufacturer of lasts in Ireland and one supplier of findings.[21] Hallidays, for instance, reported that hob-nails were often virtually unobtainable[22] and the company relied upon C. & J. Clark Ltd and its associate companies and subsidiaries for toe puffs, reinforcement board, stiffener paste, bottom wax, crepe rubber solution, wetting solution, shoe carton board and labels, and stains, inks and finishes.[23] This dependence upon one supplier was perhaps exceptional but it does indicate the kind of items which the Irish footwear factories usually obtained from foreign manufacturers.

In the autumn of 1940, the supply situation took a turn for the worse. Supplies from Britain were declining as manpower shortages and shipping losses began to take effect and the Irish factories were reporting widespread short time working.[24] The more popular leathers were in short supply and prices were beginning to rise sharply.[25] A further deterioration in the supply situation was threatened in November 1940 when the British government announced that exports of a wide variety of items would be controlled from the beginning of 1941. Among the items which would require export licences were all types of leather, cork, fibreboard and rubber; cotton and flax yarn; abrasive wheels and papers; and other finishing materials.[26]

Between 1941 and 1944, the supply situation steadily worsened. Machinery breakdowns were beginning to create problems because virtually all the equipment in use in the Irish footwear factories was of British or

American origin and spares were either unobtainable or subject to long delays in transit. After the Japanese successes in South-East Asia, many rubber or rubber-based materials became virtually unobtainable; as sole leather was already in particularly short supply, the availability of soling materials was becoming the major restraint upon output. The scarcity of metallic grindery continued to be a major problem, and early in 1944 leather shortages were exacerbated by a serious strike in the Irish tanneries. Cut-backs in the electricity supply were also beginning to affect the footwear industry. In March 1944, the Electricity Supply Board announced that the scarcity of imported fuels necessitated a 15 per cent cut in the supply of electricity to all industrial concerns,[27] and by June the cut-back had been increased to 25 per cent.[28] Towards the end of 1944, however, the supply situation began a gradual improvement, although some essential items were to remain in short supply long after the war had ended.

These shortages led directly to a drop in output. As can be seen from Appendix I, total output fell fairly slowly during the early years of the Emergency, from about 4,801,000 pairs in 1939 to 4,562,000 pairs in 1941. This decline was more or less offset by an increase in imports because quota restrictions were lifted during the war. After 1941, however, the supply of footwear to the Irish market began to decline. Home production fell to 3,907,000 pairs by 1943, which represented a reduction of roughly 20 per cent on the 1939 level, and the supply of imported footwear was drastically curtailed. Although there was an increase in home production of the order of 100,000 pairs in 1944, the output of the Irish factories did not again begin to approach the 1939 figure until 1945. The overall effect was to reduce the quantity of footwear on sale in Ireland by about one million pairs between 1939 and 1943. Before 1939, footwear manufacturers had been able to produce more shoes than they could reasonably hope to sell; by the middle of the war, it was clear that they could sell every pair they could make.

For footwear manufacturers, wartime conditions meant a continual struggle to keep their factories operating. Short time working was increasingly prevalent,[29] and the overall impression is one of continual improvisation and substitution as more items became unavailable. Faulty machinery, for example, could no longer be serviced by the British or American manufacturer and during the war many footwear manufacturers expanded their own repair workshops or utilised the services of local blacksmiths to rectify minor faults. Major breakdowns, of course, could not be dealt with and, in this respect at least, it was fortunate that the Irish factories had not been working at full capacity in recent years; there were often spare machines on hand which could be cannibalised or used as replacements.

The process of improvisation and substitution is well illustrated by the manufacturers' attempts to maintain the supply of soling materials, which represented a particularly difficult problem. Before the war, most Irish footwear had utilised leather soles, machine-sewn or rivetted or screwed to the upper and insole. Metallic grindery was in short supply from the autumn of 1939 and this led to a greater consumption of waxed thread; when thread and yarn became difficult to obtain, shoes with stuck-on soles began to make up an increasing proportion of the industry's output. At the same time, supplies of sole leather were giving cause for concern, and a number of substitutes were being introduced. Until early 1942, most of these substitutes were rubber-based, for rubber was still readily available in comparison with bottom leather.[30] It was noticeable that Clonmel, which was mostly working with crepe rubber soles, was much less affected by stoppages than other centres. Rubber or rubber-based materials, of course, were particularly suitable for the stick-on method of construction.

After Japan entered the war, however, rubber became unobtainable and the Irish manufacturers had to devise new ways of augmenting their meagre supplies of bottom leather. A number of companies therefore began investigating the possibility of using wooden soles. Connollys used a garage business belonging to one of the directors to carve soles from beech blanks,[31] while Hallidays subcontracted this work to a Dundalk joinery firm.[32] The usual procedure was to last the upper onto a stout leather insole, to which the sole was then attached with screws.[33] Although wood was warm and gave good arch support it was not abrasion resistant nor quiet, and treads had to be fitted to the footpart and heel. These were usually made of scraps of waste leather.[34]

At first, the use of wooden soles was confined to the heavy boot sector because agricultural footwear was in very short supply. Rubber wellingtons were now unobtainable and, for reasons of state security, substantial quantities of leather boots were required for the Irish Army and the Local Defence Force.[35] There were, however, a number of production problems due to lack of experience with the new material, and it was some time before wooden-soled boots became available in reasonable quantities; Hallidays' wood-soled boots did not reach the shops until March 1943.[36] Padmore & Barnes, Winstanleys and Woodingtons also commenced production of wood-soled boots in the autumn of 1943 as a result of a further decline in the supply of bottom leather.[37] Attempts to use wooden soles for ladies' footwear, however, were rather less successful. Lighter shoes required a flexible sole and the usual practice was to make the sole and heel in two parts, joined by a flexible hinge of stout leather. At first, these shoes met with some consumer resistance; they were not uncomfortable but they often looked clumsy and the need to use uncomplicated styles and plain uppers contributed to their 'ersatz' appearance. It must be remembered that the public at this time expected shoes to be made of leather; today's public readily accepts a wider range of materials. Eventually, customers came to accept wooden soles but only because footwear of traditional materials could not be obtained.

This process of substitution appears to indicate that it was fairly easy for manufacturers to switch to different materials and different techniques in response to wartime conditions. A number of cautionary remarks have, however to be entered. Firstly, it was much easier to find substitute materials for soles than for uppers. Stuck-on or screwed-on soles could replace the traditional welted sole but leather was really the ideal material for uppers and the only viable substitutes at this time were canvas and a variety of other textile fabrics. Consequently, the Irish tanneries were called upon to increase their output of upper leather and, although the manufacturers could usually obtain enough leather to make full use of their supplies of soling materials, much of it was of very poor quality. There was a shortage of tanning agents, and in trying to meet the footwear industry's needs the tanners were often tempted to pass hides through the production sequence too quickly.[38] The upper leather which they produced could often be torn quite easily in the hands and was finished with a heavy grain print to disguise flaws.[39]

Secondly, the preceding remarks should not be taken to imply that there was an orderly process of substitution, with traditional materials and techniques gradually giving way to alternatives. The essential feature of the supply situation was that it was very erratic, but supplies of essential materials did continue to dribble through throughout the war. Moreover, many of the alternative materials used were also subject to limited availability. It is more realistic to say that manufacturers made use of any materials that were available at a particular time; if a supply of conventional materials became available a manufacturer would temporarily suspend the use of substitutes until it had been used up.

This brings us to the third point; the substitutes used during the Emergency were almost invariably of an 'ersatz' nature. They were often less suitable than the conventional material and usually led to a reduction in quality and/or an increase in manufacturing costs. A major drawback to the use of wood soles, for instance, was that they were more expensive than leather or rubber. Experimenting with substitutes was very time-consuming, and the difficulties of working with unfamiliar materials meant a reduction in productivity and a decline in production standards. Manufacturers persevered in the use of substitutes because they were under pressure to maintain the supply of footwear to the public, but it was always regarded as a short-term expedient to make good the shortfall in production of conventional footwear. As soon as the supply situation began to improve, the Irish footwear manufacturers quickly returned to traditional materials and techniques.

In short, the new materials used during the Emergency were substitutes rather than alternatives. The manufacturers were preoccupied with the exigencies of the moment and none of their improvisations could be considered to represent a significant technological advance. This, of course, is hardly surprising; traditional materials and methods were the product of long experience, and the Irish industry had not needed to develop research and development skills because of the service provided by BUSMC and the other machinery manufacturers. The use of substitutes, therefore, was subject to limitations and, insofar as it led to technological change, it was usually a retrogressive rather than a progressive step. The only exceptions were the use of rubber soles and the cemented process; in terms of durability at least, rubber soles possessed a significant advantage over the traditional material, whilst cementing offered a viable low cost alternative to stitched construction. If rubber had remained available, and if suppliers had been able to meet the demand for cements, the stuck-on rubber sole might have been widely adopted by Irish manufacturers (and accepted by the Irish public) rather earlier than was in fact the case. After the end of the war, the manufacturers went back to using leather soles, and rubber-soled shoes did not come to represent a significant proportion of Irish footwear production until the early 1950s. This delay may be partly attributable to the fact that during the war the public had come to associate substitutes with inferior quality and it was slow to respond to developments which in fact represented a technological advance.

Up to this point, we have looked at the nature of the problem and the importance of improvisation and substitutes in fairly general terms. However, while every footwear manufacturer was adversely affected by supply problems to some degree, the experiences of individual manufacturers did in fact vary considerably. As we have seen, one of the greatest difficulties was the uncertainty of the supply situation, and flexibility was essential if a company was to make the most efficient use of the available materials. Short-run production was the norm and production bottlenecks would be reduced to a minimum if management and operatives could adapt quickly to changing conditions.

A wide variety of expedients were adopted by footwear manufacturers to keep their factories running during the war. Apart from the use of substitutes like rubber and wood, a number of specific examples come to mind. Hallidays established a laboratory which operated as a kind of 'emergency general store', carrying out experiments into the manufacture of rubber solutions, cellulose cements, leather dressings, pigment paints, shoe creams and edge and bottom finishes.[40] These were items which hitherto had usually been imported. Hallidays also produced cellulose cements from scrap cinema film, while Padmore & Barnes manufactured rubber solutions in small quantities.[41] Other industries were encouraged to produce items which were in short supply or had not been previously manufactured in Ireland. In 1943, for example, the Irish Oil & Cake Mills Ltd of Drogheda began making leatherboard from waste leather. Unfortunately, it is not known how significant a contribution this represented, nor how many factories were supplied, but it is known that it was sending shipments to John Halliday & Son, which in return was offering technical assistance. Samples were passed on to the Avalon Leatherboard Co. Ltd of Street (a subsidiary of C. & J. Clark Ltd) and a number of improvements were suggested.[42] There is also some evidence to suggest that some of the Dundalk factories were able to obtain leather which had been smuggled across the border from Northern Ireland. The quantities involved were probably relatively small, but it all helped to keep the factories working. When cutbacks in the supply of electricity to industrial concerns were announced early in 1944, Woodingtons and Hallidays made a significant saving by operating the factory only during the hours of daylight and cutting motive power requirements wherever possible.[43]

It is obvious from the preceding remarks that the response to wartime conditions depended very much upon the resourcefulness of the management. In addition, there was the question of the company organisation within which the management was operating. The ideal was a flexible organisation, operated by a management which was both willing and able to take important decisions on a day-to day basis. One would like to know more about the role of management during the war, but the available evidence suggests that John Halliday & Son was the most enterprising of all the Irish footwear companies.

Arthur Halliday was a very able businessman, especially in the vital fields of buying and labour relations, but the company also devoted a considerable amount of attention to its structure during the Emergency. A detailed analysis was prepared in 1942 and 1945.[44] Because John Halliday & Son was still a small company by most criteria, Arthur Halliday retained personal control of most of the major managerial functions. But this was essentially a supervisory control and the delegation of responsibility to junior executives meant that the factory could continue to function efficiently if he was not available for an on-the-spot decision.

This enabled Arthur Halliday to concentrate upon developing alternative sources of essential materials. It has been noted that Ireland's dollar reserves were rising during the war because of the drastic cutback in imports, but they could not be used because of the British embargo on neutral companies. Yet Arthur Halliday was able to show that given enough time and effort the blockade could be circumvented. He began making annual visits to the United States to buy leather and other essential materials and was also able to purchase supplies through an agent in Buenos Aires. The cargoes were shipped to Ireland via Lisbon and although it was expensive none of the shipments were lost through enemy action or confiscation. Fortunately, the

British and American authorities were very reluctant to alienate Irish interests and, after unofficial discussions with the company, the American Ambassador in Dublin and the British Trade Commission indicated that they would turn a blind eye to Arthur Halliday's activities. Halliday bought virtually anything he could lay his hands on and, inevitably, some of his purchases proved to be unsuitable, but his efforts undoubtedly played an important part in keeping the factory running. His purchases of synthetic rubber were particularly important; this was a commodity which was almost unobtainable on the Irish market and this ability to tap American sources gave the company an important advantage over it competitors.[45] The prevalence of short time working was reduced and whereas the total volume of Irish output fell from 1939 to 1943 and was still below the 1939 figure in 1945, Hallidays' output rose continuously, from 192,113 pairs in 1940 to 342,848 pairs in 1945. As a result, the company's share of the Irish market increased from 4.5 per cent in 1939 to 8.1 per cent in 1944, although it dropped back to 7.4 per cent in 1945 as supply difficulties eased and other companies increased their output.

Many of the other factories were unable to emulate this kind of initiative because they lacked the necessary resources or because they could ill-afford the absence of key executives on buying trips. Dubarry Shoemakers, for example, did not make any purchases in the States during the war, although F.J. Scott was able to use his contacts in the British footwear industry to obtain some supplies.[46] It has been suggested that the companies which fared worst were usually those which lacked an organisation capable of the rapid decisions which wartime conditions required. Notable in this respect were Rawsons and Woodingtons — both of which were in the hands of the English owners who visited their Irish factories infrequently, yet who retained a very large measure of personal control. During the war, even relatively senior executives lacked the power or confidence to make decisions on their own initiative. This was a particularly serious problem at Drogheda, for J.H. Woodington died in April 1943 without leaving a will. Control passed to his widow who also died intestate and the English shareholding was divided amongst the surviving relatives. Both the owners and the Irish management now lacked the power to take decisive action, and there is only one reference in the surviving records to purchases in America — a vital shipment of two tons of hob-nails, which arrived in October 1943, but which, significantly, had been ordered in 1941, before J.H.Woodington's death.[47]

The performance of individual companies also depended to a considerable extent upon government activity in the industrial sector and, again, there are a number of indications that the effects of government regulation were not uniform throughout the footwear industry. Government intervention took place in three key areas. Firstly, there were the Department of Supplies' efforts to facilitate the acquisition and distribution of essential materials to the manufacturers. Secondly, there were the controls on wages and conditions of employment. Thirdly, there were the controls on prices and other measures calculated to prevent the market responding to conditions of unfulfilled demand; these included the introduction of rationing and the restrictions on profits.

During the Emergency, the Department of Supplies played an active role in procuring and distributing materials. The case of Irish Shipping Ltd has already been mentioned and in July 1941 the Department became involved in the purchasing of American leather — presumably with the tacit agreement of the Allies.[48] In both instances, the contribution made by the Department was probably fairly small because the footwear industry had to compete with many other industries for cargo space. Perhaps more important was the informal agreement with Britain in late 1941 which permitted the export of Irish hides in return for tanning agents. Irish hides were relatively plentiful, but the tanners were unable to process them because they had always imported a large proportion of their tanning agent requirements.[49] The British leather industry, on the other hand, was suffering from a hide shortage, and the agreement benefited both countries.

The Department of Supplies was also responsible for the distribution of materials to the footwear industry. Home-produced leather, for example, was distributed on a quota system. The quotas, however, were fixed according to pre-war production levels and, consequently, they varied considerably from one company to another. For companies like Dubarry Shoemakers, which was of fairly recent origin and was still building up production when the recession struck, the quota allowance was fairly small. For Woodingtons, on the other hand, the allowance was fairly generous because this company had 'artificially' maintained output levels during 1937-38 by producing for stock. Similarly, when the Department became directly involved in importing American leather in mid-1941, it was announced that it would be supplied on a quota basis with those factories which had not stockpiled receiving first priority.[50] This was probably in the best interests of the industry as a whole but it did mean that those companies which had built up emergency stocks during 1939-40 were unable to benefit from their forethought. However, this provision soon became immaterial because very few companies had any reserves left by 1942.

The purpose of the Department of Supplies' direct intervention to control the distribution of materials was to prevent companies with better resources and better contacts from securing an unfair advantage over less favourably placed competitors, and it must be conceded that it was generally successful; none of the Irish footwear factories was forced to close permanently as a result of supply difficulties during the Emergency. The Department of Supplies therefore made a significant contribution to the government's primary economic objective — the maintenance of employment levels at a time when emigration opportunities were severely curtailed.

This objective led, as we have seen, to a wide range of controls over employment levels, wage rates and trade union activity. Manufacturers had to be restrained from cutting manning levels, and therefore wages had to be held down and unnecessary stoppages eliminated. In general, the controls were fairly successful in maintaining employment levels, although there were significant short-term fluctuations; the overall trend was one of decline until 1943, followed by recovery.

TABLE 9

Employment in the footwear industry, 1939-45

	Total number employed in mid-October	Average employment through year
1939	5,644	5,150
1940	5,095	4,879
1941	5,464	5,017
1942	5,193	4,818
1943	5,152	4,785
1944	5,392	4,960
1945	5,625	5,225

Source: *Census of Industrial Production.*

Average employment therefore fell much slower than volume of output; between 1939 and 1943, there was a decline of roughly 6 per cent in average employment while the volume of output fell by more than 18 per cent. The Standard Wage Orders were also influential in preventing a rapid increase in wages, although Table 10 shows than the slow growth rate of average earnings was partly the result of a reduction in the hours worked. Although relatively few footwear operatives were on piecework, it will be recalled that the contract rate for day work included a substantial bonus component for production in excess of an agreed norm; the many interruptions which characterised footwear production during the Emergency therefore tended to push average earnings down towards the minimum day work rate.

The regulations, however, did not succeed in eliminating labour disputes. Indeed, 1942 was the worst year for strikes in the history of the footwear industry.[51] In Britain, industrial disputes during the war centred around the dilution of skills which resulted from the scarcity of labour. In Ireland, on

TABLE 10

Average earnings and hours of work, 1939-45

Employees aged 18 and over

	Average earnings per week		Average hours worked		Index of average earnings per week	
	Males £	Females £	Males (hours)	Females (hours)	Males (1953 = 100)	Females
1939	2.85	1.70	43.0	43.7	38	36
1940	2.81	1.77	40.0	40.9	37	37
1941	2.95	1.80	40.5	40.5	39	38
1942	2.98	1.75	37.2	38.6	39	37
1943	3.22	1.78	36.2	34.7	43	37
1944	3.54	2.04	37.7	38.7	47	43
1945	3.80	2.27	40.8	41.3	50	48

Source: *Census of Industrial Production.*

the other hand, industrial unrest was primarily due to short-time working and the government's wage controls, which combined to cause a steady fall in real incomes. Whereas the the cost of living index rose by an average of 11.6 per cent per annum between 1939 and 1945,[52] average earnings only increased by 5-6 per cent per annum.[53] Initially, NUBSO had accepted the government regulations as being in the best interests of its members but the decline in real incomes soon began to cause industrial unrest and there were reports that Union members were leaving the industry because of inadequate earnings.[54] Dissatisfaction with the wage freeze could usually be contained if manufacturers maintained employment levels. Most manufacturers complied with the government's directives and opted for work-sharing instead of redundancies, but in 1942 it became apparent that some companies were unwilling to pay for the maintenance of an under-utilised labour force; they managed to evade the regulations and continued to lay off workers.

After Union-backed protests, matters came to a head when Edward Donaghy & Son and the Edenderry Shoe Co. took action to prevent Union interference. NUBSO officials were dismissed and the two companies refused to consider their reinstatement until they had resigned from their Union posts. Donaghy quickly backed down after threats of strike action, but the dispute at Edenderry was more prolonged. After negotiations between the company and the Union, during which Len Smith, the Union President, stated that Edenderry's action was regarded as a direct challenge to the Union's authority, a strike began and the dispute was referred to the Chief Conciliation Officer under the terms of the 1941 Trade Union Act. It then transpired, however, that he had no power to intervene; although the Union had obtained a negotiating licence, the Federation of Boot Manufacturers had made no application and hence the dispute could not be referred to the Arbitration Board for investigation and settlement. Len Smith visited the Federation in Dublin to urge its officials to obtain a licence and eventually they did so. The Arbitrator was called in and after eleven weeks the dispute was resolved in the Union's favour. The sacked official returned to work and the Edenderry Shoe Co. undertook to refrain from interfering with Union organisation in future.[55]

Nevertheless, while it would now be possible to utilise the conciliation machinery to prevent future disputes of this nature, a number of leading Union officials evinced continuing concern over the attitude of some manufacturers towards trade union activities and their apparent readiness to use the prevalence of unemployment and short-time working to weaken the Union's position and influence. In April 1943, the General Secretary of NUBSO, George Chester, told the Union Conference that the best interests of its members required a separate and independent union for Éire. The proposal was accepted by the conference, but it was resisted by the Irish leadership; in view of the difficulties which their members were facing, they felt it was no time to be severing links with the bargaining power of a large and long-established Union.[56] The executive did not reverse its decision but left it in abeyance, to be reviewed after the war.[57]

Some industrial unrest was probably inevitable in view of the difficulties which faced manufacturers and operatives during the war, but it should be emphasised that a breakdown in relations such as occurred at Edenderry was exceptional. Other manufacturers maintained a reasonably good relationship with employees and Union officials, and the Union was not so preoccupied with disputes that it was obliged to neglect its other responsibilities to its members. In particular, it was able to attend to social welfare schemes, the need for which had been apparent for some time.

The initiative was taken by the Dundalk branch of NUBSO, which discussed the desirability of forming a benevolent fund and requested advice from a number of British trade union branches which were already operating such schemes.[58] The fund came into operation in June 1942, and was run for the benefit of the three Dundalk factories. Circulars were sent out and about 200 operatives joined the scheme. Each member paid a small weekly sum which entitled him to benefit after 26 weeks' payment, with a maximum of eight weeks' benefit per year. Sick benefit was fixed at five shillings (25p) per week, starting after five weeks' absence, and dependents were to receive five guineas (£5.25) on a member's death. The fund was to be managed by a Committee of six members who were to be elected at the Union's Biennial Conference. The fund proved to be very successful and by June 1943 it was found that sufficient funds had accumulated to permit an increase in benefit to six shillings (30p), payable after three weeks. The membership grew steadily, reaching 550 by the end of the war, and the fund was to play an important part in the anti-tuberculosis crusade of the late 1940s.[59]

The Benevolent Fund Committee was also represented on Hallidays' Factory Council, which had been set up in 1936, and in the autumn of 1942, it requested that the company set up a pension and life assurance scheme for its wage-earning employees. Hallidays already possessed a Hospital Fund which had commenced in 1938,[60] and the directors were happy to agree to the Union's proposal. A scheme was prepared by the Irish Assurance Co.; all employees between the ages of 18 and 59 were eligible and contributions were fixed at 1s 6d (7.5p) per week. The pension was to be calculated at the rate of £1 for each year of employment and payments were to start at 60 and cease at 70 years of age. If death intervened, all contributions were returned to the member's dependants, together with a lump sum of £100. By the end of the year, the scheme had been joined by 95 per cent of the male and 55 per cent of the female operatives, and membership was later made a condition of employment at Hallidays' factory.[61]

The pension scheme was an indication of Hallidays' attitude towards labour relations and it is evident that the response to labour problems, like the response to supply difficulties, depended very much upon the attitude of the management. Hallidays recognized that antagonising the government, the labour force and the union was counter-productive and concentrated upon maintaining the good relationship which the company had established in the 1930s. Although Hallidays' attempts to keep the factory running did occasionally lead to discord, the company only suffered one short strike during the Emergency.[62] Hallidays showed that alternatives to redundancy could be found which actually improved the company's position. In 1942, for example, efforts were made to improve the educational standards amongst its employees. Arthur Halliday had complained that many of his juveniles had received insufficient instruction in elementary school subjects and, after discussions with the local technical school, it was agreed that juveniles would receive non-vocational training from 4pm to 6pm each day. Initially, the programme was to run for six months from the beginning of 1943 and Hallidays was to contribute £200 to cover expenses.[63] Hallidays claimed to be the only company in Ireland which paid employees for non-vocational training in working hours at this time, and the scheme was to prove of great value. In the short term, it reduced the prevalence of short-time working and spread a greater proportion of the available work amongst adult employees; in the long term, it placed the company in a stronger position to cope with post-war conditions.

In addition, Hallidays actually began to increase the size of its labour force. Between 1942 and 1946, the number employed nearly doubled, from 324 to 631.[64] In particular, large numbers of juveniles were taken on and, although they could not be fully employed immediately, there were obvious attractions in training extra labour in preparation for the boom which was expected to follow the end of the war.

The provision of a pension fund and the improvement in the educational standards of the labour force therefore offered both short-term and long-term benefits and clearly the management felt that the *net* cost was fairly small; we shall see that profits were strictly controlled by way of an excess profits tax. In view of this, one can ask why other companies did not follow Hallidays' lead. Certainly, none of the other companies appear to have devoted much thought to the improvement of their long-term prospects. The answer, one suspects, is partly to do with the calibre of the management at Hallidays; for example, Arthur Halliday's assistants included Philip McLoughlin, who later became managing director of J.H. Woodington. It will also be suggested, however, that the restrictions on Hallidays' profits were particularly severe, and this may have helped executives to formulate the question, 'If we cannot earn a reasonable profit, what else can we do to improve the company's prospects?' In other words, the government regulations may have presented a challenge which was met by a successful response. But it must be confessed that these suggestions are based on incomplete evidence and one would like to know much more about the considerations which lay behind decision-making during the Emergency.

It has already been noted that the cost of living index rose by roughly two-thirds between 1939 and 1945. Government price controls, therefore, were rather less successful than the wage freeze. This was largely due to the fact that important materials were still obtained from abroad; and while Irish materials were subject to price controls, it was still much more difficult to regulate the prices of imported goods. As far as the footwear industry was concerned, the rising cost of materials meant that the Department of Industry and Commerce was obliged to allow manufacturers to make some increases in ex-factory prices. After 1941, as can be seen from Table 11, ex-factory prices in fact rose somewhat faster than the price of sole leather — the only important material for which detailed figures are available.

Additional measures were therefore considered and, in October 1942, the Reference Tribunal's powers were widened to include the regulation of profits. As can be seen from Table 12, the extension of these controls in the latter half of the war period did have an influence upon the footwear industry's profits. Up until 1943, increased prices rather more than offset increased materials costs and, as relative labour costs declined throughout the war, manufacturing profits showed a slow relative increase. After 1943, however, the trend was reversed and manufacturing profits fell until 1945.

The experiences of individual manufacturers, however, did not always

TABLE 11

Index of prices of sole leather and leather footwear, 1939-45

	Index of sole leather prices (1953 = 100)	Index of ex-factory prices (footwear wholly/mainly of leather) (1953 = 100)
1939	35	35
1940	41	39
1941	41	42
1942	42	47
1943	47	53
1944	51	57
1945	53	58

Source: *Census of Industrial Production.*

coincide with the general trend, and this was particularly true in the case of profit restrictions. Information on the operation of these controls is unfortunately scarce but it appears that they did not consist of a blanket restriction on gross or net profits. Instead, the Reference Tribunal had discussions with representatives of individual companies and varied their restrictions according to the circumstances in which different firms were operating. For example, according to Arthur Halliday, Hallidays' profits were restricted to a figure equivalent to its best performance during the period from 1937 to 1939. Any revenues above this figure were subject to 100 per

TABLE 12

Manufacturing costs and manufacturing profit in the footwear industry, 1939-45

	Net sales	Materials	Materials as % net sales	Wages and salaries	Wages and salaries as % net sales	Manufacturing profit	Manufacturing profit as % net sales
	(£000)	(£100)	%	(£100)	%	(£100)	%
1939	2,024	1,086	53.7	588	29.0	350	17.3
1940	2,211	1,243	56.2	603	27.2	366	16.5
1941	2,409	1,348	56.0	627	26.0	434	18.0
1942	2,481	1,296	52.2	643	25.9	541	21.8
1943	2,741	1,446	52.8	695	25.3	600	21.9
1944	3,044	1,700	55.9	770	25.3	573	18.8
1945	3,497	2,051	58.7	838	23.9	608	17.4

Source: *Census of Industrial Production.*

cent excess profits tax, and this tax remained in force until about 1948.[65] As we shall see, this was to prove a very burdensome restriction because Hallidays had been returning very low profits in the late 1930s.

Woodingtons' profits, however, were fixed according to its performance during 1941 and the rate was set so as to cover normal overheads and permit a 10 per cent return on the capital employed in the business. There was some dispute as to what the capital employed actually was; the Tribunal rightly believed that Woodingtons was over-capitalisd and that it possessed large cash reserves which were not, and could not, be used in the business. Eventually, the employed capital was assessed at £85,000, compared with a book value of £100,000, and it was calculated that a gross profit of 22 per cent would suffice to leave a net profit of £8,500 (10 per cent).[66] This restriction was soon relaxed, however; in May 1943, a letter from the Department of Supplies informed the company that its selling prices were to be constructed so as to yield a gross profit not exceeding 27 per cent of turnover, but the Minister reserved the right to fix or control the actual price of different lines.[67] This seems to have been the usual rate for the other Irish companies, although E.J. Connolly has stated that Connollys' profits were restricted to 14 per cent on wholesale and 25 per cent on retail sales.[68]

The effect of these controls is indicated in Table 13. At Woodingtons, labour costs fell considerably and while there was a relative increase in materials costs, the company was still able to show a steady improvement in pre-tax profits. Hallidays, however, was unable to pass on increased materials costs, and profits in most years represented a low rate of return on turnover. This, however, did not seriously threaten the company's existence; any type of profit control is difficult to operate because firms can often avoid rather than evade the restrictions. In Hallidays' case it meant that, rather than declaring substantial net profits, there were obvious advantages in using income for other purposes; and the strictness of the controls upon this particular company provided part of the incentive for measures designed to secure its future prosperity. The improvement and expansion of the labour force has already been mentioned and this explains why Hallidays' labour costs did not decline in the later stages of the war. On a number of occasions too, Hallidays resorted to selling boots and shoes at a loss to keep profits down. Yet even this had its positive aspects because it helped spread costs and enhanced the company's reputation with wholesalers, retailers and government officials.[69]

Controls on prices and profits, therefore, were less effective than the regulation of wages and industrial relations. Yet it must be emphasised that the price of finished goods would have risen much faster if it had been allowed to respond freely to market pressures because demand for footwear far outstripped the supply. The government did what it could to restrict

TABLE 13

Production costs and pre-tax profits, 1939-45:
John Halliday & Son and J.H. Woodington

	Net sales	Materials	Materials as % net sales	Manu-facturing wages	Manu-facturing wages as % net sales	Pre-tax-net profit	Manu-facturing profit as % net sales
	(£000)	(£000)	%	(£000)	%	(£000)	%
John Haliday & Son							
1939	157	75	48.0	31	19.7	9	5.9
1940*	130	74	56.9	30	23.1	6	4.3
1941	151	93	61.6	35	23.2	7	3.6
1942	182	115	62.6	37	20.1	22	9.3
1943	213	149	70.0	40	18.8	16	5.9
1944	262	181	69.0	49	18.7	11	3.2
1945	275	199	72.4	51	18.6	13	3.5
J.H. Woodington							
1939	97	37	37.8	27	27.9	7	7.2
1940	97	46	47.6	26	26.9	7	7.2
1941	117	69	58.5	21	17.8	9	7.8
1942	107	65	51.5	22	21.0	10	9.7
1943	113	61	53.6	24	20.8	12	10.3
1944	127	69	54.6	26	20.5	17	13.0
1945	133	69	52.1	28	21.4	16	11.9

* 11 months.

Source: *Annual Reports and Accounts.*

demand. In July 1942, all types of footwear had been brought under the scope of the Clothing Rationing Scheme.[70] Boots, bootees and shoes required two coupons for adults' sizes and one coupon for children's, while all slippers, sandals, goloshes and other types of footwear required one coupon per pair. Rationing was steadily tightened up in subsequent years and by June 1944 the number of coupons required varied from two for children's shoes and sandals to six for women's boots and shoes with leather uppers and soles and eight for men's boots and shoes with leather uppers and wooden or leather soles.[71] For most people, however, the problem was that it was often difficult to find any shoes to buy with their coupons, and a black market appeared in a number of towns. Bend leather allocated to the repair trade was finding its way on to the black market and was being made up into women's shoes and sandals. The quality left much to be desired,[72] but there was a healthy demand for this type of footwear and sandals with first grade bend soles could be seen in shop windows at prices of up to two guineas (£2.10). This was extremely expensive, for Hallidays' highest-priced women's shoes retailed at 22s 6d (£1. 12½p) at this time, and it gave some indication of what might have happened if the government had not acquired a wide range of regulatory powers.

By 1944, therefore, virtually every aspect of industrial activity was subject to government regulation and it must be concluded that government intervention was basically successful. The task facing government officials was a difficult one. Often lacking specialised knowledge, they were required to strike a balance between competing claims of different industries; between employers and employees; and between producers and consumers. Inevitably, there were inconsistencies, but underlying every decision was the basic objective of government economic policy during the Emergency — the maintenance of employment levels, which in turn depended upon the maintenance of the existing structure of Irish industry. It seems probable that the footwear industry would have moved towards oligopoly if business activity had remained uncontrolled. The companies with better resources, better contacts and above all better management would have been able to improve their position while weaker companies would have been forced out of business. It might be argued that this was what the industry needed; the pre-war problems of excessive production capacity and too many companies competing for a small home market were to return after 1945. Yet a move towards oligopoly could not be countenanced by the government because it would have caused a reduction in employment levels. In the event, none of the Irish footwear manufacturers went out of business during the war, but wartime restrictions inevitably made it very difficult for them to operate efficiently and earn reasonable profits. In short, the extent to which the Irish footwear industry could benefit from neutrality was limited; the scarcity of essential supplies was a fundamental problem and both government officials and the manufacturers themselves tended to be preoccupied with essentially short-term remedies.As a result, few manufacturers were in a position to prepare themselves for the return of 'normal' trading conditions after 1945.

5

RECOVERY AND CRISIS
1945-55

The return of peacetime conditions created new opportunities for economic growth in Ireland; the existence of unfulfilled demand offered the prospect of a consumer boom. The Fianna Fáil government sought to achieve rapid economic recovery from the Emergency, and its efforts met with considerable success.[1] Between 1945 and 1949, GNP was rising at an average of 5 per cent per annum.[2] The wartime controls were gradually lifted. Controls upon wages and conditions of employment were rescinded by the Industrial Relations Act of September 1946, which also provided for the return of free collective bargaining, and for the registration of National Agreements under the supervision of the Labour Court.[3] The stringent controls on prices and profits were retained as a check upon inflation but were also lifted in 1948.

However, the recovery and expansion of the late 1940s was not maintained; it was a direct result of wartime shortages and consequently was of a 'once-for-all' nature. Between 1949 and 1955, GNP increased at a rate of only 1.75 per cent per annum.[4] This figure does of course include agriculture, which made a particularly poor showing, but industrial output only rose by 3 per cent a year between 1949 and 1955, and output per worker by less than 2 per cent a year.[5] The early 1950s were characterised by balance of payments crises, high unemployment and rising emigration, which reached a peak in 1955 and necessitated a thorough examination of economic policy. This performance was only marginally better than Britain's and compared unfavourably with the other European nations.[6]

The disappointing performance of the Irish economy was partly due to the fact that the post-war period was a time of political instability by Irish standards. Fianna Fáil's long period of office came to an end in 1948 and for the next three years Ireland was governed by an inter-party coalition led by John Costello. Although Fianna Fáil regained power in 1951, it was again defeated at the polls in mid-1954, being replaced by a second coalition government which remained in office until 1957.[7] As a result, as Dr Garret Fitzgerald has noted, 'Policy tended to be dominated by short-term considerations of political expediency and by a negative desire to prevent some undesirable development rather than by any positive aim of seeking economic growth'.[8]

Another factor underlying the relatively poor economic performance of the decade between 1945 and 1955 was the low rate of industrial investment in Ireland. During the war — and indeed until controls on prices and profits were lifted in 1948 — Irish industry had been obliged to operate on very low profit margins. Price-fixing was politically desirable and some degree of control was undoubtedly necessary to prevent inflation, but it did make it difficult for Irish industry to generate investment capital for reorganisation and expansion by way of ploughed back profits. In 1953, Seán Lemass remarked that 'the fundamental cause of the persistence of abnormal unemployment and emigration in Ireland is the continuing low level of capital investment by private enterprise'.[9] Government grants and other incentives which might have offered an alternative source of capital were not forthcoming in the immediate post-war period. The government did of course make efforts to encourage economic growth — notably its long-term recovery programme, published in January 1949, and the establishment, in the same year, of the Irish Development Authority — but industrial grants were not introduced until 1952 and were initially restricted to the more under-developed areas in the west of Ireland.[10] Thus government encouragement was essentially small scale in its scope and was largely concerned with the specific problems faced by the designated areas rather than with ensuring the well-being of the economy as a whole. Moreover, this type of government involvement came too late to enable Irish industry to expand quickly in response to post-war opportunities and was not of any real significance until the expansion of the grants programme and the appearance of additional incentives in 1956-7.

This failure to invest in turn meant that Irish industry was unable to satisfy consumer demand. The public was not only demanding more goods, it also wanted a wider choice. The years of austerity had made the public increasingly desirous of many of the luxury items which were becoming commonplace in Britain and America. The government was under pressure to relax tariffs and quota restrictions (especially when an election was imminent), and the result was that imports were pushed up to record levels. Ireland's dollar reserves began to disappear and, like the rest of the sterling area, Ireland suffered a shortage of hard currency. To offset the rise in imports, the government made efforts to encourage exporters and a new trade agreement was negotiated with the United Kingdom in 1948,[11] but there were few Irish industries which could really compete in overseas markets. As a result, there were major balance of payments crises in 1951 and 1955 and, to quote again from Fitzgerald, 'the basic disequilibrium between competitive Irish exports and the imports demanded by an Irish public increasingly conscious of the disparity between its living standards and those of the British public were disastrously exposed.'[12]

Admittedly, the 1951 crisis was precipitated by external factors beyond the control of Irish planners and industrialists. The immediate cause of the crisis in Ireland was the onset of the Korean War which caused prices to rocket as manufacturers stockpiled materials. The Irish government recommended manufacturers to build up stocks and ordered the banks to make available the necessary finance, and, in the event, this proved to be a miscalculation. Heavy buying of imports was not matched by any improvement in export sales and the balance of payments deficit became a major problem.[13] Moreover, there followed a recession during which some companies had to write down the value of the materials which they had purchased at peak prices. Fanning has documented the Department of Finance's considerable success in offsetting the effects of the crisis which ensued[14] but the fundamental problem remained and there came another major balance of payments crisis in 1955. This crisis, unlike its predecessor, was purely domestic in origin and caused a drastic re-thinking of economic planning in Ireland which led up to the publication in November 1958 of the First Programme for Economic Expansion.

Thus the first post-war decade was not a time of vitality and growth in the Irish economy; opportunities for expansion were missed and the lack of government direction, coupled with the unfortunate influences of external factors, led to stagnation and recession once the initial post-war boom in demand was over. Moreover, the development of a more sophisticated market for consumer goods implied a greater demand for imports, which led to the major crises of 1951 and 1955. It is against this background that we have to consider the post-war development of the footwear industry.

A brief look at Appendix I shows that the performance of the Irish footwear industry between 1945 and 1955 was very disappointing and clearly lagged behind the growth rate of Irish industry as a whole. Although the value of output rose by an average of 6.4 per cent per annum, this was almost entirely due to inflationary pressures; despite government attempts to limit increases the manufacturers were obliged to raise their prices to cover wage rises and rapid increases in the cost of raw materials. Clearly, in a period of relatively rapid inflation, pairage is a better guide to the performance of the footwear industry and, as can be seen, there was a considerable fall in the volume of output between 1946 and 1955. However, output did not fall steadily; the footwear industry experienced a series of rapid and fairly substantial fluctuations.

In Ireland, as elsewhere, the end of the war did not bring about an immediate return to normal trading conditions. As we have seen, the government found it necessary to continue restrictions on industrial activity and, in the case of the footwear industry, the controls on prices and profits were actually tightened up in the latter part of 1945. At J.H.Woodington, selling prices were cut by 4 per cent in October.[15] Hallidays was also under pressure from the Department of Supplies to keep prices down and, in June 1945, the company complained that the controls did not permit an adequate return on capital.[16]

Nevertheless, problems in obtaining supplies had already begun to ease by the middle of 1945. There were, of course, a number of essential items which remained in short supply for some time to come, notably machinery and metallic grindery, for both Britain and the United States were suffering from steel shortages. Moreover, some types of leather, especially the better qualities, were still in short supply. However, most materials were available in sufficient quantities to enable the manufacturers to discontinue the use of substitutes and make substantial increases in output; in both 1945 and 1946, the total pairage was up by 12.7 per cent on the previous year's performance.

This increase in production could be easily absorbed by the Irish market, and the manufacturers experienced little difficulty in disposing of their products. The return of conventional materials was welcomed by the public, and there was a particularly healthy demand for the better quality and more elaborate lines which had been phased out during the Emergency. Heavy boots also had a ready sale, for there was a continuing shortage of agricultural footwear. Suitable leathers had only recently become available and, for reasons which are not entirely clear, Army and L.D.F. contracts were still keeping the boot manufacturers busy. Indeed the demand for civilian boots was sufficient to persuade Hallidays, which had concentrated upon the development of its ladies' shoes during the war, to take the apparently retrograde step of announcing that its first priority for 1946 was the restoration of heavy boot production to pre-war levels.[17]

This expansion, together with some increases in imports, was sufficient to push total output for the Irish market to a record level by the end of 1946. Yet it is clear that the supply of footwear, for a while at least, was not improving fast enough to please the government. Companies like John Halliday & Son were still supplying their customers under a monthly quota arrangement,[18] and coupon rationing continued up to the end of 1947, albeit on a much less restrictive level than in the United Kingdom.[19] Some of the reasons for this unsatisfactory growth rate have been touched upon but it is worth noting that a number of manufacturers were restive under the system of controls operated by the Department of Supplies and regarded inadequate profit margins as the fundamental cause of their inability to generate sufficient capital for post-war organisation and expansion. The Department's close watch upon the activities of the footwear manufacturers became particularly burdensome when materials prices began an upward movement shortly after the war's end and there were widespread demands for relaxation of the

Recovery and Crisis

controls.[20] By the end of 1946, gross profit margins were increased to 17.5 per cent for wholesale and 30 per cent for retail business but demand remained at an abnormally high level, partly because of purchases by visitors from the U.K., and the government decided to relax import restrictions. Import duties were suspended and, from mid-1946 to the end of 1947, quotas for leather footwear were set at the relatively high level of 625,000 pairs per six month period.[21] Equally significant was the decision to issue supplementary licences in addition to the quota allowances. Applicants for licences were put in touch with the manufacturers, who had to notify the Ministry of Industry and Commerce within 14 days if they were in a position to supply the specified orders; if they were not, the goods required could then be obtained from overseas suppliers.

The practical effect was a boom in imports, because British leather producers received government subsidies, and British footwear was very competitive. In 1947, imports totalled 2,141,980 pairs and represented 27.7 per cent of total output for the Irish market, which climbed to the unprecedented figure of 7,724,368 pairs.[22] In the short term, the relaxation of import controls had the desired effect of improving the supply of footwear to the public, but it quickly proved damaging to the well-being of the Irish manufacturers. The intention was doubtless to tighten up restrictions again once home production increased, but the adjustment of import restrictions to balance discrepancies between supply and demand was difficult to effect with any accuracy. Early in 1948, the market reached saturation point; supply exceeded demand and Irish retailers were left with large stocks on their hands. Consequently, they immediately stopped buying and, although the import quota for leather footwear for the second half of 1948 was cut to 125,000 pairs, the recession continued to deepen. Rather than increasing their output, the Irish manufacturers were obliged to reduce output, and short-time working reappeared in a number of centres during the autumn and winter of 1948.[23] In March 1949, Edward Donaghy announced that it was cutting output capacity by one-third, and about 70 of the company's employees were made redundant.[24] Although most manufacturers anticipated an improvement during 1949 as imports and manufacturers' stocks were sold off, all but two or three factories were still on short time in June[25] and production for the Irish market continued to fall until the end of the year — by which time, of course, the footwear industry was beginning to suffer from the general recession in the Irish economy.

Government intervention to improve the supply of footwear brought the expansion of the immediate post-war period to an abrupt halt and continued to have an unfortunate effect upon the Irish manufacturers for some time after steps had been taken to remedy the situation. It may well have been preferable to have continued the restrictions on imports while at the same time offering incentives like the relaxation of prices and profits controls and the provision of capital which would have stimulated a steady expansion of home production. Yet it must be conceded that the government was in a very difficult position. De-restriction of the Irish footwear industry meant price increases which were politically undesirable at a time when rising prices and low wages were meeting with increasing criticism and, with an election imminent, it is hardly surprising that Fianna Fáil was eager to make a rapid improvement in the supply of consumer goods.

It must also be stated that the difficulties of the footwear industry were partly due to factors which, for various reasons, were beyond the government's control. To begin with, there were continuing problems with the supply of materials and machinery, although they were of course a great deal less severe than they had been during the war. Manufacturers were experiencing long delays in delivery of machinery which they needed for expansion or to replace equipment which had deteriorated during the Emergency, and the growing shortage of dollars meant that Irish manufacturers were no longer able to make large purchases in America.[26] This clearly placed limitations upon the potential growth rate of the Irish factories and made some increase in footwear imports inevitable. More important, however, was the continuing imbalance of the footwear industry towards the heavy boot sector; in May 1949, Hugh Crilly, the NUBSO official responsible for the northern half of the Irish republic, could report that virtually all the growth in output which had been achieved after the war, had taken place in this sector.[27] But there was an increasing demand for lighter types of footwear, and the government was obliged to relax its import restrictions because the Irish manufacturers were unable to meet this demand.

Thus the footwear industry, for a variety of reasons, did not make the most of the post-war opportunities for expansion. By the end of the decade, there were some grounds for cautious optimism; supply problems were lessening and sales were picking up as retailers disposed of accumulated imports. Moreover, the new coalition government was evidently determined that it should not repeat Fianna Fáil's miscalculation and the import quota for leather footwear for the whole of 1950 was set at just 20,000 pairs.[28] But as the Irish economy moved towards crisis point, there was no chance of a breathing space for the footwear industry. Falling real incomes and high unemployment speeded up the rate of emigration and led to a further contraction in the size of the market. Moreover, the boom in raw materials prices was also causing problems. Most footwear manufacturers responded to the government's recommendations in favour of heavy stockpiling of materials during the early stages of the Korean War. Hallidays' stocks jumped from £158,800 in 1949 to £225,655 in 1951, although it is not possible to distinguish between materials and finished goods. Woodingtons had also been buying heavily and materials stocks had doubled during 1950.[29] The manufacturers were ready to follow the government's recommendations because the industry had not been prepared for war in 1939 and it was feared that an escalation of the conflict would lead to similar supply problems. But heavy buying inevitably had an effect upon cash flow and in most cases it meant a greater reliance upon bank drafts and overdrafts. Woodingtons' credit limit rose from £45,000 in May 1950 to £100,000 in June 1951 and it was obliged to provide various securities, including a floating debenture on the firm's assets.[30] Stockpiling was also taking place in many other countries during 1950 and the result was a sharp increase in materials prices. Most imported leathers advanced 60-80 per cent during the second half of the year, and there were also substantial increases in the cost of rubber.[31] The Irish footwear industry still relied upon imports for about half its leather requirements and, although the post-war increase in demand had led to the establishment of a number of new Irish tanneries after 1948,[32] heavy buying of foreign leather pushed imports above £1 million in 1950. The price of home-produced leather was also pushed up by the abnormal demand.[33]

Another factor which caused problems for footwear manufacturers in the late 1940s was the steady increase in labour costs. During the Emergency cost of living-linked increases had been set aside and so, once the war was over, the Union leadership began to press for wage rises which would restore the purchasing power of its members to pre-war levels. This meant an increase of the order of 70 per cent and was initially resisted by the manufacturers. A decision was deferred until labour relations had been normalised, and on 23 September 1946 the Industrial Relations Act came into effect and superseded all the restrictions on wages and trade union bargaining which had been imposed under the Emergency Powers Orders. The Labour Court was established and was empowered to register agreements between manufacturers' associations and trade unions which were considered to be representative of the industry as a whole. A registered agreement then became binding on all manufacturers, whether federated or not. Disputes over wages and the conditions of employment were to be referred to the Labour Court, which would arrange for negotiations to take place under the auspices of its officials. A recommendation would then be published and, although it was not legally binding, it was hoped that the Court's decisions would became generally accepted.[34] A settlement was finally reached between the manufacturers and the Union in December 1946 which provided for a 60 per cent increase over pre-war rates. Over the next five years, further increases were negotiated and the Union was able to register them with the Labour Court, thus ensuring that they were legally enforceable throughout the industry.[35] Minimum day rates for adult workers rose by 26.8 per cent (men) and 29.0

per cent (women) between 1946 and 1951, and there were proportionate increases in juveniles' rates. These minimum rates were adjusted in accordance with changes in the cost of living rather than with changes in labour productivity, and rising labour costs created difficulties for manufacturers; fierce competition for sales meant that the increase could not be entirely passed on to the consumer.

Fortunately for the manufacturers, their difficulties were not compounded by labour troubles. As we have seen, NUBSO officials had considerable success in restoring their members' purchasing power to the pre-war level, but they were also finding life difficult in the late 1940s. It was becoming necessary to seek regular increases because of inflation and this placed greater demands upon Union negotiators. While pressing for cost of living-linked increases, they had to ensure that labour costs did not rise so sharply as to encourage manufacturers to cut employment levels. Such considerations tended to encourage conciliation and compromises rather than a militant attitude.

The need to devote more attention to the problems of the Irish membership led in 1949 to the revival of the proposal for a separate union. Another consideration was that the split between the Irish Trade Union Congress and the breakaway Congress of Trade Unions had led to increased pressure for Irish-based trade unions. There was at least the possibility that growing militancy would create difficulty for both manufacturers and Union leaders at a time when co-operation was essential to the well being of the footwear industry. NUBSO's major worry was that members might leave and join one of Ireland's general unions which lacked experience of conditions in the footwear industry.[36] The three Irish Area Officers, Paul Alexander, Hugh Crilly and Charles Ware, proposed an independent but 32 county union, and discussions with the executive followed in late 1950 and early 1951. The leadership was anxious to come to an arrangement and, although it was calculated that there was about £16,000 to the credit of the Irish membership in Union funds,[37] it was ready to give £35,000 towards the establishment of an Irish union. The stumbling block, however, was that these proposals were strongly resisted by members in the North. In April 1951 a ballot was held and the South voted in favour of independence by 1,990 votes to 932 votes. The branches in Northern Ireland rejected the proposal by a conclusive 217 votes to 45 and, when pressurised by Union leaders, they threatened to join a general union or leave the trade union movement altogether.[38] NUBSO therefore decided to retain the Ulster members, while the Irish Shoe and Leather Workers' Union was established for the Twenty-six Counties at a conference of Irish delegates in Limerick in December 1951. Paul Alexander became president and, at the request of NUBSO, also continued to serve the interests of the Northern Ireland membership, while Charles Ware was appointed vice-president and Hugh Crilly, general secretary.[39]

The new union was to follow NUBSO's policies, negotiating on a national level via biennial conferences to obtain National Agreements. This had enabled NUBSO to maintain fairly harmonious relationships, with a marked absence of official strikes in most years, and had relieved the Union from heavy financial commitments in strike pay. At the 1951 Union Conference, Hugh Crilly stated that, 'The whole success of the Union will depend upon the continuation of that policy. It will not only pay us financially but, as past experience has shown, it will pay members themselves. It is our intention . . . to try and run the new Irish union in close conformity with the organisation and complete set-up of the existing union'.[40] Generally speaking, the new union achieved this objective and, in the early 1950s, its moderate stance and willingness to co-operate with manufacturers in the best interests of the industry as a whole ensured that industrial disputes were generally infrequent and small-scale.

Nevertheless, whilst labour relations remained relatively amicable, abnormally high stock levels, rising materials prices and increased labour costs combined to place footwear manufacturers under intense pressure. Heavy competition for sales meant that increased production costs could not be entirely passed on to the consumer, but the average price of Irish footwear still rose to record levels. As can be seen from Appendix II, the average cost of leather footwear had been rising since the end of the Second World War but, between 1949 and 1951, there was a jump from 101.8p to 135.1p per pair. (Prices for imported footwear also rose very fast in this period, although they peaked rather earlier, and fell back quite sharply in 1951.)

In January 1951, the Irish government made a Price Standstill Order to try to halt this upswing.[41] The Order froze the retail price of a wide range of commodities (including leather and footwear) at the price operative on 2 December 1950, although allowances were to be made for index-linked pay rises. Not surprisingly, the Department of Industry and Commerce experienced growing criticism from the footwear manufacturers. In February 1951, for example, Hallidays commented that 'while we applaud the government's desire to restrict price increases, we, in common with many other firms, shall have to begin almost at once to curtail our scale of activity if we cannot recover in our prices the replacement value of the materials we use'.[42] To make matters worse, negotiations with union officials had culminated (December 1950) in a 10 per cent pay award, although Hallidays conceded that it was justified by the steady upward movement of prices.[43]

In fact, the government controls do not appear to have succeeded in halting the upward trend in retail prices, and the price increases led to a downturn in consumer spending. Retailers cut their orders drastically in May/June 1951 as stocks piled up on their shelves. By July, the shoe trade was reported to be at a standstill and some factories had ceased production. The experience of James Winstanley was typical of medium-sized footwear manufacturers; production was frequently interrupted by short-time working and average output fell from 2,400-3,000 pairs per week in late 1948 and 1949 to 1,600-1,800 pairs per week in 1951-2.[44] This period of depression did not reach its nadir until the middle of 1952 and, unlike 1947-8, it was not due to direct competition from imports. Imports of leather footwear were restricted to 20,000 pairs per annum between 1950 and 1954 and very few supplementary licences were issued. Imports of non-leather footwear — especially rubber boots — were of course much higher, but the Irish manufacturers were showing little interest in this sector.[45]

By the end of 1952, the footwear industry was beginning to recover and there was a noticeable improvement during 1953; output was up by 20.8 per cent on the previous year. But again this period of buoyancy was to prove short lived and the footwear industry again went into recession. In 1955 production was slightly higher than the 1952 figure but with this exception was the lowest figure to be returned since 1945. Thus the footwear industry was subject to quite sharp fluctuations and could pass quite quickly from buoyancy to a state of depression; successive peaks in 1947, 1950 and 1953 were followed by sharp cutbacks in production. This pattern did of course reflect the general economic climate but it also indicated that a restructuring of the Irish footwear industry was becoming imperative. In fact, whilst the industry continued to be plagued by problems of surplus production capacity,[46] signs of change were beginning to appear. The market for footwear was changing and the rate of technical innovation was beginning to accelerate.

The most obvious market trend in post-war Ireland was the increasingly rapid decline of demand for heavy agricultural footwear — traditionally the 'bread and butter' of many Irish manufacturers. On the one hand, the size of the rural labour force was falling; on the other hand, agricultural workers were exhibiting an increasing preference for cheap, lightweight rubber boots. Leather boots were being priced out of the agricultural market because suitable leather with good water-proofing qualities was scarce and expensive. After a brief post-war boom, the heavy boot trade entered a permanent decline. By 1955, output of heavy leather boots stood at about one-third the 1945 level, and now represented only 11 per cent of total leather footwear production in Ireland. In contrast, the Irish Dunlop Co. Ltd was now producing about one million pairs of wellingtons per year.

Amongst the urban population, there was a growing demand for lighter, better quality footwear. Fashion considerations were of increasing importance in the larger eastern towns; significantly, it was in these areas that imported leather footwear had achieved its greatest market penetration.

TABLE 14

Production of heavy leather boots, 1945-55

	Pairs
1945	1,448,040
1946	1,583,040
1947	1,598,688
1948	950,352
1949	1,002,132
1950	1,078,608
1951	960,096
1952	747,456
1953	846,408
1954	616,596
1955	533,376

Source: *Census of Industrial Production.*

Imports acquired a reputation for style and quality and could command high prices.[47] It is clear that high prices did not act as a deterrent upon sales; the evidence suggested that the Irish public would readily buy imported footwear in much larger quantities if there was any relaxation in quotas. In contrast, Irish-made footwear was often considered to be badly made and unattractive in appearance. This was not entirely fair — consumers were strongly influenced by their experiences during the war years when the industry had been labouring under immense difficulties. Yet it did suggest that the Irish manufacturers were not supplying the type and quality of footwear which a more sophisticated public was beginning to demand, and provided further evidence of the need for a restructuring of the industry.

The pattern of footwear retailing in Ireland was also beginning to change. Outside Dublin and the other large Eastern towns, the bulk of the trade was still in the hands of small independents, many of whom were not specialists in footwear; lacking capital resources, they could not place large orders in advance of sales and, consequently, did not share the risks with the manufacturers. Although small accounts were expensive to service, in aggregate they represented a considerable proportion of a manufacturer's business and therefore could not be neglected. But in the main urban centres, multiple retailing was beginning to develop. This was a much later development in Ireland than it was in Britain, where multiples already dominated the market for footwear by the 1950s,[48] and the typical Irish multiple was still a fairly small business. The largest at this time were Tylers (about 25 shops), Connollys (14 shops), Boylans (8 shops), and Densons (6 shops). Branches were nearly always located in Dublin, Drogheda, Dundalk and a few other eastern towns. With the exception of Tylers, which was a subsidiary of a large English multiple, John Tyler & Sons Ltd of Leicester, these companies were all linked with footwear manufacturers in some way. The Boylan family also owned Michael Governey Ltd of Carlow, while Densons was owned by the O'Neill family, which by this date had acquired a controlling interest in James Winstanley. The Connolly family was particularly well-known in the footwear industry. Matthew Connolly's Dundalk factory produced heavy boots until 1952, when it was sold to Hallidays. His nephew, E.J. Connolly, had entered the retail trade in 1939, and by the 1950s he owned about one-third of the shops which the family ran. The remainder were owned by his brothers. E.J. Connolly also had a wholesaling business, although it was sold in the early 1950s when he decided to commence manufacturing on his own account.[49]

Multiple retailers of course possessed a number of advantages over their independent competitors. As Silverman noted, 'they benefit from the advantages of large-scale organisation and mass buying. They usually pay cash ... and, for this reason, as well as the size of their orders, can often obtain better terms than the individual trader. They can afford the expensive sites in main streets and the lavish displays that usually go with them ... but the greatest advantage, of course, is in the size and the rapidity of the turnover. The multiple trader is largely responsible for the development of the fashion trade, and his methods of promoting quick turnover are admirably suited to it'.[50] Admittedly many of these advantages were less clear-cut in Ireland than they were in the United Kingdom because it was relatively difficult to develop volume sales but, by Irish standards, the multiples represented very sizeable accounts. In 1952, for example, accounts over £2,000 — which were nearly all multiples — represented about one-eighth of Clarks Ireland's customers, but accounted for between a quarter and a third of its total sales.[51]

In short, there was a widening gulf between the rural market for footwear, which was essentially conservative and dominated by small independent retailers, and the more vigorous market which was developing in the Eastern towns, which was characterised by a growing demand for more expensive and better styled footwear, and in which the multiples were playing an increasingly significant part. The response of footwear manufacturers to these changes in the Irish market will be considered later.

The rate of technological change was also beginning to accelerate. It should be emphasised that technical advances rarely originated with Irish manufacturers. In view of the small size of the home market, few Irish manufacturers could justify the expense of research and development departments of their own, and it was much more logical to adopt improvements which had originated elsewhere, as and when they became desirable in the context of Irish market conditions.[52] There was often a time lag before Irish manufacturers took up the latest techniques, but conditions in the late

1940s and early 1950s provided a clear incentive for adopting technical improvements which served to cut manufacturing costs or improve the quality of the product.

One result was the much wider use of rubber soling materials. Rubber was cost-competitive against leather and less sensitive to price variations; it offered greater consistency of quality, thickness and finish; and it was waterproof and more durable.[53] Raw rubber, however, is vulnerable to oil and becomes tacky with heat and is therefore vulcanised by the addition of sulphur and various other chemicals, and shaped under pressure in heated moulds. As time went by, a growing list of other additives had also been incorporated to improve the qualities of the natural product; pigments to improve the appearance, new accelerators and activators to reduce dwell time,[54] plasticizers and peptizers to increase the plasticity of the rubber, anti-oxidents and anti-ozonents to prevent oxidation and ozone influence (which makes rubber perish) and reinforcements to improve wearing qualities.[55]

Vulcanised natural rubber soles were ideal for a number of different types of footwear, including agricultural boots, women's warm lined boots, walking shoes and childen's shoes, but for lighter, higher-quality footwear synthetic rubber was often preferable. Synthetic rubber — a chemical combination of styrene and butadiene — entered commercial use in the 1940s, but it was not of any significance as a soling material until the 1950s. Its uniform properties and stable price gave it an advantage over natural rubber because this simplified costing and permitted greater consistency in quality during a production run. Synthetic rubber of a high styrene content could also be used to produce resin rubber, which was particularly useful for ladies' fashion shoes; it could be made to resemble leather and was waterproof and easily stitched or stuck. Resin rubber soling materials were sold under a variety of trade names, including Solite, Rubberlite and Neolite. Another type was micro-cellular rubber, which was made with the addition of an ingredient which turned to gas at a certain temperature in the mould. Micro-cellular soles were usually relatively bulky, but were very light and were particularly useful for walking shoes, sandals and other footwear of veldtschoen construction. However, micro-cellular rubber was difficult to mould and less durable than other types.

Rubber soles were usually cemented on, sometimes being stitched as well, but the further development of vulcanising techniques offered a new alternative. This was the direct vulcanising process, whereby the soling mixture was moulded and attached to the lasted upper in one operation.[56] But it was not as widely used as the cemented process because the steel moulds necessary had to be capable of withstanding high pressure and were, therefore, too expensive unless a fairly long production run could be expected.

During the 1950s, natural or synthetic rubbers gradually became the preferred soling material for a wide variety of footwear. Unfortunately, the 'materials used' section of the Irish *Census of Industrial Production* does not list rubber separately until 1958, but the imports of rubber soles increased roughly tenfold in value during the decade, from £15,135 in 1952 to £154,586 in 1960.[57] This implied a decline in demand in soling leather. As Table 15 shows, purchases of soling leather began to decline steadily in the early 1950s and, by 1960, the volume used was down to almost exactly one-third of the 1950 figure. During the decade, Irish leather manufacturers devoted considerable attention to improving production efficiency — usually by way of an increase in mechanisation of each production stage — but it is significant that these improvements were almost entirely confined to the upper leather sector. There was no incentive to develop new machinery or techniques for the production of sole leather, and the trend was for sole leather tanners to widen their base. Irish Tanners Ltd commenced production of upper leather and rubber soling materials in 1955 and also opened a vulcanising plant which was used by a number of footwear manufacturers.

TABLE 15

Sole leather used and average price per hundredweight, 1945-60

	By volume (cwt)	Price per cwt (£)
1945	53,801	9.2
1946	59,175	10.3
1947	68,919	10.9
1948	55,746	12.5
1949	55,206	12.7
1950	59,355	14.5
1951	53,887	16.8
1952	44,815	17.6
1953	51,639	17.5
1954	43,432	18.1
1955	39,253	19.5
1956	34,874	19.7
1957	34,438	19.3
1958	29,289	19.4
1959	26,807	20.9
1960	20,796	22.0

Source: *Census of Industrial Production*.

Increased labour costs also created pressure for technical change; as we have seen, wage increases were tied to the cost of living rather than to productivity and, in the early 1950s, labour costs were increasing in relation to net selling value. This was a factor behind the adoption of the cemented process, which required a lower labour input than the more traditional techniques. It also provided the stimulus for improvements in production efficiency. Closer study of the operatives' movements while operating their machines revealed a number of possible improvements. For instance, it was discovered that a noticeable improvement in output could be achieved if the machines were placed at a slight angle to the line of production. As has been noted, the tendency had been to divide the complex processes up into many relatively simple operations, and shoemaking machinery had been simplified to the point where picking up and setting down took up a considerable proportion of the operative's time. This provided the incentive to improve production study methods. Production study not only led to economies like the example given above, it also provided a basis for pieceworking and other incentive schemes and supplied the management with more detailed information on manufacturing costs, which led to greater accuracy in planning and costing. Another significant advance was the appearance of a new generation of shoemaking machines which were powered by individual electric motors. This was particularly important in Ireland because it made for greater flexibility; under the older eight station bench system, where several machines were operated by one electric motor, it was much more difficult to alter the production sequence and bring extra machines into production.

The main emphasis after the war, therefore, was on cutting costs, although it was essential to maintain the quality of the product. An important innovation was the slip-lasted construction, which became very popular in this period. This was an American process which was introduced to the British Isles in 1944. Slip-lasting differed from traditional constructions in that the upper was not shaped by being drafted over a last. Instead, the upper was stitched to a soft sock, a last was forced in, and the sole was then attached. Nor did a slip-lasted shoe need a conventional insole to hold the rubber in shape, and a platform, usually of cork, was used instead between sole and upper. At the time, the principal attraction of this construction was that although the closing room input was substantial, it offered major savings in male making room labour at a time when skilled workers were scarce. However, it quickly became apparent that slip-lasting produced lightweight, flexible comfortable shoes without sacrificing stylishness, and the construction quickly became very popular, especially with manufacturers of women's fashion shoes.

Many of the improvements were cumulative; if a company was to obtain the maximum benefit from an improvement at one stage of the production process, additional improvements at subsequent stages were often necessary to prevent bottlenecks. There was a growing tendency to call in outside consultants to examine production and quality control methods. Consultants often recommended improvements in factory layout and encouraged manufacturers to put a larger proportion of their labour force on to piecework and other incentive payment schemes. It was becoming apparent to most observers that a large proportion of day work was both a cause and symptom of low productivity. This was partly due to the fact that certain unskilled ancillary tasks tended to be performed by day workers, but employees might also be put on day work when the management considered that there was not an adequate flow of work to enable them to earn a reasonable wage on piece rates. In fact, the connection between day work and low productivity was so marked that a report commissioned by the Shoe and Allied Trades Research Association (SATRA) concluded that, 'the proportion of day work, without consideration of other factors, is a fairly reliable index to the productivity of a factory'.[58] In Ireland, there was another compelling reason for the adoption of piecework. As we have seen, piecework rates had initially been set too high but, in the early 1950s, when day work rates were subject to regular cost of living indexed bonuses, payment by results was beginning to appear increasingly attractive. The return to pieceworking, though, was a somewhat later development in Ireland than it was in Britain — even in 1962, only 40 per cent of the Irish operatives were on piece-rates.[59]

Another feature was that the new techniques being introduced were often associated with the trend towards specialisation. Specialisation and long production runs were now recognised as the best means of improving manufacturing efficiency. Consequently, the size of a footwear firm was becoming a significant determinant of its profitability. The larger firms were able to adopt capital intensive methods like direct vulcanising; it was an expensive process because of the cost of machinery and moulds, and it was therefore uneconomic unless fairly long production runs were anticipated — or unless a large number of styles could be designed to share the same moulds. Moreover, the bigger firms could be organised on a 'production unit' basis; if a factory could be subdivided into separate units, each concentrating upon a certain type of footwear — in terms of construction, labour input and so on — then it became much easier to achieve higher productivity and more consistent product quality. It also facilitated accurate costing and budgeting and increased the attractiveness of other innovations such as the installation of conveyor systems.

In the first post-war decade, therefore, the environment within which the footwear industry was operating was beginning to change. How then, did footwear manufacturers respond to such changes? It is not possible to examine the activities of every Irish footwear manufacturer in this important period; many records have been destroyed or, for a number of reasons, could not be made available. But, fortunately, we can draw on the detailed business records of John Halliday & Son, which include voluminous correspondence files as well as the usual minute books and accounts, and therefore throw considerable light upon the management's way of thinking. They are particularly valuable in this period because in many respects Hallidays was no longer a typical Irish footwear manufacturer but was beginning to move to a position of market leadership.

Hallidays began to prepare for the return of peacetime conditions during 1944, when plans for the further expansion of its Clarks business were put into effect. Land adjoining the Quay Street factory was acquired and, in March 1944, extensions and alterations to the existing factory were approved and a new building for children's footwear was planned at a total cost of £10,000.[60] The extensions were finished by the end of 1944 and the company pushed ahead with further expansion during 1945, including another new factory for the production of men's footwear. The decision to start manufacturing men's shoes was of particular significance because it meant entering a field in which Hallidays lacked previous experience and managerial expertise. So too, for that matter, did C. & J. Clark,[61] and Clarks was happy to see an associated company gaining experience in a field in which it had not had much success. It was recognised that entry into the market for men's footwear would not be immediately profitable but it was seen as a valuable means of acquiring experience and improving the service which the company could offer to its customers. As most of the Irish factories had surplus production capacity, it was apparent that greater availability of materials would lead to increasing competition, and it was felt that there would be significant advantages in being able to offer a complete range of footwear to retailers. Of course, a diversification of product range could be viewed as a retrograde step but it was offset by significant improvements in factory layout.

The key factor was the development of separate production units, each making a particular type of footwear. Clarks was the leader in this type of reorganisation in the United Kingdom and its expertise was readily available to John Halliday. This technique could be adopted because Hallidays was now the second largest footwear producer in Ireland; in 1947, Rawsons, which was also able to manufacture in separate production units, had an average output of 16,000 pairs per week, while Hallidays usually produced between 12,000 and 14,000 pairs per week.[62]

Hallidays also recognised the need to improve the saleability of its footwear. Quality had been a relatively minor consideration during the war, and the very restricted profits which had been permitted had 'resulted in a hopelessly careless production of inferior shoes'.[63] Consequently, great efforts were made to improve quality control procedures, often with the assistance of experts from Street. Greater attention was paid to style and fashion appeal, and expenditure on advertising was stepped up. There had been very little advertising during the war because there was no point in generating demand which could not be met, but in 1946 it was decided to spend a sum equivalent to 3 per cent of sales, of which Hallidays should contribute two-thirds and Clarks one-third.[64] Particular attention was paid to the promotion of Clarks' 'Skyline' brand which was a range of ladies' fashion shoes in four width fittings.[65] The introduction of these shoes in November 1945 was preceded by intensive market research and retailers were provided with, and trained in the use of, Clarks' foot-measuring gauge which had recently been introduced in Britain.[66] Advertising was controlled by Clarks' British agents. Initially, it was not a success — Hallidays was unable to increase production to cover the different fittings and the number of retailers supplied with 'Skyline' shoes had to be severely limited — but it was of importance because it introduced the concept that shoes should not be sold solely on price. A strong body of knowledge on health considerations was growing up and, if Hallidays could persuade the public that Clarks shoes were healthier as well as stylish, it might prove possible to sell shoes more profitably than would be the case if they relied upon competitive pricing. In other words, if the manufacturer could reach a certain standard and develop a certain reputation, it could include an element of monopoly pricing. Clarks, of course, had already been emphasising the health aspect in Britain for a good many years.

Thus Hallidays was able to devote considerable attention to post-war planning, and it was particularly fortunate in that it had ready access to outside expertise and was able to find the capital required for expansion projects. Borrowing powers were steadily increased from £30,000 to £200,000 between April 1946 and January 1948,[67] and the issued capital was increased from £77,000 to £188,000.[68] This ability to generate extra capital may seem surprising, for footwear firms were not generally seen as an attractive investment. In fact, the additional shares were not made available to new investors but were largely used to liquidate the liability to C. & J. Clark for service charges and commission. In other words, the increase in issued capital represented capitalisation of certain debts. In May 1946, Clarks accepted ordinary shares worth £35,270 at par in settlement of the debt which had accumulated since the last share issue in 1943 and, in April 1948, it acquired shares worth another £18,645.[69] Thus Hallidays' expansion plans were financed by Clarks and, by the latter date, Clarks held approximately 43 per cent of the issued ordinary capital.

Although the other footwear firms were not unaware of the opportunities and problems which were likely to result from a return to peacetime conditions, their ability to implement plans for reorganisation and expansion was often much more limited. The experience of Munster Shoes Ltd was typical of the small-to-medium sized footwear firm. During the late 1930s, it had built up quite a successful business by Irish standards and had acquired a good reputation for machine-sewn shoes and veldtschoen slippers and sandals. Output was run down during the war and the company just managed to show a profit in most years. Consequently, it was not possible to reinvest profits in order to finance expansion and, when competition within the industry intensified after the return of normal trading conditions, the company found it very difficult to keep its factory working at an economic level. As a report on the company noted in 1964, 'Profits were small, and insufficient to meet the financial demands of the business by way of installation of up-to-date plant and, at the same time, to provide sufficient working capital in a period when inflation demanded that the latter be increased with every passing year'.[70]

Dubarry Shoemakers offers another example. In 1946, Dubarry was able to install a cemented plant leased from BUSMC, but its capital resources were very slender. The managing director and chairman, F.J. Scott and H. Cullen, had together bought out the other shareholders and had repaid the Department of Industry and Commerce loan used to start up the company. All investment was to be from ploughed back profits and, initially, the sums involved were very small. Dubarry was a small company even by Irish standards and its output was usually below 1,000 pairs per week at this time.[71]

The initial response to post-war conditions was therefore an uneven one. Yet, when the crisis of 1951 highlighted the weakness of the Irish market, an increasing number of manufacturers began to turn their attention to both short-term and long-term remedies. A number of different strategies were open to manufacturers — although in fact most companies pursued all of them to a greater or lesser extent. Firstly, they could cut back promotion capacity to bring it more into line with the level of demand. Secondly, they could move away from declining sectors into more dynamic sectors of the market. This would also entail paying greater attention to the problems of marketing footwear in Ireland. Thirdly, they could develop export business to reduce their dependence upon a home market which showed little sign of any sustained growth.

During the late 1940s and early 1950s, a number of factories reduced their productive capacity as an alternative to short-time working. Edward Donaghy, as we have seen, cut heavy boot production in 1949 as a result of the continuing decline in demand and J.H. Woodington was to do the same in 1954 when it became apparent that sales were insufficient to cover factory overheads. There were advantages in operating a smaller factory if this implied a more efficient use of plant, equipment and labour. Woodingtons, for example, calculated that the reduction in capacity saved about £3,000 per annum. Admittedly, this was not a very large sum compared with total manufacturing costs — about £180,000 in 1954 — but it must be remembered that fierce competition meant that even a few pence off the ex-factory price could lead to an appreciable improvement in sales. Nevertheless, this type of rationalisation had its limitations; in particular, it meant that the manufacturer would be slow to respond if there should be any improvement in the state of the market. A competitor who possessed excess production capacity would be in a much better position to make the maximum use of a short-term upswing in demand.

Potentially more rewarding was a move into less developed sectors of the market, although the risks involved in the development of new lines was not insignificant, and by no means all the Irish manufacturers were in a position to cope with the short-term drop in profits which this implied. It has been shown that there were certain market sectors (in terms of type of shoe and price bracket) within which there was very severe competition and hence price elasticity of demand (i.e. a small reduction in a manufacturer's prices would have a significant effect upon demand from distributors). But different sectors were quite clearly defined and price competition took place *within* a sector rather than *between* different sectors.[72] A move into less developed sectors was therefore a means of getting away from the intense price competition which characterised the market for conventional mid-price leather footwear.

There was still room for expansion in the non-leather sector; Irish manufacturers had shown little interest in these types of footwear, and in 1950 they still represented only 17.2 per cent of total output. Consequently, the government had never deemed it advisable to impose stringent restrictions on non-leather imports. But, in fact, this sector was not particularly attractive to Irish manufacturers. To begin with, non-leather shoes had a much lower unit price than leather footwear and often carried a lower profit margin,[73] and so they were less profitable unless they could be manufactured and sold in large quantities. This was difficult, if not impossible, given the state of the Irish market. In addition, a very large proportion of non-leather sales consisted of rubber boots and a move into this sector was not a viable proposition.[74] The technology was quite different; it was very capital-intensive and was protected by patents. It was therefore extremely unlikely that another Irish manufacturer would be able to challenge the Irish Dunlop Co. which had access to the resources of its British parent and held the rights to the latex-dipped process.[75]

However, there were still opportunities within the general category of 'footwear wholly or mainly of leather' because output (and therefore competition) was concentrated around the medium price brackets. Again, cheap footwear was not an attractive proposition because of the lack of a volume market and, for most manufacturers, a move into less developed sectors of the market meant an improvement in quality. As Arthur Halliday noted in 1953, Hallidays' objective — in men's as well as women's — was to avoid getting tangled in the intensely competitive medium-grade trade.[76]

A move into better quality footwear necessitated improvements in production techniques and, as in the 1930s, an improvement in quality was usually achieved by way of agreements which gave Irish manufacturers access to outside expertise. For example, Dubarry Shoemakers already had something of a reputation for good quality and design but, in 1954, it was decided to enter into a manufacturing agreement with Norvic Ltd. At this time, Norvic was one of the biggest and most dynamic companies in the British footwear industry, with seven factories and about eighty retail outlets. The company was anxious to keep its brands in existence in Ireland but import quotas were very small in the early 1950s and it was agreed that Dubarry should commence production of men's shoes under licence. At the same time, Tara Shoes Ltd of Kells, an associate of Dubarry,[77] began production of Norvic ladies' fashion shoes. A managing company, Norvic (Ireland) Ltd, was set up in Dublin to oversee the project, and had particular responsibility for sales. Dubarry and Tara each paid a 5 per cent royalty on sales, and the service agreement gave them access to technical and styling information and enabled them to visit Norvic's British factories. The arrangement proved successful and ran for a number of years, until Norvic got into financial difficulties around 1970.[78]

Equally important was the use of agreements by Woodingtons. This company had originally been established to manufacture heavy boots and had been beset by a lack of leadership after the death of Mr Woodington. In the late 1940s, the controlling block of shares was acquired from his estate by the directors,[79] and, early in 1950, they took the decision to commence production of high-quality ladies' footwear to reduce their dependence upon the declining heavy boot market. Since they lacked experience in this type of footwear, it was necessary to recruit personnel from outside the company to supervise the development of the new range. Their choice fell upon Philip McLoughlin, who was in charge of quality control at Hallidays and had played an important part in the establishment of its Clarks brand business. McLoughlin was enticed to Drogheda by the offer of a directorship and was given the titles of Technical Adviser and Quality and Production Manager.[80]

Under his guidance, the sandal plant was closed down and the company began to cast around for a British manufacturer which could offer the kind of outside assistance on which McLoughlin had relied at Hallidays. Such a manufacturer was Edwards & Holmes Ltd of Norwich, which had a very good reputation in Britain but did little business in Ireland. The agreement, which came into effect in January 1951, was a very flexible one and enabled Woodingtons to get a start in the top grade ladies' market. Output initially consisted of machine-sewn lines, although cemented shoes were introduced later in the decade. The minimum quantity to be manufactured under the agreement was to be 5,000 pairs in the six months ending 30th April 1952, rising to 17,000 pairs in 1953 and 25,000 pairs in 1954 and subsequent years.

However, by 1954-5 Woodingtons was finding that there was a limit to demand for these high-priced lines and wanted to widen the range; the intention was to retain the style appeal and quality of construction associated with the Holmes brand but to use less expensive materials in order to tap a wider market. Holmes, however, was unwilling to agree to this proposal, and McLoughlin entered into another agreement with Lotus of Stafford. Lotus was interested in manufacturing in Ireland because, like Holmes, it could only import very limited quantities under the quotas then in force. Lotus had already been discussing an arrangement with Rawsons, which of course possessed considerable expertise in good quality ladies' shoes, but had been unable to come to a satisfactory agreement. After meetings between McLoughlin and James F. Bostock, chairman of Lotus, Woodingtons began production of ladies' shoes under the Lotus brand in September 1955.[81] At the same time, McLoughlin was authorised to approach the Boylan family, who as well as their substantial retail interests had also acquired Michael Governey of Carlow, and had developed a substantial business in unbranded men's shoes for multiples like Tylers and Saxone.[82] Agreement was quickly reached and Governeys began producing Lotus men's shoes some time around the end of 1955. Both these agreements were initially to run for five years and the Irish companies were to pay 3 per cent on sales, with a minimum annual payment, which rose from £1,000 in the first year to £2,500 in the third and subsequent years.

A major advantage of the Lotus agreement was that Woodingtons and Governeys would determine the specifications of the shoes which they made under the Lotus brand. Of course, Lotus had to be satisfied that quality was up to the standards it expected, but it recognised that the Irish companies were the experts on the Irish market, and allowed them to develop the range which would be best suited to their customers' needs. Although advertising was to be directed from Britain, Woodingtons and Governeys could fix prices as they saw fit and could modify British designs to suit the Irish market — and indeed, could develop their own designs for sale under the Lotus brand. For example, an expensive British design might be copied in cheaper materials to retail at, say, £2.49, and this gave access to a much larger market and enabled the Irish companies to offer attractively styled footwear at a competitive price. And, of course, this was a particularly valuable asset to Woodingtons, since the Holmes range already covered the high-price sector.[83]

Woodingtons' move into the good quality ladies' market, however, was not achieved without a great deal of effort, and it was some time before the new lines began to have a beneficial effect upon the company's profits. Indeed, the problems which Woodingtons experienced in improving quality and expanding sales in an unfamiliar market were a significant factor behind the company's poor showing in the early 1950s. Profits fell from £15-16,000 in 1945-6 to about £2,000 in 1948-9. Losses were made in 1951 and 1953 and profits remained below £5,000 until 1958. Entry into a fashion business carried a inherent risk of increased seasonality and tied up more capital in materials and finished stocks, because the manufacturer had to produce in advance of sales to cater for short peaks in demand. This explains why Woodingtons' overdraft remained at a high level after the period of heavy buying during the Korean War crisis; its credit limit increased from £50,000 in December 1950 to £100,000 in July 1951, and remained above £85,000 until 1955.[84] Moreover, given the depressed state of the Irish market, it was not possible to build up sales to the point where less remunerative lines could be dropped; in 1955, for example, heavy boots still constituted a significant proportion of total production and were of some value as a means of keeping the factory running and spreading costs. In fact, the short term effect of a switch to ladies' footwear was to necessitate a reduction in productive capacity. Between 1951 and 1953, sales of these lines averaged about 2,500 pairs per week but the factory was set up to produce twice this quantity and needed to sell 4,000 pairs to cover overheads which were running at about £800 per week. In December 1954, it was therefore deemed advisable to reorganise the factory to reduce its capacity to 3,600 pairs per week.[85] Nevertheless, Woodingtons was planning for the future, because it was quite evident that the heavy boot market was beyond recovery; two of the other heavy boot manufacturers were forced to close down in the early 1950s. S.A. Wiltshire Ltd of Dublin made a loss between 1951 and 1954 and stopped trading in 1955, and Hearne & Cahill, one of Ireland's oldest boot manufacturers, went into liquidation at about the same time.[86]

John Halliday, of course, was another concern which was benefiting from a tie-up with an English company. Hallidays did well with the slip-lasted process, and its ladies' footwear was very successful. Substantial improvements were made in production methods. In 1949, for example, a cost accountant was appointed to investigate and control labour and material costs, manufacturing and planning.[87] In the following year, specialists from BUSMC were employed to install their method of production control.[88] Hallidays also took the lead in adopting piece working. A visit by production study experts from Street in May 1951 led to a recommendation in favour of a wider use of piecework,[89] and, between 1951 and 1956, the proportion of the labour force on piece-rates rose from 40-50 per cent to 90 per cent.[90]

But, whilst Hallidays' ladies' shoes were well established in the higher quality market, the same was not true of its men's shoes. Significantly, neither Hallidays nor Clarks had much experience of the men's trade and the quality of their shoes was distinctly erratic. As Bancroft Clark remarked in 1950:

> The fitting qualities of the lasts are not standardised, the specification of edges and heel heights is not standardised, stiffener quality is poor, quality generally irregular, and as a collection of shoes they would be quite unsaleable anywhere else. Nevertheless, what has been done is laudable and has started Clarks in the men's field, which C. & J. Clark have not succeeded in doing anywhere else. The question arises as to whether we can go on letting Clarks Ireland put our name and brand on these shoes, and what steps we can take to standardise the fitting and quality to build up a range which is good enough to bear our brand.[91]

Instead of dropping men's production, it was decided to invest a considerable sum in the development of a complete range of shoes to retail at 49s. 6d. to 69s. (£2.45 - £3.49). In 1951, C.C. Arnall, who was described as 'one of the most experienced men's shoe designers in the UK', was recruited from James Allen & Sons Ltd of Edinburgh[92] and Hallidays began to consider the construction of a new factory to provide additional space and permit reorganisation of the layout in the existing buildings. In the event, this proved unnecessary, for a chance conversation led to the purchase of Connolly Shoes Ltd. Connollys had made good profits for a number of years but was hard hit by the steady decline in heavy boot sales and had been losing money from the late 1940s. The entire shareholding was purchased on 31 March 1952 at a total cost of about £30,000, and the leases on the BUSMC machinery were transferred to Hallidays.[93] However, the production of men's footwear continued to be beset by problems. There were frequent stoppages which led to delays in delivery, and the proportion of rejects and returns was often excessive.

Other lines developed by Hallidays during the late 1940s and early 1950s included a range of women's comfort shoes and a range of youths' welts, but, as they were intended for the British rather than the Irish market, they will receive attention when we come to consider the development of export business. At this point, it is sufficient to note that production for export, like the production of men's welted shoes for the home market, required a considerable improvement in quality.

This examination of the activities of the Irish footwear manufacturers between 1945 and 1955 has so far concentrated on their attempts to improve quality and reduce manufacturing costs. However, the immediate returns from such attempts remained limited because the problem facing Irish footwear manfacturers was fundamentally a *marketing* one rather than a manufacturing one. In Ireland, as in Britain during the 1950s, marketing was often the 'poor relation' and tended to take up a fairly small proportion of executives' time. Yet there were some significant improvements in marketing techniques during this period.

'Marketing', of course, should be differentiated from 'selling'; marketing involves identifying what the public wants, designing and producing to the required standard, and selling at the right price. The move into lightweight, better quality footwear, therefore, was significant in marketing terms because it involved a recognition that this, rather than heavy boots, was now the dynamic sector of the market. The move into better quality footwear, coupled as it was with a tendency towards technical innovation, was also important because it did something to tackle the problem of a lack of product differentiation. Similarly, the adoption of slip-lasting by fashion footwear manufacturers (notably Hallidays and Woodingtons) was of significance because it enabled them to sell on the basis of style rather than on price alone. This was important because most companies relied on copying or adapting foreign designs for the Irish market and produced them largely on BUSMC machinery which was available to the whole industry; this meant that competing lines from different manufacturers often seemed very similar to the consumer.

The use of branding and advertising to persuade the public that certain manufacturers' goods did in fact possess superior qualities was therefore of some importance. Hallidays was already well-known for the strength of its branding policies,[94] and was rapidly reaching the point where it became desirable to *reduce* the emphasis on the Clarks name. By the early 1950s, Clarks brand sales had so saturated the market for ladies' footwear that they were beginning to meet increasing consumer resistance. Retailers reported that customers did not have any complaints to make about Clarks shoes; it was simply that their last three or four purchases had been Clarks, or their friends all wore Clarks, and they wanted something different.[95] Hallidays therefore found it profitable to manufacture ladies' shoes for Saxone (Ireland) Ltd in the late 1940s and early 1950s. The shoes made for Saxone still carried the words 'Made by Clarks' in small letters, but the emphasis was upon the retailer's name and brand, and this had the effect of winning back some of the lost sales. A number of exclusive lines were produced for Saxone to retail at 45*s*. to 55*s*. (£2.25 to £2.75) and Saxone agreed that it would not import shoes in this price bracket unless Hallidays was unable to meet its requirements.[96] In 1955, Hallidays also began to reduce the emphasis on the Clarks name by concentrating upon the individual brands — 'Clipper', 'Country Club' and 'Craftmaster'.[97]

Hallidays' branding policies were backed by advertising which, by the standards of the time, was quite lavish. This trend was set immediately after the war with the campaign to announce the introduction of width fittings and the Clarks Fitting Gauge, and by the early 1950s the company was making extensive use of materials supplied by C. & J. Clarks' English advertising agents. Between 1949 and 1955, Hallidays was spending sums varying from £9,000 to £17,000 per year on advertising, which represented something like 2-3 per cent of turnover.

Woodingtons was also beginning to pay increased attention to the advertising of its women's lines, and both the Holmes and Lotus ranges were backed by promotional material supplied by the English associate company. As Table 16 shows, expenditure on advertising moved sharply upwards in 1954 — albeit from a fairly low level — and then remained fairly steady until the end of the decade when improved performance permitted a further increase:

TABLE 16

J.H. Woodington Drogheda (1936) Ltd: ratio of advertising expenditure to turnover, 1952-60

	Turnover	Advertising	Advertising as % T/O
	(£)	(£)	(%)
1952	179,147	473	0.26
1953	217,137	71	0.03
1954	224,216	1,344	0.60
1955	210,704	1,074	0.51
1956	229,291	1,581	0.69
1957	256,590	1,637	0.64
1958	299,085	1,495	0.50
1959	299,569	2,743	0.90
1960	329,852	3,033	0.92

Source: *company accounts.*

In Woodingtons' case, this was not merely an attempt to establish the reputation of its ladies' shoes and generate extra sales; it was also part of a drive to increase the proportion of direct sales to retailers. Large wholesalers were of considerable importance to Woodingtons,[98] but sales figures from the early 1950s clearly demonstrated the dangers of relying upon a small number of large customers. Around 1953, Woodingtons commenced making sandals with micro-cellular rather than crepe rubber soles, and they were a great success with wholesalers. One large customer wanted them as an exclusive line and Woodingtons made 10,000 pairs as a special design and stamped with the wholesaler's brand. By the following year, however, a competitor was offering identical footwear at a slightly cheaper price, and the wholesaler did not order a single pair. This provided a compelling argument for increasing direct sales.[99]

At other footwear companies, however, expenditure on advertising was more modest, both in absolute terms and in relation to turnover. Between 1953 and 1955, James Winstanley was spending about £300-£500 on advertising, which represented 0.15 per cent of turnover. Yet it should be noted that this does not necessarily imply a lack of interest in advertising on the part of management. It must be remembered that the usual publicity methods were not costly. Lavish displays and expensive colour printing were uncommon and Telefís Éireann did not commence broadcasting until 1964. A company could keep its name in front of the public without the kind of expenditure which has become the norm in more recent years.

During the early 1950s, therefore, a number of Irish footwear companies were coming to realise the importance of forceful advertising. As the example of Hallidays demonstrates, this not only enhanced the company's reputation with the public but also gave it an important advantage in its dealings with distributors; because its products were in demand, Hallidays could sell Clarks brand footwear through a limited number of selected agents. This reduced the number of small accounts and enabled the company to establish retail price maintenance. In May 1949, for example, a circular from Clarks Ireland re-stated the trading standards which it expected its authorised agents to observe:

> 1. Our shoes, including rejects, are sold on the strict understanding that they will be sold at retail prices and will not be subject to 'mark down' during their current season.
>
> 2. They will not be offered for re-sale to other distributors whether at retail prices or below.
>
> 3. Rejects or seconds will not be displayed in windows or other advertised.[100]

It was considered necessary to issue this reminder because Clarks Ireland was receiving reports that its shoes were being offered by a number of unauthorised dealers, often at reduced prices. The company asked for assistance in tracking down the source of their supplies and threatened to close the account of any agent who did not comply with its terms.[101] This was felt to be in the best interests of its customers as a whole, and is an interesting example of Clarks Ireland's attempts to build up goodwill between manufacturers and retailer — a feature which was conspicuously lacking in the

Irish footwear market. The same circular of May 1949 provides another illustration; it was noted that:

> with the re-imposition of tight quota control, we have received inquiries from distributors in many districts who are anxious to secure Clarks shoes. Only in a very few districts and then only after the fullest consultation with our old and valued customers, have we opened new accounts. We had to refuse supplies to most prospective accounts as we felt that it was against the interest of our old friends who had helped us to build up our business and whose interests are our first concern.[102]

However, Clarks' retailing policies led to a period of strained relations with the Department of Industry and Commerce when fair trading rules were introduced under the 1953 Restrictive Practices Act. Not surprisingly, unsuccessful applicants resented the agency system, for it was widely believed that they could not compete successfully against Clarks stockists. The most frequent complaints were that Clarks Ireland refused to supply the trade generally and insisted that minimum prices be observed, and the Fair Trade Commission asked for the ending of both practices. In the event, Clarks Ireland successfully resisted this pressure, pointing out that the division of a limited supply of Clarks shoes between neighbouring shops did not increase Clarks Ireland's sales, and might well increase distribution costs and lose the goodwill of existing customers.[103]

To improve the service which they offered, Hallidays and Clarks Ireland made use of the abnormal level of materials and finished stocks in 1951 to recreate an in-stock system, which enabled retailers to make small back-up orders. A postcard to the manufacturer would ensure prompt replacement as soon as a style or size was sold out. This was partly an exercise in goodwill because it was expensive to operate; however, there were some useful spin-offs. Firstly it tended to even out the flow of orders to the factory and, secondly, it created extra sales which would not have been possible with extended delivery dates or minimum quantity restrictions: thirdly, it provided the pretext for requesting weekly sales figures and other up-to-date information from retailers which enabled the manufacturer to forecast demand trends earlier and more accurately.[104]

During the early 1950s, therefore, some Irish manufacturers were beginning to devote more attention to marketing techniques. Although this implies an awareness of the nature of the problems facing the industry, the immediate results were fairly limited. While improvements in marketing helped to determine whose shoes the public bought, it seems clear that they did not succeed in persuading the public to buy more shoes. This would have to wait until there was a recovery in the state of the economy as a whole.

Nevertheless, the search for new products which were more in line with the trend in consumer demand, and the improvements of production and marketing techniques, were beginning to lead some of the Irish footwear manufacturers away from their traditional reliance upon the heavy boot sector towards lighter types, and from medium price to higher price ranges. While we should be careful not to over-estimate the extent of this trend in the early 1950s, this was clearly a more positive response to the problems facing the industry than a cut-back in output. And, in the long term, the firms with the best growth potential were those which were able, by virtue of their concentration on quality, production efficiency and brand reputation, to develop export business which would reduce their dependence upon a small home market.

The period immediately after the Second World War offered good opportunities for the development of export business until foreign competitors could put their industry back on a peacetime footing but, as we have seen, the Irish footwear industry was not able to recover sufficiently quickly to make the most of this situation. The first signs of a growing interest in export business came with the signing of an Anglo-Irish Trade Agreement on 31 July 1948[105] and the subsequent announcement in September 1949 that the British government was to permit free entry of Irish footwear in return for preferential treatment of British goods.[106] This was important because the United Kingdom offered a much larger market for footwear and there were no problems with exchange rates or language to complicate matters. For most manufacturers, exporting meant the development of UK sales, and the decision to allow Irish footwear into Britain offered opportunities for increased sales to manufacturers which, like Hallidays, Woodingtons and Padmore & Barnes, concentrated upon the better quality types of footwear. Other overseas markets looked less attractive, although the Swedish State Trade Commission announced in October 1949 that it was prepared to grant licences for the import of Irish shoes. Sweden had recently decontrolled footwear and Irish imports could undercut the home manufacturers' prices.[107]

The first manufacturer to take advantage of the relaxation of import controls in Britain was John Halliday & Son and, again, the key factor was the close relationship with C.& J. Clark. During 1949, Bancroft Clark approached Arthur Halliday with a proposal that Hallidays should commence production of certain lines for Clarks' British customers. The range he had in mind was Clarks' 'Serenity' brand, which were essentially women's comfort shoes aimed at the 35-plus market. They were only made in the wider fittings and offered extra arch support, but Clarks was careful to emphasise that comfort was not achieved at the expense of style and its advertisements referred to them as 'a stylish shoe with an unusual number of comfort features'.[108] Clarks wanted to reorganise its factories on a production unit basis and it was intended to shift the 'Serenity' unit to Dundalk in order to facilitate reorganisation of its British factories and concentrate on other badly needed lines. The agreement, which was signed in December 1949, differed in a number of ways from the existing agreement which covered manufacture under the Clarks brand for the Irish market, because C.& J. Clark wanted to retain close control over styling and quality. In effect, the 'Serenity' unit was run from Street as a branch factory and Clarks had to obtain a New Manufacture Licence (although this presented no problems as it was an export business). Hallidays provided floor space and equipment and remained responsible for the actual shoemaking, but a quality control expert was sent to Dundalk and C.& J. Clark was responsible for pattern cutting, specifying components, styling of lasts and the supply of upper and sole leather.[109]

'Serenity' production was transferred from Street during 1950 and output was gradually built up to 1,500 pairs per week by 1955, although there were periodical fluctuations due to organisational and quality control problems during the early 1950s. For Clarks, the 'Serenity' agreement meant a reduction in profit margins — a detailed analysis in October 1951 revealed that manufacturing costs in Dundalk were about 5 per cent higher than in Street[110] — but this was more than offset by the opportunity it provided for rationalising and improving the layout of its English factories. As far as Hallidays was concerned, the major advantage was that it offered the prospect of a guaranteed export market. Moreover, Clarks' responsibility for materials, patterns and other items reduced the risks, financial and otherwise, which were usually attendant upon export sales. Table 17 indicates the importance of 'Serenity' sales to Hallidays.

TABLE 17

John Halliday & Son Ltd / Clarks Ireland Ltd:
sales breakdown, 1952

	Value (£)	% of Turnover
Home sales	540,562	70.9
'Serenity' brand exports	146,657	19.2
Other exports	75,880	9.9

Source: Hallidays, H 5/6.

Inevitably, the agreement meant that ties between the two companies were strengthened because Clarks kept a much closer watch upon quality than it had done in the case of footwear intended for the Irish market. Hallidays had to be brought up to the standard which English distributors expected from footwear bearing the Clarks brand and this led to frequent visits by quality control personnel from Street.[111] The success of the 'Serenity' agreement led Bancroft Clark to suggest the building of a factory in Dundalk to manufacture youths' welted shoes for Clarks to sell in Britain. The agreement went ahead, although a new factory was not necessary because Hallidays was able to acquire Connollys' Dundalk premises. Clarks was to style the range and make available all the necessary plant and machinery under terms identical to the 'Serenity' agreement. However, production of these types did not prove anything like as successful. There were frequent manufacturing problems[112] and, between 1951 and 1955, youths' welts lost about £10,000 per year. Arthur Halliday did not feel that they offered good value for money compared with competitors' products and was reluctant to put up prices. He also noted in October 1955 that the unit was running at about 75 per cent of full capacity and, as full production would mean an end to losses, he concluded that it was a selling problem rather than a manufacturing one. Admittedly, the depressed state of the British footwear market was partly to blame but Clarks rightly pointed out that sales were being lost because of variable quality and irregular deliveries and that this was due to problems in Dundalk rather than in Street.[113]

C.& J. Clark was also asked to consider selling Hallidays' men's welted shoes in the United Kingdom. As we have seen, these lines were originally developed for the Irish market, but were experiencing fierce competition — the market leaders in men's welts were K (Winstanley), Lotus (Governeys), Rawsons, and Moccasin (Padmore & Barnes) — and, as Arthur Halliday noted in May 1955, 'Sales of men's welts in this country are in the doldrums; Rawson and Moccasin are both feeling it, and the only successful firm is Winstanley, who really are offering very good footwear at extremely competitive prices'.[114] Although Hallidays' Irish sales were picking up, access to a much larger market was needed if the men's welted unit was to become profitable. Clarks did begin to take delivery of small quantities for Peter Lord and for its overseas customers, but export sales of men's welted shoes were still restricted by quality control problems and did not come to represent a substantial part of Hallidays' business.

Hallidays also began to display a growing interest in the American and Scandinavian markets after 1949, but sales were very small in comparison with its UK business and were not really profitable. However, they were a valuable means of acquiring competitive experience, and further enhanced Hallidays' standing with the government and public as a substantial exporter.

Nearly all the other Irish footwear manufacturers took some steps to develop exports,[115] and, like Hallidays, showed a particular interest in the American and Scandinavian markets. Wisely, few firms paid much attention to European markets because Britain, Italy and, to a lesser extent, West Germany, were regarded as dangerous competitors and the design flair of Italian shoemakers was often mentioned as a particular strength.[116] Most Irish companies were reluctant to enter Europe unless they could offer footwear at a substantially lower price. A number of firms sought the assistance of Córas Trachtála (the Exports Promotion Board) which had been set up by the government in 1952 to promote Irish products in overseas markets. CTT was primarily interested in the North American market, and its most effective contribution came in the form of general information about markets, advice about means and techniques of selling, and restricted market testing, for example by carrying samples and exhibiting at trade fairs.[117]

Yet it must be conceded that in general progress was slow, and there was no-one to challenge Hallidays' pre-eminence in exporting. With the exception of Clarks, British manufacturers did not allow their associate companies in Ireland to use their brands outside the home market, and the Irish factories did not find it easy to enter export markets during the late 1940s and early 1950s. Firstly, the British, European and American markets were all suffering from the economic recession, and Irish imports had to face fierce competition from native producers. Secondly, the Irish manufacturers were often ill-equipped to cope with the problems associated with export sales. Their concentration upon the home market meant that the management lacked any experience in dealing with overseas customers and was reluctant to make the strenuous efforts needed to promote their lines. Some manufacturers did not avail themselves of the services of CTT, which were admittedly limited in scope.

Thirdly, there was the question of the suitability of Irish-made footwear for foreign markets. There were serious obstacles to the development of an export trade in the cheaper styles of mass-produced footwear because margins were usually narrower than in the higher price brackets. Consequently, the best opportunities for overseas sales were restricted to those manufacturers who could compete in the better quality categories — and it may be conjectured that few were in a position to offer lines which were likely to achieve large sales. In many instances, Irish footwear could not compete in free markets, either in terms of quality or price. In January 1953, for example, CTT reported that in the United States Irish footwear did not have any advantages which gave them the edge over domestic products. Buyers noted that some lines were simply unsuitable for the American market, and in general they found Irish goods to be overpriced. Irish footwear was often compared unfavourably with imports from Britain; manufacturers in the United Kingdom had been able to acquire a very good reputation in America but, while reputation was undoubtedly a valuable asset, British shoes had only found a volume market because they were competitively priced. In fact, they were usually being sold cheaper than American footwear of a comparable quality.[118] Without an established reputation to sustain them, the quality of Irish exports had to be at least as good as British products and the price lower. It is clear that many manufacturers could not meet these requirements and this inability to offer the right footwear at the right price was largely due to the fact that the Irish footwear industry did not possess a healthy home base. Indeed, it is often the case that an *expansion* in home demand provides the greatest stimulus to export sales by increasing investment, raising productivity and providing a cushion for entry into riskier foreign markets.[119]

In view of these considerations, it is hardly surprising that the Irish manufacturers were unable to make much of an impact in the early 1950s upon overseas markets. Nevertheless, the significance of their growing interest in exporting should not be under-estimated; as we have seen, export business could have a useful effect upon overall profitability and was a useful means of generating goodwill with the Irish government and public. Moreover, it was clearly a more desirable response to the problems of a small home market than a mere cutback in output levels, and the experience gained in export markets in the early 1950s stood the Irish manufacturers in good stead when opportunities began to improve later in the decade.

Thus, some at least of the Irish manufacturers were beginning to make serious efforts to deal with the problems which they were facing in the late 1940s and early 1950s, and there was a slow but steady move towards lighter, better quality footwear. In virtually every instance, the firms which responded fastest and most successfully to this development were those which had entered into agreements with foreign manufacturers and could readily obtain access to outside expertise. Probably at no time had a British connection been more advantageous. Of these companies, by far the most successful was John Halliday & Son Ltd, which benefitted from its particularly close liaison with C. & J. Clark, the vitality of its management and the strength of its brands. In the first post-war decade, Hallidays was steadily moving to a position of market leadership. As Table 18 shows, its share of total production rose quite dramatically over the period as a whole, although the upward trend was interrupted in 1949 and 1952. It will also be apparent how very much smaller Woodingtons' share was. In fact, by this criterion, Hallidays was very large indeed, because the footwear industry — in Britain and Europe as well as Ireland — is one of fairly small concerns, typically with around 5 per cent of the home market. Moreover, it must be remembered that Hallidays was not at all successful by its own standards in the men's market and its share of the market in other sectors was proportionately larger. In 1956, Hallidays accounted for 3.5 per cent of total men's production; 13.2 per cent of

TABLE 18

John Halliday & Son Ltd and J.H. Woodington Drogheda (1936) Ltd: share of home production, 1945-56

	Hallidays		Woodingtons	
	By Quantity %	By Value %	By Quantity %	By Value %
1945	7.4	10.6	n.a.	3.8
1946	7.5	11.0	n.a.	3.5
1947	8.8	11.9	n.a.	3.3
1948	10.5	12.9	n.a.	2.0
1949	8.1	11.5	n.a.	3.1
1950	8.3	10.6	n.a.	n.a.
1951	12.5	11.0	n.a.	n.a.
1952	9.9	10.9	n.a.	3.1
1953	11.7	14.4	n.a.	3.2
1954	12.8	n.a.	n.a.	3.6
1955	13.9	n.a.	n.a.	3.3
1956	12.6	17.1	n.a.	3.5

Source: company accounts; *Census of Industrial Production.*

children's footwear production; and 22.5 per cent of ladies' footwear production (by volume).[120] It is easy to see why an agency for Clarks' women's and children's shoes was generally regarded as an essential part of a successful retail business in Ireland.

The only company which matched Hallidays in terms of size was John Rawson & Son Ltd. In the 1930s, Rawsons was by far the larger of the two but, by the 1950s, the gap had virtually disappeared. Moreover, Hallidays was growing in terms of total assets, while Rawsons entering a period of slow but steady decline which continued until its eventual liquidation in the mid-1960s (Table 19).

Woodingtons and Padmore & Barnes were both considerably smaller than the big two, but were still substantial companies by Irish standards. Another company which deserves a mention here is the Edenderry Shoe Co. Ltd of Edenderry, Co. Offaly. This was a company which possessed very close links with its associated companies in Britain,[121] and during the 1950s it was a growing force in the market for ladies' fashions and casual shoes. In particular, a number of commentators noted that it was beginning to make considerable inroads into Rawsons' share of the market. Unfortunately, Edenderry was a private company in the 1950s[122] and information on its activities is not available. At this time, its issued capital totalled £70,000, which placed it between Woodingtons and Padmore & Barnes in size. Most of the other companies were considerably smaller; Donaghys and Birr Shoes, for example, had an issued capital of £29,000 and £19,000 respectively, although again it is not possible to provide more detailed information.

TABLE 19

Issued Capital and Total Assets, 1950-56 (£000)

	John Halliday & Son Ltd		John Rawson & Son Ltd		J.H. Woodington Drogheda (1936) Ltd		Padmore & Barnes Ltd	
	Issued capital	Total assets	Issued capital	Total assets	Issued capital	Total assets	Issued capital	Total assets
1950	180	358	180	379	100	172*	47	113
1951	180	417	180	470	100	178	47	108
1952	180	402	180	373	100	161	47	116
1953	180	464	180	388	100	205	47	120
1954	180	398	220	410	100	171	47	125
1955	180	456	220	393	100	168	47	118
1956	195	433	220	378	100	186	47	142

*It will be recalled that Woodingtons' assets were inflated by the excessive valuation placed upon goodwill. By 1950, goodwill had been reduced to a book figure of £11,000 but this was still abnormally high by footwear industry standards. Hallidays and Padmore & Barnes did not include a goodwill valuation in their accounts, while for Rawsons the 1950 figure was £1,250.

It is also interesting to compare the profitability of different firms during this period.

TABLE 20

Return on capital, 1945-55

	John Halliday & Son Ltd NP : TA (%)	John Rawson & Son Ltd NP : TA (%)	J.H. Woodington Drogheda (1936) Ltd NP : TA (%)	Padmore & Barnes Ltd NP : TA (%)
1945	9.1	n.a.	11.5	36.8
1946	5.8	n.a.	11.5	15.5
1947	8.9	n.a.	8.1	12.1
1948	6.3	n.a.	1.6	10.2
1949	5.3	n.a.	1.5	14.4
1950	7.8	10.7	2.9	11.5
1951	4.6	15.7	2.8	13.0
1952	6.5	13.9	Loss	11.2
1953	10.6	9.7	2.0	15.0
1954	11.3	8.7	Loss	10.4
1955	11.8	n.a.	0.6	4.2

Note: NP: TA — ratio of pre-tax profits to total assets.

As the table shows, Hallidays' profitability was not maintained after 1945. However, the poor return on capital in 1946 and 1948-9 was partly due to the capitalisation of debts, and the steady improvement after 1953 suggests that the company was beginning to benefit from improvements in marketing and production efficiency. The incomplete series for Rawsons shows a relatively good performance in 1952 and 1953 but thereafter a decline set in and this trend was to continue into the 1960s. Padmore & Barnes was still showing a good return on capital, but in 1954 S.J. Davis died and the company was sold to the British-based Airborne group. This was to have an unfortunate effect upon the Kilkenny company's fortunes. These two examples clearly indicate that connections with a British company *per se* were not a guarantee of success in the Irish market. This point will require further consideration in a subsequent chapter but it is worth noting that the value of a British connection depended upon the kind of service which the British company was able and willing to offer; in both these instances, the problems of the Irish company were largely due to the failings of the English management.

Two other points should be made. Firstly, the profits made by Irish firms were very small in absolute terms. Hallidays' net profits before tax had reached £54,000 by 1955 and Rawsons' best figure was £61,000 in 1953. Woodingtons' profits were below £10,000 for most of the period and Padmore & Barnes, the company with the best rate of return, only once exceeded £15,000 between 1946 and 1955. These figures provide a useful and essential reminder that, even by Irish standards, the footwear producers were fairly small businesses. Secondly, it must be stated that, even in the case of Hallidays, Rawsons and Padmore & Barnes, the return on capital was often considered insufficient to permit a reasonable reinvestment rate. In Britain and other countries, footwear manufacturers regarded a 20 per cent return on total assets as an acceptable figure, and the four Irish companies surveyed did not approach this level. If, as seems likely, these companies were amongst the most successful, it is clear that some of their competitors must have achieved a very low return on assets. Yet it must be conceded that the British industry was also in difficulties in the early 1950s, and in 1951-2 the average return on total assets recorded by 12 leading footwear manufacturers in the United Kingdom was around 12 per cent.[123]

How, then, are we to assess the footwear manufacturers' efforts to improve their footwear during the first post-war decade? Clearly, the economic environment was often uncertain or downright depressing, and government regulations sometimes exacerbated the difficulties facing footwear producers instead of easing them. Not surprisingly, the response to post-war conditions was uneven. It depended upon the size of the individual concern and its ability to draw upon the technical expertise of outside consultants or associated companies. It also depended to a considerable degree upon the calibre of

1 The closing room at James Winstanley's Dublin factory in 1910, where the component parts of the uppers were sewn together using heavy-duty sewing machines.

2 Another view of James Winstanley's Dublin factory just before the First World War. This is the making section, where the completed uppers were lasted (stretched over the last), and the sole attached. Unlike closing, this was men's work.

3 The Blake sole-sewing machine, widely used in Irish factories from the late nineteenth century until after the Second World War.

4 Seán Lemass was Fianna Fáil's leading spokesman on economic affairs in the 1930s. He was Minister for Industry and Commerce from 1932 until 1939, when he moved to the newly created Department of Supplies. © RTE.

5 John Halliday & Son's boot factory at Bramley, near Leeds, in 1887.

6 'Pulling over' ladies' shoes at John Rawson & Son's Dundalk factory in the 1930s. Treadle-operated pincers stretched the upper over the last from heel to toe and across the forepart. Adjustments could be made for straightness and tension by the use of levers at the top of the machine. In the foreground is a steam heater, used to 'mull' or condition the upper prior to stretching.

7 Another view of Rawsons' factory in the 1930s. In the shoe room, finished pairs were touched up, ironed, cleaned and boxed ready for dispatch.

13 Hallidays' factory, 1948: the cutting room. Templates were used to cut out the various component parts of the uppers.

14 Hallidays' factory, 1948: preparing soles and insoles. The presses used to cut the heavy sole leather can be seen in the background.

15 Hallidays' factory, 1948: the lasting department. Methods had changed little since the interwar years.

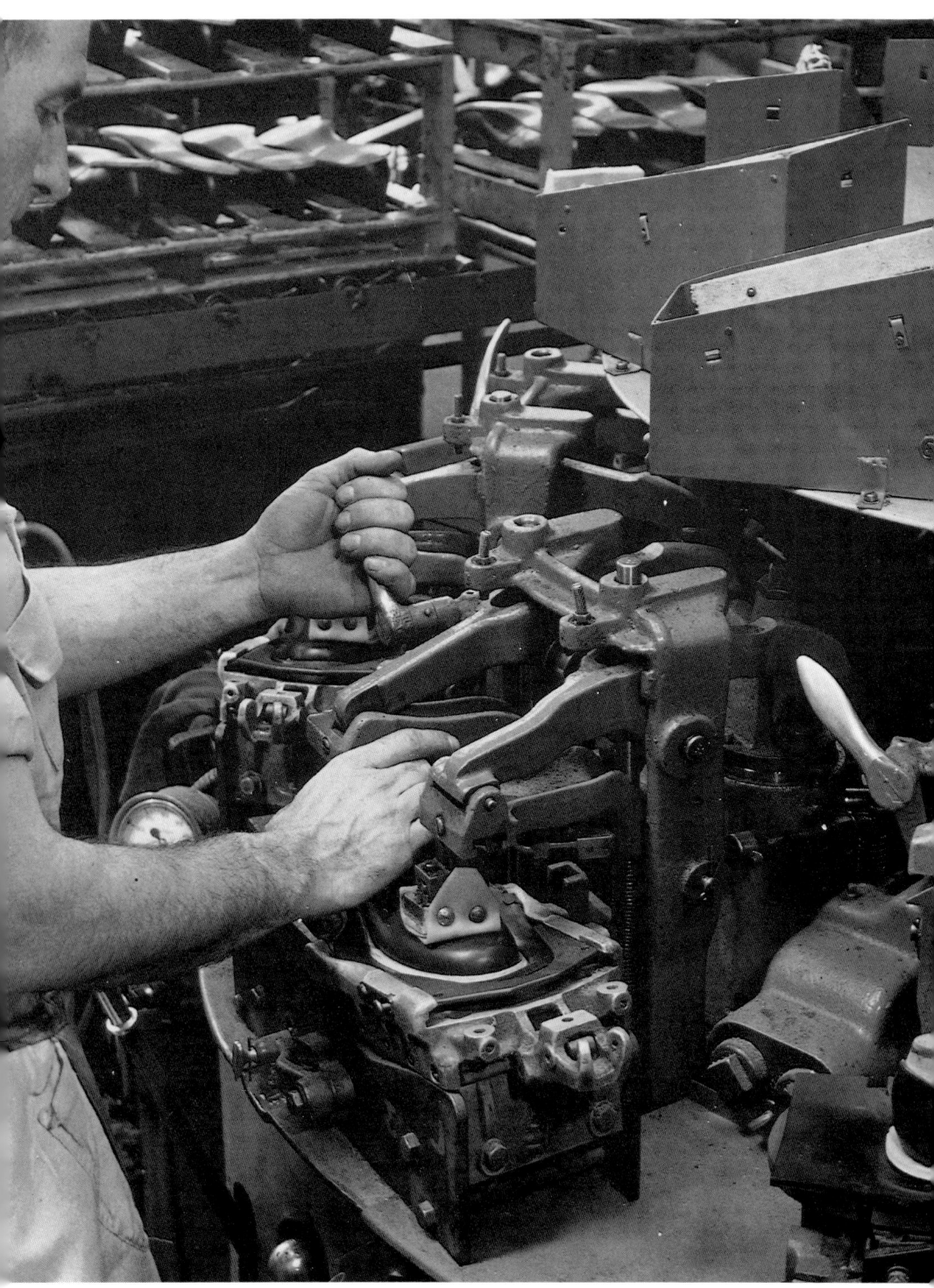

16 The cemented process became increasingly popular with manufacturers in the later 1950s as the public began to demand lighter, more flexible shoes. Here, soles are being attached on a multi-station press, using infra-red heaters to activate the cement.

17 A direct vulcanising machine, which vulcanised and moulded rubber soles and bonded them to the upper in one operation. Developed by C. & J. Clark, it was extensively used by Hallidays in the late 1950s and early 1960s to produce men's and children's shoes. After the upper was fitted over the metal last, the moulds were brought together and filled with the rubber mix. The temperature gauges for the heaters can be seen on the top of the machine.

18 Padmore & Barnes' 'Wallabee' shoe, a hand-sewn mocassin. Twelve million pairs have been sold around the world since production commenced in the mid-1960s.

19 Wallabee shoes being made on a backpart pre-forming machine at Padmore & Barnes' Kilkenny factory in the later 1960s. This machine was used for shaping the back part of the shoe before the last was inserted.

management. A move into the market for better quality footwear, for instance, made heavy demands upon management and supervisory staff. New skills had to be acquired and new standards met. The quality control and production study procedures which this necessitated tended, somewhat paradoxically, to be very labour intensive in terms of management time. Management's inability to cope with the demands of marketing was also particularly significant; as we have seen, management was generally better equipped to cope with production problems than with marketing ones in the 1950s.

A few footwear companies were unable to cope with the challenge posed by post-war conditions and closed down, but others began to respond to the need for a restructuring of the industry and took action to set their long term prospects on a firmer base. We must of course be careful not to overestimate the extent to which this had been achieved by 1955 — all in all, it was some time before the improvements which had been put in hand began to show through, and the footwear industry did not really emerge from the doldrums until the Irish economy as a whole began to pick up in the late 1950s. But, once this occurred, the footwear industry was able to enter upon a period of rapid and sustained growth.

6

ECONOMIC PLANNING AND RENEWED GROWTH
1955-61

The balance of payments crisis of 1955 represented something of a turning-point in the economic history of Ireland. Until then, the policy of protection and self-sufficiency which had dominated economic affairs since 1932 had not really been questioned. Indeed, it was clear to the vast majority of observers that such a policy was essential to generate industrial growth and provide some answer to the perennial problem of unemployment in Ireland. The difficulties which many of the developing industries experienced could be regarded as the inevitable result of forcing the pace of industrialisation or of the abnormal economic conditions pertaining throughout the 1930s and 1940s. By the mid-1950s, however, it was apparent that, while Irish economic growth was reasonably encouraging in absolute terms, it was much less satisfactory in comparison with most other industrialised nations, which were now benefiting from the return of relatively normal trading conditions. Between 1950 and 1961 the growth rate of GNP in Ireland was significantly lower than that of Europe and America, and was only one-third of that of the EEC countries. It was, however, marginally better than Britain's growth rate.[1]

The government's attitude to self-sufficiency was slowly beginning to change. Considerable attention was being devoted to the nature of Ireland's problems and the crisis of 1955 injected new vigour into Irish policy making. The later 1950s saw the appearance of a number of new incentives designed to encourage both new and existing industries. The grants programme which had operated in the underdeveloped western areas since 1952 was recognised as a means of encouraging industrial expansion throughout the country. In 1956, the programme was extended, although there were still differentials to encourage the location of new industries in the underdeveloped areas.[2] In June 1957, an additional scheme for technical assistance grants was introduced. Initially, these grants were fixed at 50 per cent of the cost of each project, although they were reduced to 33 per cent at the end of 1957.[3] Small grants towards market research aimed at the development of exporting were also made available through Córas Trachtála.

Another development which resulted from the need to stimulate private investment was the relaxation of the Control of Manufactures legislation in

1958. The Acts of 1932-4 had placed numerous restrictions on the activities of foreign nationals and this became a problem when the Irish Development Authority began to canvass for investment from overseas. The 1958 Industrial Development (Encouragement of External Investment) Act represented a sharp reversal of public policy and most of the controls upon companies intending to produce commodities which were not already being made in Ireland were removed. At the same time, controls were removed from companies which were primarily producing for export. The alarming balance of payments deficit of 1955 had emphasized the Irish public's growing demand for imported consumer goods and it was also apparemt that any increase in Irish industrial output implied an increase in raw material imports. The extent to which a deficit on the visible trade balance could be offset by invisible earnings from remittances, dividends and tourism was strictly limited, and the Irish government introduced a number of measures intended to stimulate the growth of export business. The most important of these was the introduction of tax relief on exports under the Finance Act of 1956. This Act provided for the remission of most of the income tax and corporation tax due on new or increased export business for the term of five years, and the amounts and periods of remission were extended by the Finance Acts of 1957-8.[4]

Yet up to 1958, growth rates were still disappointing and, in real terms, the average increase in national income between 1955 and 1958 barely exceeded one per cent per annum.[5] Industry was still suffering from depressed trading conditions and there was no sign of an upward movement in the index of industrial production.[6] There was widespread criticism of the government's role; in particular, it was claimed that there was far too much unproductive investment. The disappointing growth rate led in November 1958 to the publication of the first *Programme for Economic Expansion*, which covered the period from 1959 to 1963.[7] This programme was intended to shift the deep-seated pessimism which had resulted from prolonged stagnation during the 1950s, and its primary objectives were to direct investment into more productive channels and to raise the growth rate of national income to two per cent per annum — a fairly modest target compared to the figures achieved by most countries at this time.[8] Although there was a time lag before industrialists responded to the government's initiative the programme had a profound psychological effect.[9] In fact, an average growth rate of about four per cent per annum was achieved between 1959 and 1963.[10] The visible balance of payments deficit was reduced and the 1960 figure of £73.5 million was the lowest recorded in the post-war period.[11] While total imports were moving upwards fairly steadily, from £204.6 million in 1951 to £226.2 million in 1960, exports nearly doubled, from £81.5 million to £152.7 million, with a noticeable acceleration in the growth rate after 1958.

This trend was largely due to the international boom in manufactured goods, but another important factor was the existence of surplus production capacity in Irish industry, which permitted a fairly rapid increase in input without additional capital investment.

The *Programme for Economic Expansion* was also intended to improve the competitiveness of the private sector in readiness for the adoption of freer trading conditions, because the government was beginning to reconsider the value of protection to the Irish economy. This trend was given further impetus in January 1957 when the Organisation for European Economic Co-Operation (OEEC) initiated negotiations for a European free trade areas. After the EEC was set up by the Treaty of Rome (March 1957), most of the other OEEC members joined together in the European Free Trade Association (EFTA), but Ireland eventually decided not to participate. Trade with Britain was already covered by special trade agreements and the recent balance of payments crisis meant that, in the short term at least, it was not desirable to initiate any reduction in import restrictions. In fact, protection was actually stepped up between 1955 and 1958; special levies were imposed on a wide range of goods in March 1956 and July 1957 at a rate of 37.5 per cent *ad valorem* (25 per cent preferential). The purpose of these levies was to curb imports rather than to stimulate industrial expansion in Ireland and they were intended as a temporary measure, although in many cases they were replaced by custom duties — including duties on quite a few commodities which previously had been exempted. Most of these additions took place in 1958 when the free trade area was under negotiation and, as Meenan notes, 'There may well have been some design of increasing tariffs so as to obtain a better bargaining position when free trade became obligatory'.[12] Nevertheless, the Irish government was still interested in developing closer links with the rest of Europe; Irish industrial development had been influenced by the fortunes of the British economy and Britain had had a very unsatisfactory growth rate. In July 1961, when it became apparent that Britain would apply to join the EEC, Ireland decided to follow suit and, in a number of important policy statements by the Minister for Industry and Commerce, it was announced that tariffs would be reduced by 10 per cent from 1 January 1963, with subsequent annual reductions.[13]

The period between 1955 and 1961 therefore, was characterised by a growing government involvement in economic development and a re-assessment of previous policies. State grants programmes were extended to provide an alternative to private investment and, for the first time, investment by overseas companies was actively encouraged. The excessive concentration upon the needs of the home market, which had characterised government involvement in earlier years, was giving way to a new emphasis upon exporting, and this was coupled with the realisation that Ireland would have to be prepared for the eventual relaxation of tariff and quota controls — although the immediate needs of the Irish economy meant that little could be done in this direction in the short term.

In general, the experience of the footwear industry was similar to that of the Irish economy as a whole. In 1955, output was at its lowest level since the war, but between 1955 and 1959 the annual growth rate average 3.4 per cent. In 1960-1 it quickened to 13.7 per cent per annum. The value of production (at 1961 prices) rose by 2.9 per cent per annum in 1955-9 and 11.7 per cent in 1960-1. Average ex-factory prices remained fairly steady; a significant factor here was the stabilisation of materials prices after a period of violent and erratic increases. This growth in home production was matched by a fairly steady increase in imports, which rose from 139,848 pairs in 1955 to 234,384 pairs in 1961. Imports of non-leather footwear fell slightly, while leather footwear imports rose sharply thanks to a relaxation of the quota restrictions. Overall, imports' share of the market remained fairly steady at about 4 per cent.

By the footwear industry's standards, this was a relatively prolonged period of growth; in previous years, increased output had quickly been followed by cutbacks as unsold stocks built up. In the late 1950s, however, there was a noticeable increase in per capita consumption.[14] Especially after 1957, most companies were reporting that trade was very good, with several months' orders in hand. Clearly, the second half of the decade saw a marked improvement in the fortunes of the Irish footwear industry and the causes of this trend require some consideration. Was it the result of important developments within the industry itself or was it largely due to external factors, such as the renewed attention of the Irish government to economic affairs or the general improvement in domestic and foreign markets?

In Chapter 5 it was shown that quite a number of companies made considerable efforts to improve their performance, and there were further developments towards the end of the decade. Particularly significant was the adoption of scientific leather measurement (SLM) at two factories.[15] Nevertheless, the exact significance of such improvements is not easy to determine. Firstly, their effect in terms of productivity requires careful consideration. Such improvements help to explain why the size of the labour force did not increase in proportion to the rapid rise in output between 1955 and 1961. As can be seen from Appendix VI, there was therefore a steady increase in per capita output. This increase, however, was also partly due to the existence of surplus production capacity; when trading conditions improved, manufacturers were able to make more efficient use of previously under-utilised labour and machinery and this, as well as improvements in the techniques of production, lay behind the growth of per capita production. Secondly, one hesitates to suggest that improvements which were primarily concerned with production techniques led directly to increased sales and increased per capita consumption; marketing remained a weak link. In Ireland, as in Britain, management's conception of the role and scope of marketing was often fairly unsophisticated and it always tended to deal much better with production problems than with marketing problems. The timing of the period of growth suggests that it was primarily due to the general recovery in the state of the Irish economy rather than to factors operating within the footwear industry itself. In other words, increased sales (and especially increased per capita consumption) depended upon rising real wages and living standards rather than upon the manufacturers' ability to persuade the public to buy more shoes.

Irish footwear manufacturers were also doing much better in overseas markets by the late 1950s. Again, demand was significantly influenced by factors operating *outside* the industry. There was an international boom in demand for manufactured goods and the Irish government actively encouraged exports by way of Córas Trachtála (CTT) and the 1956 Finance Act. By 1960, nearly all the Irish footwear manufacturers had taken some steps to develop exports, usually with the assistance of CTT. In general, exporting was still primarily directed at the British market, although seven companies were selling via agents in the United States and Canada.[16] Continental markets were still regarded as an unattractive proposition; CTT noted that Irish footwear would have to drop 20 per cent in price to be competitive in West Germany, while in the Netherlands, where the market was suffering from over-production and it was very difficult to sell imports, it was calculated that Irish prices were 15 per cent out of line.[17] Between 1955 and 1961, total exports tripled from 414,288 pairs (£700,201) to 1,301,712 pairs (£2,053,576), and by the latter date they represented 18.7 per cent of total production. In other words, exports were growing significantly faster than home sales.

A variety of factors lay behind the improved performance of the footwear industry in the later 1950s, and it has been necessary to emphasise the importance of outside influences. Yet there is no doubt that the improvements made by footwear manufacturers facilitated a rapid response once trading conditions improved. While materials costs rose by 24.9 per cent between 1956 and 1961 and labour costs by 28.5 per cent, 'remainder of net output' (manufacturing profit) rose by 97.7 per cent. It should also be noted that there was a noticeable improvement after 1958; between 1956 and 1958, manufacturing profits were increasing at an average of 7.7 per cent per year, compared with an average of 27.8 per cent for 1959-61.[18]

The experiences of individual companies did of course vary considerably, and it is worth considering the major developments in more detail. Within the area of production efficiency, reference has already been made to the introduction of scientific leather measurement. Briefly, the SLM procedure commenced with in-factory measurement to check the leather area figures supplied by the tanner. A second measurement was then made of the *useable* area of the hide, and these two measurements were combined to produce a 'true leather coefficient' — a figure of 92, for example, meant that out of a nominal 100 square feet, 92 square feet were useable. Next, it was necessary to work out how many items could reasonably be expected to be cut from each hide or skin. This was calculated for each type of shoe and produced a scale number based on the average hide or skin size and relating to the mid-point of the range of shoe sizes required. The scale number and the true leather coefficient could than be combined to give an exact cutting allowance for each style of shoe and which could then be scaled up or down according to the size of shoe being made. SLM was, inevitably, a fairly complex procedure, but it offered some significant advantages. It provided data on average leather requirements which eliminated much of the guesswork involved in costing a new line of shoes; by introducing an element of pre-planning, it helped speed up the clicking process and reduced waste; and it could be used as the basis for incentive payment schemes. Padmore & Barnes introduced SLM in 1956 at an initial cost of £2,520,[19] and also employed the consultancy firm of Weston Evans & Co. to make a survey with a view to reducing production costs.[20] Hallidays introduced a similar system at about the same time.[21]

Hallidays also employed BUSMC experts during 1958 to conduct a thorough overhaul of production and quality control methods in its men's factory, which was still unprofitable and giving cause for concern.[22] The BUSMC team concluded that there was no reason to believe that men's and youths' footwear could not be produced at competitive prices and was able to suggest a number of major improvements which could be made. For the most part, these consisted of eliminating wasteful or unnecessary operations and improving quality control methods to reduce the proportion of rejects.[23] As a result of the BUSMC survey, Hallidays was able to make substantial improvements and, by August 1958, Clarks Men's Sales in Street was able to report that quality was far more consistent and that there had been a significant reduction in the number of pairs which had to be returned to Dundalk.[24]

Another important consideration was re-investment. Like many other sectors of Irish industry in the 1950s, the footwear industry tended to show a low rate of investment. This did not seem too serious in the late 1950s because the existence of surplus production capacity meant that a considerable increase in output could be realised without further investment. In the long term, however, it seemed likely that further growth would be retarded unless the rate of investment could be stepped up.

This consideration led Hallidays to follow a policy of heavy re-investment during the late 1950s and early 1960s. The dividends paid never represented more than 20 per cent of net profits[25] and total capital employed rose from £456,000 in 1955 to £839,000 in 1961. The issued share capital rose from £180,000 to £359,000 by way of annual bonus issues. This re-investment policy provided the funds needed to continue Hallidays' reorganisation on a production unit basis. A new children's factory of 10,000 square feet was built in 1956,[26] and in 1959 the need to reorganise women's production and increase output of 'Serenity' shoes for C. & J. Clark led to the acquisition of a 20 acre site on the Rampart River in Dundalk.[27] A 20,000 square foot factory with a total capacity of 4,000 pairs per week was completed in December 1960,[28] and early in 1962 the chairman announced that another factory for women's production was to be built on the Rampart River site.[29]

Another company which was reorganised on a production unit basis at this time was Munster Shoes Ltd. This company's record had not been impressive since the war and, during 1957, it was realised that swift action was needed if the company was to be established on a profit-making basis. It was decided to eliminate uneconomic lines and outmoded methods of production, and to introduce a conveyor system. This meant returning to BUSMC about 170 machines which had been in use since the company's inception and confining production to cemented footwear. Specialisation in a fairly restricted product range was seen as the key to profitability. The main production unit was to concentrate upon ladies' styles while a subsidiary unit was established to produce girls', children's and infants' shoes. These alterations appeared to have the desired effect and, by the early 1960s, the company was able to report that both units were working near full capacity and that an export trade in ladies' fashion styles was slowly being built up.[30]

On the selling side, the trend towards lighter shoes continued and was increasingly associated with the use of rubber soles. There was also growing interest in the use of prefabricated rubber heels. At Woodingtons, heavy boot production was allowed to decline steadily as the volume of the Holmes and Lotus business grew. By February 1960, Philip McLoughlin was able to report that the heavy boot unit no longer made a significant contribution to the company's profits, and recommended its closure.[31] The unit ceased production in May 1960 and was replaced by a children's unit.[32] Another manufacturer which benefited from the trend towards lighter footwear was the Edenderry Shoe Co., which was a growing force in the late 1950s. Like Hallidays and Woodingtons, it owed much of its success to the use of agreements. An agreement was signed on 21 May 1958 with Joyce Inc. of Cincinnati, Ohio (a subsidiary of the United States Shoe Corporation) which gave Edenderry exclusive rights to manufacture and sell ladies' shoes in

Ireland under the 'Joyce' brand.[33] Equally important, however, was an agreement made with the Saxone Shoe Co. in 1956. Under this agreement, Edenderry was to make Saxone 'Jumping Jacks' children's shoes and had access to the technical experience of Saxone's parent company in the United Kingdom, but it quickly became much wider in scope as Edenderry became established as the major supplier to Saxone's retail shops in Ireland.[34] According to Arthur Halliday, Jack Abbott of Saxone was one of the best fashion shoe buyers in Europe and he wanted shoes made quickly to his exact specifications. The volume of business involved was sufficiently large to enable Edenderry to concentrate on meeting his requirements and this association proved very valuable.

The experience of Rawsons and Padmore & Barnes, however, demonstrated that a connection with a foreign company was by no means a guarantee of success. By the later 1950s, Rawsons was entering a gradual decline which was largely due to the fact that the company was 'controlled from a distance'. The local management was unable to act on its own initiative and had to refer to the parent company in Leicester for decisions on all but the most trivial matters. The Leicester management, which did not possess detailed knowledge of Irish market conditions, was increasingly unable to offer the kind of support needed and, as a result, companies like the Edenderry Shoe Co. were able to nibble away at Rawsons' market share.

Padmore & Barnes was another company which, to say the least, had a chequered history during the 1950s. Like Rawsons, Padmore & Barnes was very dependent upon its British parent for decision making and financial and technical back-up. After S.J. Davis' death in 1954, the Northampton and Kilkenny companies were sold to Airborne Shoes Ltd, a British company with a growing reputation for ladies' fashion shoes. Airborne made a number of significant improvements at Kilkenny; efforts were made to bring quality and styling up to the standard associated with the Airborne name, and the introduction of scientific leather measurement also took place during Airborne's ownership. Nevertheless, Airborne's ignorance of Irish conditions led to a number of serious errors. Men's sales, which still constituted the bulk of sales from Kilkenny, were allowed to decline sharply because Airborne was not interested in this sector of the market. In addition, a gentlemen's agreement was made which gave Tylers exclusive selling rights for Airborne brand ladies' shoes in Ireland. Unfortunately, the Irish management were not consulted or they would have pointed out the weakness of multiples in Ireland and the need to retain the goodwill of independent retailers. Moreover, Tylers was unsuitable as an agent because it was not regarded in Ireland as a high fashion house.

Padmore & Barnes' problems reached a peak in 1958 when the Airborne group was itself in difficulties, largely as a result of cash flow problems. In

March 1958, Padmore & Barnes was instructed to declare an 80 per cent ordinary share dividend. This was simply a tax saving device which resulted in a tax saving of £10,000 to the British owners but, although the dividend was never drawn, it shook the confidence of Padmore & Barnes' Irish bankers, the Hibernian Bank Ltd. Then, in May 1958, Padmore & Barnes was sold to two London financiers, Seymour Kraft and Edmund Stekel, who were engaged in a number of illegal commercial activities. A technical mistake relating to directors' qualifications attracted the attention of the *FinancialTimes* and an article in that journal in December 1958 placed Stekel and Kraft in great difficulties.[35] Their interests were passed to two associates, A.E.S. Hoffman and J.L. Burden, whose activities also came under criticism. An investigation was initiated by the Company Fraud Department of New Scotland Yard and Kraft, Stekel and Burden were charged with fraudulent conversion and making false statements.[36]

Padmore & Barnes relied upon a substantial overdraft, which, in the late 1950s, was running at £20,000 to £30,000, and, in May 1959, the Hibernian Bank, by now thoroughly alarmed, instituted bankruptcy proceedings to safeguard its interests.[37] A Receiver was appointed and it quickly became apparent that urgent and drastic action was necessary if the factory was to survive. Local interests were opposed to the liquidation of the company because of the lack of alternative employment opportunities in Kilkenny, and a consortium of local businessmen, headed by Mr Thomas Crotty raised the sum of £15,240 which was needed to purchase the company's assets. Negotiations were completed in July 1960, and on 31 August the Receiver withdrew and handed control of the business back to the directors.[38] The Munster & Leinster Bank agreed to an overdraft of £30,000, secured by a floating charge debenture.[39] It was decided to continue the manufacture of men's shoes, which still made up a substantial part of production, and the new management was able to continue making ladies' fashion shoes under the Airborne brand. An annual royalty payment of £1,000 was agreed upon and Mr M.S. Simpson, the new chairman of the Airborne Group, was asked to remain a director of Padmore & Barnes.[40] These arrangements continued until the Irish company was sold to Hallidays in December 1963.

The late 1950s and early 1960s saw some interesting developments in selling techniques. There was some evidence of greater interest in advertising and, in 1956, Clarks Ireland Ltd pioneered the use of radio advertising, albeit on a fairly small scale. Initially, it was decided to concentrate upon promoting children's footwear and a fifteen minute slot before school time was booked once a week. The intention, according to an information sheet distributed to retailers, was to create 'parent interest' in the fitting qualities of its children's shoes. Later in 1956, the emphasis was switched to its men's 'Craftmasters', and a new series of programmes on the history of footwear was prepared. By

1959, the programmes had been widened in scope and included 'Serenity' as well as 'Craftmasters'. They were introduced on Radio Éireann by Eamonn Andrews.[41]

Another interesting trend in the late 1950s was a move towards direct selling from manufacturer to retailer, which came about as a result of the difficulties associated with dealing with a small number of large wholesalers. In its report on the footwear industry, the Committee on Industrial Organisation noted that, in 1960, retailers accounted for 40 per cent of ex-factory sales, wholesalers 30 per cent, multiples 20 per cent, with the remainder distributed amongst a large number of non-specialist shops.[42] Since 1950, the wholesalers' share had fallen by about 5 per cent, while multiples had become of greater importance.

Individual manufacturers' sales did, however, display variations from the general trend. At one extreme was Woodingtons, which had been making strenuous efforts to reduce the importance of sales to wholesalers and sold the bulk of its Holmes and Lotus pairage direct to retailers. By 1959, Woodingtons' sales to wholesalers represented only 13.5 per cent of total turnover. At the other extreme was the Stedfast Shoe Co. which was specialising in unbranded women's shoes in the 29s. 11d. (£1.49) and 49s. 11d. (£2.49) price brackets. By a policy of close liaison with its customers, Stedfast was able to prove that it was possible to run a successful business on the basis of cheap unbranded footwear for distribution through a few large wholesalers. Stedfast was exceptional, however, for experts in both Ireland and Britain agreed that there were many hazards inherent in the unbranded sector and that it was usually less profitable than the manufacture of branded shoes. According to a survey of the unbranded sector by C. & J. Clark Ltd in 1972, the few firms which were successful were all efficient, low-cost, low overhead companies making cheap footwear and the key to their success was the ability of the management; they were run by men who had a large stake in the company, retained close personal control over all aspects of production and possessed considerable ability in identifying and producing the kind of shoes which their customers wanted.[43] Although relating to a much later date, the Clarks survey provides a clear exposition of the factors which enabled Stedfast to do well in a sector which was generally regarded as an unattractive proposition. At Stedfast, the key role was played by Ian McLerie, the managing director, who, with his father, owned a controlling interest in the company.

Another point worth mentioning in this context is that Hallidays was beginning to display an interest in forward integration by the end of the 1950s. Backward integration to control supplies had little appeal. Component manufacturers in Britain possessed a distinct advantage, and the only last maker in Ireland was a subsidiary of a British company. In addition, the fierce independence of Irish footwear manufacturers made it unlikely that they would accept control of their supplies by a competitor. There were, however, strengthening arguments for a move into retailing, because it was apparent that multiples would acquire an increasing share of the home market in future, Hallidays began to consider the acquisition of retail outlets because it stood to lose a valuable part of its business if a competitor should acquire control of the multiples. In 1958, Hallidays' board noted that there appeared to be a good opportunity because Dolcis wanted to sell its three Irish shops. Tylers, with about 30 shops, might also be about to sell some of them. But while it was agreed to keep a close watch on the situation, nothing was done at this time, largely because of the opposition of Arthur Halliday himself. Halliday felt that the acquisition of retail interests would lead to the loss of goodwill with existing customers and result in the dilution of management strength. Moreover, as Hallidays had no retailing expertise, it would become heavily reliant upon Peter Lord for advice and assistance. Arthur Hallidays' arguments were persuasive and were justified by subsequent events; a dominant retailing group along the lines of the British Shoe Corporation did not develop in Ireland, and in fact none of the other Irish footwear manufacturers displayed much interest in multiple retailing. However, Hallidays' interest in forward integration was renewed in the mid-1960s when the removal of the Control of Manufactures legislation made it possible for British companies to acquire retail interests in Ireland.

The late 1950s also saw a very rapid growth in overseas sales, and here again Hallidays and Clarks Ireland took the lead. In 1950, export business made up about 10 per cent of Clarks Ireland's turnover; thereafter, as Table 21 shows, the proportion increased rapidly. By 1961, Clarks Ireland was

TABLE 21

Clarks Ireland Ltd: destination of sales and share of total Irish footwear exports, 1953-61

	Total sales (£000)	Home sales (£000)	Export sales (£000)	Home sales as % total sales %	Export sales as % total sales %	Clarks Ireland exports as % total Irish exports %
1953	1,016	637	378	62.7	37.3	64.0
1954	1,125	687	438	61.1	38.9	54.0
1955	1,182	679	502	57.5	42.5	54.7
1956	1,896	798	1,098	42.1	57.9	53.8

Source: Company accounts; *Trade and Shipping Statistics*.

exporting direct to the United States, Scandinavia and Holland and, via C. & J. Clark's sales organisation, to Hong Kong, South and East Africa, Rhodesia and New Zealand,[44] but the bulk of its export sales still consisted of 'Serenity' and youths' lines for Clarks' British customers. This was particularly important because, as we have seen, 'Serenity' sales were only slightly less profitable than home sales and provided opportunities for specialisation and long production runs. In this period, Clarks Ireland's export business was expanded at the expense of home sales, which did not grow at anything like the same rate.

This emphasis on exporting was still unusual in the Irish footwear industry. Although most companies participated to some extent in the export boom, the quantities involved were usually insufficient to attract good agents and build up a brand reputation in overseas markets.[45] Consequently export orders tended to be on a 'one-off' basis and were often viewed as a windfall rather than an important element of future growth. As was shown in Chapter 5, this was partly due to the fact that such exports were often of marginal profitability because of the need to offer Irish footwear at attractive prices in more competitive markets.

One result of Clarks Ireland's dominance in exporting was that its attitude to the relaxation of protection was rather different from that of its competitors. Hallidays and Clarks Ireland welcomed the possibility of Ireland's joining a European free trade area because it would enable them to stop making uneconomic lines in Dundalk and supply them from the United Kingdom.[46] As a substantial exporter, Clarks Ireland had already demonstrated its ability — in women's footwear at least — to compete under freer trading conditions and hoped to increase its market penetration on the Continent when tariffs were removed.[47] Other manufacturers felt that the industry was ill-prepared to face tougher competition in the home market and that the lack of a strong home base would prevent the development of sufficient export business to offset the decline in home sales. This problem was to receive considerable attention in the early 1960s while Ireland's application to join the EEC was awaiting attention.

The response of Irish footwear producers to improved trading conditions therefore varied considerably, and this was reflected by their performance. As can be seen from Table 22, there was a particularly dramatic improvement in the performance of Woodingtons and Munster Shoes. Woodingtons' profits rose sharply after 1958, although the return on capital was still fairly poor. At Munster Shoes, the improvements which had been put in hand, coupled with the advent of more favourable trading conditions, contributed to the company's return to profitability in 1961. Hallidays was clearly the most successful company; its profits were substantially larger than Rawsons'

TABLE 22

Sales, net profit and return on assets, 1956-61

John Halliday & Son Ltd

	Sales (£000)	NP+T+I (£000)	As % of sales	As % of total assets
1956	1,116	48	4.3	11.1
1957	n.a.	68	n.a.	14.9
1958	1,253	86	6.9	16.2
1959	1,399	90	6.4	14.8
1960	1,607	86	5.4	12.1
1961	1,896	152	8.0	18.1

J.H. Woodington Drogheda (1936) Ltd

	Sales (£000)	NP+T+I (£000)	As % of sales	As % of total assets
1956	229	0.2	0.1	1.6
1957	257	4	0.1	2.0
1958	299	12	4.0	5.6
1959	300	12	4.0	5.6
1960	330	8	2.4	3.9
1961	279	11	3.9	6.2

John Rawson & Son (Ireland) Ltd

	Sales (£000)	NP+T+I (£000)	As % of sales	As % of total assets
1956	n.a.	33	n.a.	8.7
1957	n.a.	n.a.	n.a.	n.a.
1958	n.a.	n.a.	n.a.	n.a.
1959	n.a.	n.a.	n.a.	n.a.
1960	n.a.	n.a.	n.a.	n.a.
1961	n.a.	29	n.a.	6.5

Padmore & Barnes (Ireland) Ltd

	Sales (£000)	NP+T+I (£000)	As % of sales	As % of total assets
1956	272	5	1.8	3.5
1957	n.a.	-1	—	—
1958	n.a.	n.a.	n.a.	n.a.
1959	n.a.	0	n.a.	6.6
1960	n.a.	-6	—	—
1961	n.a.	10	n.a.	8.1

Munster Shoes Ltd

	Sales (£000)	NP+T+I (£000)	As % of sales	As % of total assets
1956	n.a.	n.a.	n.a.	n.a.
1957	n.a.	n.a.	n.a.	n.a.
1958	n.a.	n.a.	n.a.	n.a.
1959	256	-2	—	—
1960	225	-4	—	—
1961	316	10	3.2	8.8

Note: NP+T+I = Net profit plus tax plus interest. Sources: Company accounts.

by this date, and by the standards of the Irish footwear industry, they represented a very good return on capital employed. Much of Hallidays' success was due to its close liaison with C. & J. Clark, for the English company not only provided vital technical asistance but also was becoming a major customer. Padmore & Barnes' performance was erratic, to say the least, but by 1961 the new ownership had ensured a return to profitability. Unfortunately, information on Rawsons' profit record is incomplete but it does give an indication of the long-term decline which the company was experiencing; Rawsons was unable to take advantage of improved trading conditions to boost turnover and profitability.

Although the fortunes of individual companies varied considerably, the late 1950s saw a marked improvement in the fortunes of the Irish footwear industry. Nevertheless, while 1961 was, by any criterion, the best year in the industry's history, it was followed by something of a recession in 1962-3,[48] and the Committee on Industrial Organisation's report on the industry was soon to issue a warning that footwear manufacturers were ill-prepared for any relaxation in protection.

7

THE PROSPEROUS SIXTIES
1961-70

Towards the end of the 1950s, the rate of growth of the Irish economy began to show a marked improvement. This trend was partly caused by the boom in international demand, but it was also a result of the modification of government policies to stimulate home demand and clear the way for the development of overseas markets. During the 1960s, economic policy making was increasingly dominated by the need to prepare for free trade. It has been noted that the Irish government felt obliged to follow suit when Britain applied to join the EEC in 1961. Membership of the EEC was attractive because it would give Irish manufacturers access to the large European market and it was hoped that this would offset the inroads which foreign competition would make into the Irish market once protection was removed. In retrospect, it seems probable that this application was premature; as yet, few Irish manufacturers were efficient enough to compete in a free market.[1] Fortunately, the Irish application was contingent upon Britain's entry and de Gaulle's veto gave the Irish economy a valuable breathing space.

Yet it was now apparent that the ending of protection could not be deferred much longer. As a preliminary, a closer relationship was sought with the United Kingdom. Under the Anglo-Irish Free Trade Agreement of December 1965, the Irish government agreed to remove import quotas on British goods in July 1968 and replace them by duties which would be annually reduced until they disappeared in 1975. In return, Irish industrial goods were to be given immediate duty-free access to the British market. Although the timetable for ending protection was subsequently extended, it was apparent that changing conditions would provide a severe test for the Irish economy. The government did its best to prepare the economy for free trade. The *Second Programme for Economic Expansion*, which covered the period from 1964 to 1970, was published in two parts, in August 1963 and July 1964.[2] It was more ambitious than its predecessor and set detailed projections for the expected increase in resources and the way in which they would be used.[3] Overall, the growth rate envisaged was fairly modest; the target for 1960-70 was an annual increase in GNP of 4.4 per cent or 50 per cent in all.[4] Industry, however, was expected to make the major contribution, and the programme called for an average increase in industrial output of 7 per cent per annum.[5] The projected growth rates were considered to be well within the capabilities of most industries.

At the same time, the scope of the grants scheme was steadily widened. The export assistance grants made by CTT were progressively raised from £145,000 in 1959-60 to £375,000 in 1965,[6] and the technical assistance grants offered by the Department of Industry and Commerce were raised from one-third to one-half of the cost of approved projects in July 1962. By this date, the scheme embraced such projects as the employment of consultants to examine management organisation, financial structure and distribution of goods in the home market; attendance of management and supervisory personnel at full-time training courses; and visits abroad to study industrial organisation.[7] In addition, a scheme of adaptation grants was introduced in 1963 to help industry to prepare for free trade. Grants of up to 25 per cent of cost were made available by An Foras Tionscáil (AFT)[8] where firms had to modernise factories or equipment, enlarge the scale of operations or embark on new lines of production.[9] Assistance could also be obtained from the Industrial Credit Co., which offered loans on very favourable terms.[10] Another government sponsored body was the Committee in Industrial Organisation. It was set up in 1962 to investigate the state of Irish industry and recommend improvements which could be made to prepare for the coming of free trade. During the next few years, it produced a large number of reports on different industries; reference has already been made to the *Report on the Leather Footwear Industry* (published 1962) and the *Report on the Leather Industry* (published 1964).[11]

Over the decade as a whole, Irish economic growth was considerable, if erratic. Between 1958 and 1969, the average increase in GNP was 4.2 per cent per annum, while industrial output rose by 9.1 per cent per annum, but the major gains were made between 1959 and 1961 and between 1966 and 1968. Moreover, while the targets set by the *Programme for Economic Expansion* had been reached, in other respects the performance was less satisfactory. There was little acceleration in the growth rate of productivity in industry in 1961-68 compared with 1949-61,[12] and it was apparent that the gains made by manufacturing industry were achieved through a transfer of resources from other sectors and a move towards full employment, rather than from productivity gains. In many respects, this mirrored the British experience in the 1960s. Indeed, the increased emphasis upon exporting tended to make Ireland more susceptible to fluctuations in the economic performance of the United Kingdom.[13]

But, whilst the achievements of the 1960s had enabled Ireland to keep pace with Britain, they had not been sufficient to close the gap. Although this was in many ways a very creditable achievement, it must also be remembered that the growth of the British economy during the 1960s was generally considered to be unsatisfactory in comparison with the rest of Europe.[14] If Ireland were to join the EEC, as appeared increasingly probable by the end of the decade, her performance would have to be judged against that of Europe rather than Britain. The removal of most of the quota restrictions in 1970, coupled with escalating inflation rates, led immediately to a recession in Ireland. The value of imports (and therefore the balance of payments deficit) grew rapidly, and Irish industry's share of the home market was permanently reduced. As negotiations proceeded for Ireland's entry into the EEC, it was becoming apparent that the 1970s would represent the severest test which the Irish economy has yet faced. This, then, is the background against which we have to consider the performance of the Irish footwear industry during the 1960s. What were the problems facing the industry? What changes were made, and to what extent was the industry prepared for free trade by the end of the decade? And how did the experience of the footwear industry compare with that of Irish manufacturing industry as a whole?

The Committee on Industrial Organisation's *Report on the Leather Footwear Industry* was published in May 1962. Although based on extensive consultations with the manufacturers, it was intended as an independent analysis, and provided an extremely detailed survey of the state of the industry, and the problems which required attention if it was to be competitive in a free market. Many of the problems have already been discussed in detail in previous chapters, but it is worth noting the major recommendations which were made by the Committee.

1. Co-ordination of adaptation and development plans and co-operation between manufacturers to put them into effect.

2. Reduction of the range of production in individual factories. Modernization of plants and enlargement of the scale of operation.

3. Better marketing.

4. Examination of the possibility of providing industry-wide research and information facilities and setting up a central design advisory service.

5. Consideration of the training needs of existing and new employees.

6. Establishment of a body to improve production and marketing.

7. Retention and expansion of the Industrial Credit Co. and the grants scheme, and financial assistance towards training and research facilities.

8. Establishment of an adaptation council for the footwear industry.[15]

Following the Committee's recommendation, the Footwear Adaptation Association was established in March 1963 and, within a short time, its

The Prosperous Sixties

members included all the major footwear manufacturers in the Republic. The Association participated in the establishment of the Irish Footwear Fashion Council, assisted in the improvement of training facilities and, in co-operation with CTT, became involved in the promotion of Irish footwear in overseas markets.[16]

There had, of course, already been substantial progress in some directions before 1961, but the Committee on Industrial Organisation clearly felt that there was still a long way to go before the industry was ready for free trade. It estimated that if its recommendations were not followed up the Irish footwear manufacturers would lose up to 50 per cent of the home market under free trade, while about 1,000 workers, or roughly one-sixth of the labour force, would be made redundant. If the footwear industry followed the course suggested by the Committee, it was estimated that it would be left with about 75 per cent of the home market and this, together with the expected improvement in export sales, was expected to make large-scale redundancies unnecessary.[17]

By the time the Committee on Industrial Organisation presented its report, it was already becoming clear that the rapid growth which had been achieved between 1959 and 1961 was not being maintained. Although the total pairage produced continued to rise in absolute terms, there was a marked reduction in the rate of growth between 1961 and 1963. During the 1960s, output was much higher than in previous decades because of the growth of export business, but it was apparent that the industry was still subject to quite marked short-term fluctuations. Total production rose sharply again in 1963-4, rather more slowly in 1964-5, and then fell back slightly in 1965-7. The upward movement was then resumed and continued until 1970 (see Figure 2).

One important influence upon growth rates of course, was the rate of growth of the home market. The size of the population continued to expand, albeit slowly, from 2,818,341 in 1961 to 2,884,002 in 1966, and 2,978,248 in 1971.[18] In addition, per capita consumption was increasing,[19] largely as a result of the growth of fashion demand; the Irish public was becoming increasingly sophisticated during the 1960s. Real incomes were growing and consumers were much more exposed to outside influences which tended to increase their expectations. For example, the number of Irish homes with television sets was growing fast, [20] and in many parts of the country viewers were able to receive British television programmes as well as those of Telefís Éireann. Television had an influence far beyond that of a mere advertising medium.

The Irish footwear market did of course retain many of its traditional features. Despite the appearance of multiples in some large towns, the market was still dominated by small independent retailers, who lacked the resources to place advance orders and carry large stocks. The extent to which Irish

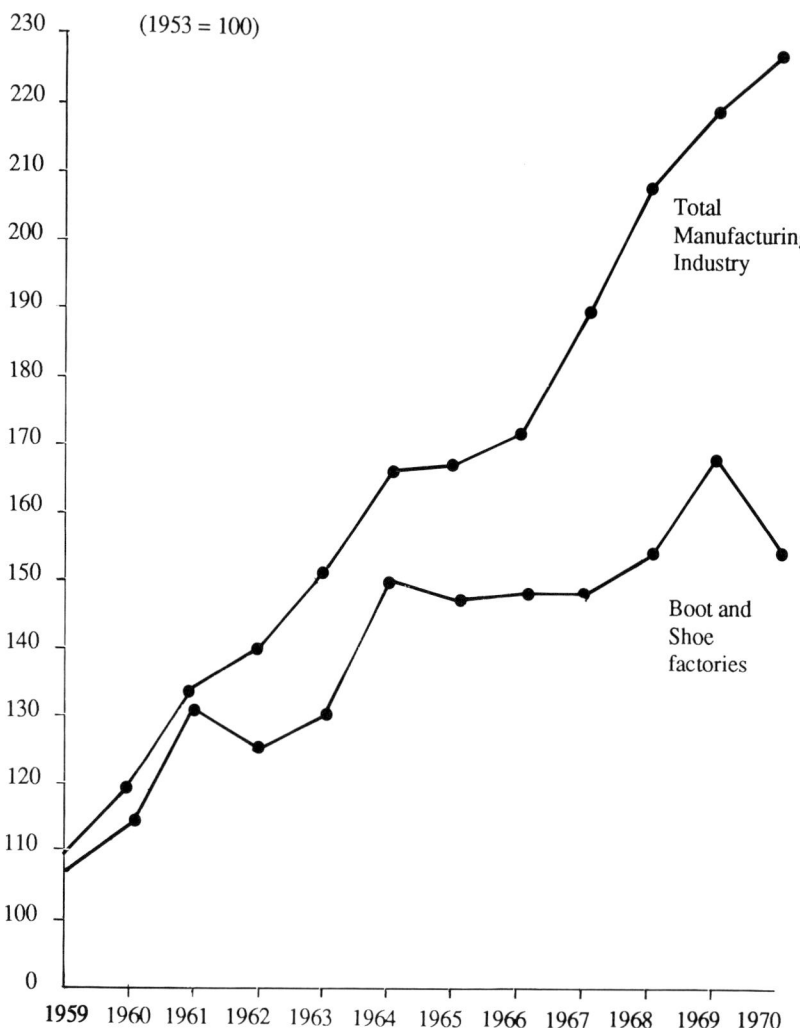

FIGURE 2: Index of production,
boot and shoe factories and total manufacturing industry, 1959-70

Source: *Irish Trade Journal and Statistical Bulletin.*

market conditions restricted opportunities for multiple retailing is indicated by Table 23.

TABLE 23

Distribution of footwear sales in Ireland and the United Kingdom, 1964

	Ireland (%)	U.K. (%)
Large multiples (100+ branches)	—	36
Medium multiples (10-99 branches)	10	11
Small multiples and independents (1-9 branches)	81	20
Department and grocery stores	5	13
Co-operative Societies	—	6
Mail order	—	10
Other	4	4
	100	100

Sources: Hallidays, H 9/4; A. Vermeulen, 'Economic Aspects of the Shoe Trade in the Next Decade', *British Boot and Shoe Institution Journal* 12 (1964/5), 274.

The definitions are, of course, those used in the United Kingdom. 'Small multiples and independents' include nearly all Irish multiples — only Tylers and Connollys possessed more than 10 shops. Multiples and large independents accounted for much of the increase in sales which took place during the 1960s, largely because they were concentrated in the eastern towns where the bulk of this growth took place. But, as can be seen from Table 24, the growth of these large retailers did not lead to a rapid decline in the number of outlets.

The number of non-specialist shops declined, especially in the towns, but manufacturers still had to service a considerable number of small accounts. The scattered rural market did not encourage the large retailers to expand their activities into these areas, and even companies like Hallidays,

TABLE 24

Retail outlets for footwear in Ireland, 1966/71

	1966	1971
Specialist footwear shops	377	384
General drapery shops	669	644
Grocery — all descriptions	406	320
Other	235	180
	1,687	1,528

Source: *Census of Distribution*, 1966 and 1971.

which sold a large proportion of its fashion shoes in urban markets,[21] still had to consider the needs of its small customers.[22] In 1964, 21 per cent of Hallidays' customers made purchases totalling less than 2,000.[23] The growth of large retailers, therefore, merely served to emphasise the dichotomy between urban and rural areas, and did not obviate the problems associated with servicing small accounts. Thus, while the home market was undoubtedly expanding in absolute terms, it was still small in comparison with other European countries and retained characteristics which made for excessive production and distribution costs and led to significant short-term fluctuations in demand. Nevertheless, the growth of the home market helped create a healthier base for the development of export business.

Exports were of increasing significance to the Irish footwear industry. In 1959, for example, production for export represented slightly more than 16 per cent of the total volume of production; by the mid-1960s, the figure had reached 20-22 per cent. Total exports more than doubled in the same period, from 827,772 pairs in 1959 to 1,985,736 pairs in 1970.[24] But this overall growth did in fact conceal considerable fluctuations from year to year. In particular, the growing importance of export sales made Irish footwear manufacturers more susceptible to the fluctuations of the British business cycle.

Britain was by far the most important export market for Irish footwear, accounting for about nine-tenths of overseas sales between 1959 and 1964. As can be seen from Table 25, the pairage sold to British customers rose rapidly between 1959 and 1961, as a consequence of boom conditions in the British footwear market. The better quality women's and girls' styles sold particularly well. By the end of 1961, however, footwear sales in Britain were falling; the recession deepened during 1962 and continued into 1963.[25] In 1962, therefore, the pairage produced for export by the Irish manufacturers fell by 14 per cent. There was a substantial recovery in 1963-4, but the experience of the Irish footwear industry in 1964-5 again indicated the dangers inherent in this increased reliance on the British footwear market. Taken as a whole, 1964 was a very good year, total production was up by nearly one million pairs on 1963 and about half of the increase in output went to British customers. In October, however, came the British government's announcement that all imports would be subject to a 15 per cent levy, and this was a heavy blow to the Irish footwear industry.

Although grants were made available by the Irish government, the price of Irish-made footwear in Britain rose by approximately 4 per cent and sales fell off. The reduction of the levy to 10 per cent in April 1965 in fact added to the Irish manufacturers' problems, because the British government gave two months' warning of its intentions and this provided an additional incentive to British importers to postpone their purchasing.[26] The total

TABLE 25

Destination of Irish footwear exports, 1959-70
(footwear wholly/mainly of leather)

('000 pairs)

	United Kingdom	United States	Canada	Other	Total
1959	737	68	21	1	828
1960	947	72	39	2	1,085
1961	1,177	66	59	1	1,302
1962	1,001	61	55	1	1,118
1963	1,125	78	44	11	1,259
1964	1,596	92	63	13	1,764
1965	1,436	79	72	18	1,604
1966	1,448	78	84	30	1,640
1967	1,429	81	70	82	1,663
1968	1,842	98	89	177	2,206
1969	1,731	215	181	104	2,231
1970	1,381	353	157	95	1,986

Source: *Trade and Shipping Statistics.*

pairage exported to Britain in 1965 was down 10 per cent on the previous year and the downturn would have been much worse if sales had not picked up during the autumn season. There was no real improvement until 1968, when exports to Britain rose sharply to a new peak of 1,842,276 pairs.

However, the reappearance of import controls in Britain in October 1968 represented a new threat to the Irish footwear industry. In an attempt to cope with Britain's continuing balance of payments problem, it was announced that imports into Britain were to be subject to a deposit of 50 per cent, which was to be lodged with the British government for a period of six months. Although the Irish banks provided much of the capital needed to pay the deposits, the cost of financing the loans led to increased pressure on profit margins.[27] The 1968 restrictions did not have as serious an effect as did those of 1964-5. Irish footwear manufacturers, in common with many of Britain's other suppliers, felt that an import deposit scheme was the least objectionable type of control; it was, for example, clearly preferable to the imposition of quotas. Yet it was becoming clear that reliance upon the growth of British sales represented an uncertain basis for future expansion and a number of footwear manufacturers — notably Padmore & Barnes, which by this date had become a subsidiary of John Halliday & Son — began to devote increasing attention to the development of other export markets in the late 1960s. Another factor was the growth of consumer resistance to Irish products in the six counties of Northern Ireland. This had been a problem before, but, in the 1960s, manufacturers in the Irish Republic had succeeded in building up a very valuable trade with Ulster. In 1966, 256,332 pairs of shoes were sent to the North, representing about 18 per cent of total sales to the United Kingdom. This achievement was a temporary one, however; with the renewed unrest of the late 1960s, sales to Northern Ireland fell sharply, to 97,908 pairs in 1969 and 60,012 pairs in 1970.[28]

Britain remained the largest overseas market for Irish footwear throughout the 1960s, but, as can be seen from Table 25, sales to the United States and Canada began to grow very rapidly towards the end of the decade. In the past, Irish manufacturers had not been particularly successful in North American markets. They managed to sell a respectable quantity of men's and youths' shoes but their ladies' styles were generally considered to be inferior in design and construction. In the late 1960s and early 1970s, however, North America was experiencing a consumer boom and a prominent feature of this boom was a swing towards more casual fashions. This was particularly true of men's footwear. Formal styles like the black or brown Oxford had hardly changed since the early decades of the twentieth century; now more casual styles quickly caught on, combining chunky styling with comfort features. Soft leather uppers predominated and a wider range of colours appeared. Such styles were becoming acceptable for work as well as for leisure.

Irish manufacturers, which had not done particularly well with formal styles, were better equipped to meet the new demand. Exports of men's footwear rose very quickly in the late 1960s and a useful trade in women's casuals (but not women's fashion styles) was also developed. The total pairage exported to the United States nearly quadrupled between 1968 and 1970, whilst exports to Canada nearly doubled; by 1970, North America accounted for just over 25 per cent of Irish footwear exports. Sales to Scandinavia, West Germany, the Netherlands and France also increased, albeit at a much slower rate, and other markets were found in Australia, South Africa and the West Indies.[29]

Export business, therefore, made a major contribution to the growth of the Irish footwear industry during the 1960s. The gains which were made during 1959-61, 1963-4 and 1967-8 were much larger than the subsequent downturns; taking the period from 1959 to 1969 as a whole, total exports rose by about 110 per cent and contributed to an increase in total production of about 44 per cent. The growth of export sales in the 1960s was thus a major reason why Irish footwear factories were working much nearer full capacity than had hitherto been the case. Between 1962 and 1964, the industry was working at 94-5 per cent capacity and, even in the recession of 1965, the figure remained around 90 per cent. Similarly, in 1969-70 which (as we shall see) was also a period of recession, production was around 88 per cent of full capacity.[30]

How, then, did individual companies expand to meet this demand? Since it was no longer possible to achieve a significant increase in output by the utilisation of surplus production capacity, there was a need for additional capital investment. Footwear companies began to take more interest in the grants scheme which had been set up by the government. The number of approved projects increased rapidly after 1963, and most of the footwear companies made some use of grants during the decade. By 1970, 24 footwear companies had received grants under the adaptation grants scheme, while 18 had received technical assistance grants. Most of the projects related to the acquisition of new machinery or the employment of specialists to improve production efficiency and quality control, but in a number of cases footwear manufacturers also received assistance towards the cost of improving or replacing old and unsuitable buildings.[31] Ploughed-back profits also played a part in providing the capital for expansion. Profits were larger in the 1960s and the footwear industry was able to improve its rate of investment. Even so, many companies continued to distribute ordinary dividends amounting to more than half the net profit after tax and Hallidays' policy of never distributing more than 20 per cent was clearly unusual. The company continued to make annual bonus issues varying from 1 for 6 to 1 for 10 until 1966, by which date the issued share capital had risen to £747,000.

Ample reserves meant that Hallidays was actively looking for new investment opportunities. In 1963 a second factory was completed on the Rampart River site. This was a modern conveyorised factory, with a potential capacity of 13,000 pairs per week. This was not only substantially larger than any of Hallidays' existing production units; it was also larger than the total output of many Irish footwear firms.[32] Hallidays also began to expand by a process of horizontal integration, acquiring a controlling interest in Stedfast Shoes Ltd and Padmore & Barnes Ltd in the autumn of 1963.

Stedfast was one of the first companies in Ireland to introduce footwear with vulcanised soles[33] and had concentrated upon unbranded men's, women's and children's footwear to retail at 29s. 11d. (£1.49) and 49s. 11d. (£2.49). However, the company had attempted to produce a very wide range to satisfy the demands of its customers and had not been very profitable since 1958.[34] In September 1961, therefore, the directors approached Hallidays to find out if the Dundalk company would be interested in taking over Stedfast as a going concern. In fact, Hallidays was in the middle of its building programme and was unable to undertake any additional commitments at this time.[35] Stedfast attempted to remedy its problems by concentrating on medium grade, 39s. 11d. (£1.99) ladies' fashion shoes, but this venture was not particularly successful and, after further discussions in October 1963, it was announced that Hallidays was to acquire a 51 per cent interest in Stedfast for a total consideration of £14,655.[36]

Hallidays had already been approached with a view to taking over

Padmore & Barnes in 1960 when the Receiver, the Industrial Credit Co. and local businessmen were attempting to keep the Kilkenny factory in operation.[37] In fact, we have already seen that the company was acquired by a local consortium but it sold a considerable proportion of its shoes under the Airborne brand and relied upon the technical assistance and, in particular, the design expertise of the English company. During the early 1960s, it became apparent that Airborne was unable to provide the kind of service which Padmore & Barnes needed; in 1963, Airborne brand sales fell by 49 per cent and profits dropped alarmingly. In December of that year, Hallidays acquired the ordinary capital of Padmore & Barnes at a cost of £52,000.[38]

Why then did Hallidays want to acquire these companies? Neither had been profitable, the quality of their footwear was substantially below that of Hallidays' own and, in addition, Padmore & Barnes' reputation had been tarnished in recent years. Nevertheless, for a company looking for investment opportunities, these companies did possess a number of advantages. An obvious point is that the directors of Stedfast and Padmore & Barnes were eager to come to an agreement in order to re-establish their companies on a more competitive basis. This in itself was unusual in Ireland, where family ownership tended to lead to an excessive attachment to independence; this often meant that owners were not prepared to countenance a takeover until the business was in deep trouble. Management ability was another factor; although both companies were weak in middle management, Ian McLerie's ability in the unbranded sector was unquestioned, while Padmore & Barnes had a very good shoemaker in Paddy Roberts, who had been appointed to the board in recognition of his success as factory manager. Moreover, both Padmore & Barnes and Stedfast had already undergone modernisation programmes. Padmore & Barnes had introduced time study methods and improved the layout of the factory, while Stedfast had a modern factory equipped with up-to-date conveyors and machinery. The acquisition of Padmore & Barnes and Stedfast, therefore, offered the opportunity of a considerable expansion of productive capacity for a relatively small investment. Stedfast, for instance, had a total capacity of 12-13,000 pairs per week, so the cost of acquiring a controlling interest in the company was considerably less than the expense involved in setting up a new manufacturing unit of equivalent size — especially when the cost of training labour is taken into account.

Most important, however, was the fact that the type of footwear produced by Padmore & Barnes and Stedfast was *complementary* to Hallidays' existing output. Stedfast, of course, had concentrated upon the unbranded sector, in which Hallidays had shown little interest. To some extent, Padmore & Barnes could be seen as competition for Hallidays in that it was also producing men's and women's comfort shoes, men's welts and women's fashion shoes but, whereas Hallidays sold through a limited number of agents, Padmore & Barnes was a 'mass distribution' operation, supplying any retailer who wanted its shoes.[39] Eric Gross, who had taken over as managing director of Hallidays in 1959, was keen to develop this type of operation, using Padmore & Barnes' 'Moccasin' brand, because of the growing threat from a rival manufacturer, G.B. Britton & Sons, of Kingswood, near Bristol. In 1955, Brittons had acquired machines from Clarks' engineering subsidiary, C.I.C. Engineering, and in the next few years it emerged as the market leader in the production of direct vulcanised footwear for men and boys. Its 'Tuf' brand boots and shoes were brilliantly marketed and enormously successful, and its 'Gluv' brand soon followed, retaining the direct vulcanised sole, but intended as suit shoes rather than work shoes. By the early 1960s, Brittons was a force to be reckoned with in the United Kingdom, and began to turn its attention to Ireland and other overseas markets.[40] To fight off the challenge, Eric Gross wanted to develop a limited range of footwear which could be produced in large numbers and sold through as many outlets as possible. To distinguish the product from 'Tuf' and 'Gluv' he proposed that polyurethene should be used as the soling material, rather than vulcanised rubber. Clarks had been experimenting with polyurethene for some time, and Gross believed that a hard formulation would emulate the feel of leather soles. (Market research indicated that men still preferred leather to rubber, especially for smarter wear.) This, then, was the concept and strategy which lay behind Hallidays' acquisition of Padmore & Barnes in 1964.[41]

Hallidays was also displaying a growing interest in retailing. Despite its heavy investment programme, retained profits were still in excess of capital expenditure. By the end of 1965, therefore, Hallidays was considering how to reinvest £200,000 to £300,000 so as to yield 20 per cent on total assets. Other opportunities for horizontal integration in manufacturing were not available, and, in any case, it would be unwise to make any further acquisitions until Padmore & Barnes and Stedfast had been fully integrated into the group structure and were showing an acceptable return on assets. Backward integration to control supplies was still unattractive because of the comparative advantage possessed by British companies but retailing looked increasingly attractive to Hallidays' board. It offered an important source of feedback on design and fashion trends and, consequently, could contribute to group profits as a whole as well as being potentially very profitable in itself. In addition, Hallidays was worried that the financial weakness of retailers might lead to their being taken over by a rival manufacturer. The leading multiples and large independents were under-capitalised and few in number, yet accounted for a relatively large proportion of retail sales; and, if other manufacturers turned to forward integration, Hallidays might face a drastic reduction in sales. In 1962, for example, when it was rumoured that the Saxone Shoe Co. might be planning to sell its eight shops in the Irish Republic, Hallidays decided to make an approach to the owners, commenting that 'It would not suit us for this business to come under virile non-Clark ownership'.[42]

Nothing came of this approach, but early in 1965 it was announced that Hallidays' board had approved an entry into the retail field.[43] Arthur Halliday, however, reserved his opinion, for he still believed that a presence in retailing represented an undesirable diversification of management effort, and would offend existing customers. Although in a minority, his arguments were sufficiently forceful to persuade the board that an entry into retailing required further careful consideration. It was decided that a minimum of three to six shops should be acquired, and that special attention should be given to the acquisition of shops in Dublin.[44] In addition, considerable thought was given to the type of shop which would be suitable. A survey carried out by the company in June 1965 noted that the standard of many retailers' displays was poor and that there was a general lack of young fashion shops like Dolcis or Lennards in the United Kingdom. The survey concluded that 'there appears to be great scope for a modern approach to marketing and retailing' but cautioned that 'the biggest danger probably lies in being too clever'.[45]

After 1965, therefore, Hallidays was displaying considerable interest in retailing, but it was not until 1969 that a suitable opportunity appeared. One reason for the delay was that the threat of other manufacturers acquiring control of the important multiples did not materialise. Hallidays' rivals showed little interest in forward integration as a means of improving their competitiveness under freer trading conditions. In 1968, however, the abolition of restrictions on foreign ownership presented the possibility that British manufacturers and multiples would acquire shops in Ireland, supplying these outlets from their factories in the United Kingdom. This introduced a new urgency into Hallidays' search and, in 1969, a 51 per cent interest was acquired in Denson Ltd. Densons was owned by the O'Neill family (who continued to own a 49 per cent shareholding) and had eleven shops, including eight in Dublin. A C.& J. Clark Ltd Planning Report later noted that 'The purchase of a majority shareholding in Densons makes good strategic sense for Hallidays. It provides the basis for sharing in the development of multiple footwear retailing that is expected to take place in Ireland over the next 10 years'.[46] However, recent financial results had been very poor — profits amounted to barely 2 per cent of capital employed — and it was evident that a major improvement was necessary before the company could act as a vehicle for significant growth. In addition, Hallidays was at pains to assure its existing customers that Densons would not receive preferential treatment; the retail chain would continue to trade independently and the terms of trade would be the same as for any other customer.[47]

Hallidays' interest in horizontal and vertical integration, however, was clearly unusual in the Irish footwear industry and was only made possible by the high rate of profit retention. Despite continuing heavy investment, Hallidays' reserves came to exceed its requirements and, after 1966, it was able to reverse its policy. The preference shares were paid off and large dividends were declared — notably a 25 per cent ordinary share dividend in 1968 and one of 12.5 per cent in the following year. While the profits of most footwear manufacturers were improving in the 1960s, no other company possessed this kind of capital reserve. Instead of looking for suitable opportunities for investment in other companies, most manufacturers were likely to direct any capital available for investment towards the improvement of their own factories.

In general, Irish footwear manufacturers showed little interest in merger or co-operation during the 1960s. Although the Committee on Industrial Organisation was in favour of amalgamation, few of the Irish footwear manufacturers were willing to follow this recommendation. The Hanover Shoe Co. Ltd, Cork and Whispies Shoes (Ireland) Ltd, Edenderry, were both merged with their parent companies,[48] but there were few examples of actual takeovers. Munster Shoes Ltd, however, was acquired by the Tyler retail group and later sold to Woodingtons in 1969 when the latter company required extra production capacity.[49] Woodingtons had also acquired the premises (and part of the labour force) of Birr Shoes Ltd after its liquidation in 1966.[50] The only other companies involved in takeovers were Hilliard and Palmer Ltd and Limerick Shoes Ltd, which were both acquired by an English company, G.B. Britton & Sons of Kingswood.[51]

Similarly, there was little interest in vertical integration and such ties as existed between manufacturers and retailers continued to be indirect. Tylers' acquisition of Munster Shoes Ltd, however, did represent an interesting (and unique) example of backward integration by a retailer. For a number of years, Tylers had depended upon Munster for a large part of its requirements in Ireland and had gradually acquired a substantial number of shares in the manufacturing company. By 1966, Munster was a subsidiary within the John Tyler group. Tylers' ownership, however, was short lived; in 1967, Munster Shoes began to incur serious trading losses and the investment was written off.[52]

In short, there were relatively few examples of horizontal or vertical integration outside the Halliday group. But all the Irish companies were displaying a much greater attention to the marketing of their footwear. The growth in the volume of sales — which was by no means confined to Hallidays — could not have been achieved without significant improvements in marketing. There was a greater acceptance of the term in its widest sense; identifying and designing the type of footwear which the public wanted, producing it to the required standard, and then selling it at the right price with the aid of forceful advertising. On the design side, there was still little scope for originality and designers tended to copy foreign designs, but increasing use was made of the facilities provided by organisations like the Shoe and Allied Trades Research Association (SATRA),[53] and there was some evidence of market research to identify the kind of footwear which the public wanted. There was also a much greater use of advertising in the press and on television. Clarks Ireland Ltd continued to dominate press advertising (accounting for nearly half the industry's total expenditure in 1967)[54] but other manufacturers had taken the lead with the newer medium; G.B. Britton, for example, was making extensive use of television advertising as part of its entry into the Irish market. But the effect of advertising on sales, of course, remains in doubt; Clarks Ireland Ltd may have felt confident that it could sell its shoes without heavy expenditure in the more expensive medium.

On the selling side, an interesting innovation was the establishment of a joint exporting organisation by James Boylan & Son, Edward J. Connolly, Dubarry Shoemakers, George & Co., and Tara Shoes. The new company, Instep Ltd, was set up in July 1967 with F.J. Scott as its chairman,[55] but it did not prove particularly successful because of the problems of reconciling the interests of its constituent companies. In the following year James Winstanley and J.H. Woodington concluded a similar agreement, with Britain as the main target.[56] This venture was rather easier to operate because at this date Winstanleys specialised in men's and Woodingtons in ladies' fashion shoes, and there was less likelihood of a conflict of interests.

Once again, it is apparent that Hallidays possessed the most sophisticated view of the scope and role of marketing. By the 1960s, Hallidays was basing its strategy on a suitable product for each factory rather than attacking the market with a wide range of shoes. This followed on from the decision to specialise on a 'production unit' basis, and was also influenced by the need to find a suitable role for Padmore & Barnes and Stedfast within the group framework. The initial intention, as we have seen, was to use Padmore & Barnes for a 'mass distribution' operation, producing a small range of men's shoes to retail at 59s. 11d. (£2.99). The project acquired fresh significance when it became apparent that G.B. Britton was to commence manufacturing in Ireland on its own account; in January 1965, A C. & J. Clarks' marketing plan advised the Irish management:

> The Éire market is so small that if G.B. Britton are allowed to gain a firm share then Clarks Ireland Ltd's sales must suffer. Therefore we recommend that you should deliberately set out to block Britton's progress before they can get established . . . this can be done by freely imitating their type of footwear and their marketing approach.[57]

In August 1965, however, when Daniel Clark became managing director of John Halliday, he determined to abandon the project. One important consideration was the introduction of the British import levy in October 1964; U.K. sales would have been essential to justify the heavy capital investment required. Principally, though, it was technical problems which led to the abandonment of the project. The polyurethane process was unproven, and trials with the hard formulation required revealed unacceptable and incurable cracking problems. Polyurethane was later to become a highly successful soling material, especially for the more casual styles, but in the interim there remained the problem of finding a suitable product for Padmore & Barnes. The company had experience in conventional men's welted shoes and, as a temporary measure, considerable effort was put into developing welted sales outside Ireland, especially through Clarks' overseas sales organisation in North America.[58] However this took time to build up and did not offer a product in any way distinctive or different from the competition.

Padmore & Barnes' success story commenced when Daniel Clark persuaded his cousin, Lance Clark, to take over as managing director of Padmore & Barnes. Before moving to Kilkenny, Lance Clark had been export manager for Clarks Overseas Shoes in Europe, and knew most of the leading continental footwear manufacturers. In 1967, he found a suitable product in West Germany, a moccasin construction shoe developed under the name of 'Grasshopper' by Sioux Schuhfabriken of Walheim.[59] This shoe was probably the best selling line in Europe in the middle to late 1960s; it combined a 'nature form' last and other comfort features with good quality materials and hence was relatively expensive. A move into the higher price brackets was attractive at this time because of the appearance of footwear manufacturing in low labour cost countries like Poland, Spain and Portugal, which was likely to lead to increased competition for the lower to medium price brackets. As labour costs represented roughly one quarter of total manufacturing costs, manufacturers in such countries could possess a significant advantage over Irish producers, and it therefore made sense for Padmore & Barnes to go for product innovation at premium prices. Lance Clark was able to secure an agreement whereby Sioux supplied technical know-how, knives and patterns against a royalty of 1*s*. (5p) per pair for the first 200,000 pairs and 6*d*. (2.5p) per pair for subsequent production. An important feature was an addendum permitting sales outside Ireland for a fee of 1*s*. (5p) per pair on all sales.[60] During 1968, the older construction methods were phased out and the changeover proceeded fairly smoothly, although considerable attention had to be paid to the re-training of operatives and supervisory staff, and experts from Street were called in to refine production methods.[61]

The management of Padmore & Barnes expected the new range to do well, but sales in Britain and Ireland quickly fell off after the initial launch. It was then decided to launch the new shoe in North America and the brand name was changed to 'Wallabee' because 'Grasshopper' was already registered in the United States. Initial comments were not favourable, for the shoes looked very strange to American buyers, but market trends were now moving in Padmore & Barnes' favour. Wallabees arrived in the North American market at exactly the right time to exploit the shift towards more casual footwear and quickly became immensely successful. The moccasin construction soon became popular in other markets too, notably Australia where a small but lucrative trade was built up.[62] Padmore & Barnes had to increase production capacity to cope with the flood of orders and the pairage produced per week rose from 3,000 pairs in 1968 to 7,500 pairs in 1969 and to 10,000 pairs by end of 1970.[63] In 1970, Padmore & Barnes exported approximately 300,000 pairs, representing 78 per cent of total output of 387,000 pairs, and worth just over £1 million.[64] The company's record in North America was particularly impressive; the 249,000 pairs exported in 1970 made up very nearly half of total Irish footwear sales in Canada and the United States.[65]

During the 1960s, Padmore & Barnes was transformed from a small factory producing a mixed bag for the home market to a vigorous export-orientated company, able to reap the economies associated with specialisation. The selection and exploitation of a distinctive product was the key to this success, and it suggested that management was adopting a much more sophisticated approach to marketing. Yet — as is often the case — an element of luck was also involved.

Clearly, the sudden success of the new range in North America came as a considerable surprise to Padmore & Barnes. American customers thought of the shoes as Wallabees rather than Clarks, and liked dealing direct with a small Irish firm. As a result, Padmore & Barnes had an unusual degree of control over what was, in theory, a Clarks operation. In fact, one could argue that the really impressive feature was not the original decision to make moccasin-type footwear, but the speed with which the Kilkenny management, led by Paddy Roberts, responded once the American breakthrough had been made.

Although it earned good profits, Stedfast Shoes was a good deal less successful than Padmore & Barnes, largely because it manufactured unbranded footwear. In this sector, the major customers were the wholesalers and large multiples, which expected to have a say in the choice of styles being manufactured, and this made it very difficult to specialise upon a narrow product range. As we shall see, Stedfast's profitability declined steadily from 1964 to the end of the decade, and the trend was not halted until the establishment of a new subsidiary, Fane Shoes Ltd, in 1970. Fane also concentrated upon unbranded women's shoes but in a rather lower price bracket, and specialised in the use of synthetics.[66] An added advantage was that the Irish government was persuaded that this was in the nature of a new operation and consequently Fane Shoes was eligible for 100 per cent tax relief on all export sales. However, Stedfast Shoes continued to present problems to the management of John Halliday & Son and the company was eventually liquidated in 1975.[67]

It is apparent that other manufacturers were rather less sophisticated in their approach to marketing than were John Halliday and its subsidiaries. Executives at Hallidays had a fairly low opinion of the branding policies of some of their competitors:

> The general strategy is to attack with a wide variety of brands. Very often these brands are no more than a label, to avoid nameless shoes.[68]

It is probably fair to say that, in general, the marketing function continued to be a weak spot in many Irish companies. The 1971 survey of the Committee on Industrial Progress complained of a lack of 'market orientation' and noted that marketing functions received a relatively small proportion of management time in comparison with production functions.[69] Nevertheless, there is no doubt that considerable progress was made during the 1960s and, in the larger companies at least, relatively detailed marketing plans were being drawn up. This was due, at least in part, to the fact that it was becoming much more common for footwear executives to possess specialist skills — either in marketing or in other production or administration functions. Coupled with this was a growing tendency for footwear manufacturers to 'buy in' managerial talent. In this context, it is interesting to note that a significant number of key positions were filled by executives who had received their initial training at John Halliday or C. & J. Clark. In particular, one might mention Jim Daly, Ian McLerie's accountant at Stedfast in the early 1960s; Philip McLoughlin, managing director of J.H.Woodington from 1952 to 1971; Stephen Lowry, McLoughlin's successor who became President of the Federation of Irish Footwear Manufacturers; and Kenneth Connolly, managing director of Blackthorn Shoes.

There were also significant improvements in productive efficiency. A growing number of firms adopted scientific leather measurement as a means of keeping waste to a minimum and as a basis for improved costing and budgeting methods. In addition, there was a much greater understanding of the techniques of work study, cost control, budgetary control and forecasting. The number of conveyor systems in use was growing steadily and most firms continued to improve the layout of their factories.

Technological improvements also made a contribution. Pressure for technological change was created as a result of the need to make Irish footwear cost-competitive in readiness for free market conditions, and there was a growing tendency for Irish manufacturers to adopt new techniques which were being introduced in Britain and America at this time. There was little in the way of new constructions, but substantial improvements were made in the methods of performing existing processes. In the 1950s, such improvements had largely been directed towards simplification, which usually meant sub-dividing operations into a larger number of simple tasks; in the 1960s, the emphasis was towards the combination of several processes by the use of sophisticated machinery. The new generation of lasting machines, for instance, was able to combine pulling over, toe lasting and forepart lasting in one operation.[70] Similarly, much of the stitching process (a traditional bottleneck) could be eliminated by the use of machines which heat-welded and imitation-stitched synthetic uppers and linings.[71] Attention was also paid to speeding up the various processes. Multi-station injection moulding machines enabled a large of number of soles to be produced in rapid succession,[72] and moist heat setting machines greatly reduced the time a shoe had to be left on the last to retain its shape.[73] A much wider use of pre-assembled and pre-finished components also reduced lasting time and helped to remove bottlenecks. The move towards synthetic materials continued during the 1960s. By now, rubber or rubber substitutes had largely replaced leather as a soling material and synthetic heels were becoming more common. This was partly due to fashion trends. The stiletto styles fashionable in the 1960s, for example, required the use of plastic heels.[74] Another important development in synthetics was the injection mounting of PVC soles, which replaced the direct vulcanisation process for rubber. Although PVC tended to distort on cooling and had only 70-75 per cent of rubber's durability, it did possess a number of advantages. It was available in a wide range of colours; scrap material could be re-used; it had an indefinite shelf life and could be ordered in large quantities; it could be injection moulded into cold moulds (which reduced preparation times); and its dwell time (time spent in the mould) was also shorter, at about one minute compared with three to five minutes for rubber. PVC soles were widely used for men's and women's casual shoes in the 1960s and, towards the end of the decade, further advances were made, this time with the use of polyurethane soling materials — polyurethane could be injected at a much lower pressure, which meant that the cost of moulds was substantially reduced.[75]

In the early 1960s, synthetics also began to be used for uppers and linings. One factor here was the fear that the supply of leather would be unable to keep up as the demand for leather footwear from the emergent countries began to grow. Synthetics also offered the advantage of uniform characteristics and relatively stable prices; skilled grading of the material was unnecessary, several pairs of uppers could be cut in one operation, and costing was simplified.[76]

The Prosperous Sixties

During the 1960s, the DuPont Organisation invested a very large sum in the development of Corfam — a breathing (poromeric) uniform material, initially marketed for high-grade uppers. There was considerable interest in the new material, but in fact Corfam did not prove particularly successful; one problem was that its permanent deformation (adjustment to foot shape) was inferior to that of leather, and, consequently, it was less comfortable. Leather remained the ideal material, and it is noticeable that research and development into synthetic upper materials concentrated upon imitating leather as closely as possible. Researchers in Britain, for example, were working on sheet material of reconstituted skin fibres; this offered the advantage of uniformity, but resembled leather more closely than purely synthetic products. Little progress was made however. Thus there was a general feeling that synthetic upper materials still had to prove themselves and leather remained the most popular material for better quality shoes throughout the decade. In the cheaper price brackets, synthetics made rather more headway. Total Irish output of these types rose by 57 per cent between 1965 and 1970, which meant that overall the non-leather footwear sector was experiencing by far the fastest growth rate. Imports of non-leather footwear also showed a dramatic increase, although this was largely due to the removal of quotas on this type of footwear in 1966.

During the 1960s, technological progress began to give a clear advantage to the larger firms which were able to benefit from the economies of scale and specialisation. Many of the new techniques were unsuited to short production runs, and the rate of technical progress meant that machinery quickly became obsolete. There was a growing tendency for manufacturers to buy the simpler machines and lease the more complex types which their mechanics could not service or which had a relatively short working life, but, nevertheless, the greater sophistication of such machines meant that the cost of leasing was increasing rapidly. This gave an advantage to those companies with the managerial and supervisory strength to pay careful attention to efficient utilisation.

For most footwear manufacturers, the 1960s brought a significant improvement in productivity and profitability. To begin with, it is apparent that the industry experienced a considerable increase in per capita output; between 1959 and 1969, output per person employed rose from 993 pairs to 1,481 pairs per year, although the upward trend was briefly halted in 1962, 1965 and 1970.[77] Improved per capita output was of course partly due to technological change; but it was also due to influences on the demand side which made possible a more optimal use of existing production capacity. The footwear industry was, on average, working at about 90 per cent of full capacity in the 1960s; and this was much better than in previous decades.

It should also be noted that the rate of growth of per capita output was not accelerating; the rate of growth achieved between 1961 and 1970 was, if anything, slightly slower than in the previous decade and this was insufficient to close the gap between the labour productivity of Irish firms and that of their British counterparts. In 1965, for example, SATRA was requested by the Footwear Adaptation Association to institute a comparative productivity survey. Twenty-four Irish factories were visited and the information obtained was related to SATRA's reference data on productivity in British firms. Overall, it was found that per capita output in Ireland was 78 per cent of the British average, and two Irish firms compared favourably with the average British firm.[78] Between 1965 and 1968, there was an improvement of about 13 per cent in per capita output in Ireland but this did no more than maintain the relative position. However, SATRA's data also suggested that the big Irish firms were now significantly more efficient than the cluster of small firms which still accounted for perhaps half the output of the Irish footwear industry.[79] The improved labour productivity of the 1960s, therefore, should not be over-estimated; but it was sufficient to have a significant effect upon profitability.

In general, the profits returned by Irish footwear firms were considerably better than in previous decades. During the 1960s, the industry's gross manufacturing profit averaged about 21 per cent of turnover, compared with a figure of approximately 15 per cent for the 1950s.[80] There were of course short-term fluctuations in profitability which followed sales trends and, whilst the fortunes of most footwear manufacturers followed a similar pattern, there were considerable variations in the rate of return they achieved (Table 26).

TABLE 26

Pre-tax profits of Footwear Adaptation Association members, 1962-65

	1962 (No. of firms)	1963 (No. of firms)	1964 (No. of firms)	1965 (No. of firms)
Loss	5	3	4	4
Profit < % of turnover	1	6	1	1
Profit 1-6%	15	10	10	14
Profit 6-11%	4	6	8	5
Profit 11-16%	2	2	3	2
Profit 16-20%	—	—	1	—
	27	27	27	26

Source: Footwear Adaptation Association, *3rd Annual Report* (1965), 21.

The Prosperous Sixties

Evidence on the decade as a whole is not easy to come by, but Table 27 provides a useful summary. The John Halliday group displayed the most consistent return on capital, despite the heavy investment programme and the increase in issued capital; in fact, earnings per share remained fairly steady throughout the decade. By 1966, the company figured in the *Irish Times* list of the top fifty companies.[81] In 1968, it was the thirty-seventh largest company in Ireland and had the third highest return on capital of the top fifty.[82] This, in an industry which in most countries is characterised by a large number of small firms, was clearly a remarkable achievement. Padmore & Barnes' results were very erratic during the early 1960s as a result of the change of ownership and the shortcomings of the agreement with Airborne, but after its acquisition by Hallidays the company made a rapid improvement. During the second half of the decade (and especially after the switch to specialised export orientated production) it proved by far the most successful of Hallidays' investments. Stedfast likewise showed a rapid improvement after the takeover but, as we have already seen, it was not maintained and the return on capital was falling steadily between 1965 and 1970. Clearly, the failure to find a suitable product for Stedfast was having a serious effect upon profitability.

Improved profits were not confined to the John Halliday group. Edenderry and Woodingtons were also showing a much better return on capital and, although detailed figures cannot be given, this experience was shared by a number of other companies, including James Winstanley, Dubarry and (after the takeover by G.B. Britton) Hilliard & Palmer. A few companies, however, did not share in the general improvement. Munster Shoes' record in the early 1960s was disappointing to say the least and, while there may have been some improvement after the instigation of the adaptation programme in 1964, the subsequent history of the company does not suggest that this was long maintained. Birr Shoes was another company which did badly in the early 1960s, and was liquidated in 1966 with an estimated deficit of £27,000.[83]

More dramatic, perhaps was the demise of John Rawson & Son (Ireland) Ltd. Rawsons was still the second biggest footwear manufacturer in Ireland but its share of the home market had been steadily dwindling. This was partly due to the growing success of competitors like the Edenderry Shoe Co., but it was also due to management weaknesses at Rawsons. Ben Rawson had always retained a large part of the responsibility for management decisions and his death in 1964 left something of a power vacuum which prevented executives from taking the kind of steps needed to maintain the company's position *vis-à-vis* its competitors. The failure to improve productive efficiency led to relatively high labour costs which were pricing the company's products out of both home and export markets.[84] After a temporary improvement in the return on assets in 1963-4, a decline again set in, and was

TABLE 27

Profitability of seven Irish footwear companies, 1959-70

	John Halliday & Son*		Padmore & Barnes		Stedfast Shoes		Munster Shoes		John Rawson & Son		Edenderry Shoe Company		J.H. Woodington	
	(a)	(b)	(a)	(b)	(a)	(b)	(a)	(b)	(a)	(b)	(a)	(b)	(a)	(b)
	(%)	(%)	(%)	(%)	(%)	(%)	(%)	(%)	(%)	(%)	(%)	(%)	(%)	(%)
1959	6.4	14.8		6.6	0.9	2.5	loss	loss					4.0	5.6
1960	5.4	12.1	loss	loss	3.4	11.0	loss	loss					2.4	3.9
1961	8.0	18.1	1.8	8.1	1.7	5.6	3.2	8.8		6.5			3.9	6.2
1962	8.0	17.0	5.5	20.1			1.5	3.9		8.1				9.6
1963	9.7	19.3	0.8	3.0			1.1	2.1		15.8				9.6
1964	8.6	19.3	6.0	24.7		25.1				15.7				
1965	9.0	18.8			11.0	28.2				6.2		19.5		
1966	9.7	18.7				17.8				loss		11.6		
1967	9.1	16.1				17.1						7.3		
1968	9.8	20.4		27.1		13.5						10.8		
1969	11.2	24.1		31.5		10.2						13.5		
1970		9.0				8.5						12.6		

*Group after 1963

(a) Pre-tax net profit: turnover; (b) Pre-tax net profit: total assets.

Source: Annual Reports.

exacerbated by the general downswing in sales which took place in 1965-6. The final blow was the fire which totally destroyed the main factory in August 1967. In view of the company's previous poor performance, it was not thought practicable to re-establish the business and, after unsuccessful attempts to merge or to form an association with other companies, it was decided to recommend that the company be liquidated. Despite letters of protest and a demonstration by 400 out of the 500 employees, the shareholders supported the recommendation and the company was liquidated in October 1967 with all liabilities being met in full.[85]

The 1960s, therefore, saw an overall improvement in profitability; even during the downturns, the industry's profits were still appreciably higher than at any time during the 1950s. But clearly, there was substantial variation between individual companies. While an improved performance was by no means confined to the John Halliday Group, none of its competitors could match its record of a consistently high rate of return on assets, and some companies were making very small profits or even losses during periods of unfavourable trading conditions. The Footwear Adaptation Association and the 1971 survey by the Committee on Industrial Progress both concluded that, while there was a significant improvement over the decade as a whole, the industry generally was still experiencing an inadequate rate of return on turnover and assets.[86] Towards the end of the decade, when the Irish economy finally began to move towards free trade, only Hallidays could look forward to the future with any confidence and most footwear manufacturers were pressing for retention of controls for as long as possible.

The performance of the industry in 1970 appeared to justify the gloomy predictions of those who argued that the industry was not yet ready for free trade. 1970 brought together a number of complex problems. Firstly, manufacturing costs were rising sharply; materials costs and overheads were increasing and the twelfth wage round[87] led to increases which the industry felt were unduly high. Secondly, foreign footwear industries were also in difficulties; this made for increased pressure on the British market which was still Ireland's major export market. This problem was compounded by growing sales resistance to Irish goods in Ulster. Thirdly, there was a flood of imports when quota restrictions were removed by the Irish government. The process had started in 1966 when quota controls on rubber footwear were removed. Importers quickly realised that this freed from quota not only footwear made from rubber but also footwear made entirely of plastics or other synthetic materials. Imports of this type of footwear increased from 30,456 pairs in 1966 to 883,428 pairs in 1970. Non-leather footwear's share of total consumption rose from 25 per cent to 37 per cent and this increase was very largely due to the growth of imports. Thus imports were already beginning to cut into the Irish manufacturers' share of the home market. But all-plastic footwear was still concentrated in the lower price bracket and, as Irish manufacturers concentrated upon footwear with leather uppers, such imports did not *directly* compete with home produced goods. In July 1970, however, quotas on leather footwear were replaced by duties at the following rates:

The British rate was to fall by 4.5 per cent or 9*d*. (3.75p) on 1 July of each year, thus being removed by 1975. The reduction to 18 per cent due on 1

TABLE 28

Tariffs on leather footwear, July 1970

Full	Special Preferential	U.K.
54% or 45p (whichever is the greater)	36% or 30p (whichever is the greater)	22.5% or 18.75p (whichever is the greater)

January 1971, however, was postponed until after the publication of the report on the footwear industry by the Committee on Industrial Progress and further postponements were made by agreement between the British and Irish governments. The full and special preferential rates were also to be reduced after Ireland's entry into the EEC.[88]

Despite this gradualist approach, however, there was an immediate increase in imports when quota restrictions were lifted. Between 1968 and 1970, imports of all types of footwear nearly trebled and their share of the Irish market rose from 10 per cent to 23 per cent. This seemed to support the footwear manufacturers' argument that tariffs alone were insufficient to prevent a decline in their share of the home market, no matter what the actual rate of duty was. Even more worrying was the fact that imports were now directly competing with home-produced goods. Much of this increase took place within the leather footwear sector[89] and, whereas imports of leather footwear had previously been confined to the most expensive types, there was now an influx of medium-priced footwear similar to that produced by the Irish factories.[90]

The effect of increasing competition from imports, coupled of course with the effect of the aforementioned factors, was a severe slump in the turnover and profits of the Irish footwear manufacturers. John Hallidays' group profits fell from £528,000 in 1969 to £236,000 in 1970 and would have been even worse but for Padmore & Barnes' success in the North American markets. At Woodingtons, the setback was, if anything, more severe, and substantial losses were made in 1970-1. The Edenderry Shoe Co., however, suffered only a slight decline in profitability in 1970-1.

This worrying situation led to the setting up of the Committee on Industrial Progress, to which frequent reference has already been made. Its *Report on the Footwear Industry* was published in 1971[91] and the authors' basic conclusion was that, while there had been considerable improvement in a number of key areas during the 1960s, this improvement had not been sufficient to make the industry competitive in a free market. Moreover, the prosperous 1960s were in some respects the result of wider factors affecting the prosperity of foreign manufacturers also, and, when market conditions changed, the inherent weaknesses of the Irish footwear industry were again exposed. The Committee concluded that some of the recommendations of the 1962 Committee on Industrial Organisation had not been implemented and complained that some manufacturers were more interested in persuading the government to retain the controls for as long as possible rather than in making serious efforts to increase the competitiveness of their factories. The Committee did perhaps overstate its case, and it must be remembered that its brief was to identify what was wrong with the industry rather than compliment it on the substantial improvement which had already been achieved.

But, clearly, the period from 1961 to 1970, although the most successful in the history of the Irish footwear industry, ended on a gloomy note, with predictions that its share of the home market would gradually dwindle and that growing competition and inflationary pressures would lead to the demise of the Irish companies, or their acquisition by foreign rivals.

8

CONCLUSION: IRELAND AND THE EEC

On 1 January 1973, Ireland joined the European Economic Community. For some observers, membership of the EEC offered exciting prospects for further industrial growth. European markets were large and prosperous, and Ireland seemed an attractive base from which to mount an export drive.[1] But, as McAleese noted, the dangers of exposing the Republic's domestic market to further competitive pressures had to be weighed against the potential benefits.[2] The liberalisation of trade with the United Kingdom was already leading to market penetration by foreign firms, and it was expected that much more severe competition would result from EEC membership.[3] In the event, the expected benefits did not materialise because the recession of 1974 had a severe impact upon EEC countries, and it provided a further indication, if any were needed, of the Irish economy's vulnerability to outside factors.

This recession reached a low point in mid-1975 in Ireland, and led to the demise of some of the country's oldest and best-known footwear firms. Edward Donaghy, for example, went into liquidation in May 1975.[4] The Cork Shoe Co. also appointed a Receiver in May 1975 and finally closed down in April 1976, although the buildings, plant and much of the labour force were taken over by the privately owned Youngline Shoes Ltd.[5] Even the Hallidays Group was not immune; although it had acquired the minority interest in Stedfast Shoes in January 1971, Stedfast continued to realise an inadequate return on assets and was liquidated in June 1975.[6]

Other companies, however, were able to adapt to changing conditions and survived the various crises which beset the footwear industry during the early 1970s. John Halliday & Son Ltd and Padmore & Barnes Ltd became wholly-owned subsidiaries of C. & J. Clark Ltd; there were now no restrictions on foreign ownership, and Clarks acquired the 38.5 per cent minority interest in the Hallidays Group in 1971, for a total consideration of £1,483,600.[7] The Dundalk company, which now became known as Clarks Ireland Ltd, continued to dominate the Irish market, and Padmore & Barnes' export success with its Wallabee brand moccasins led to a phenomenal rate of expansion. By 1975, the Kilkenny factory was producing 23,000 pairs per week and employing 650 people, and exports now accounted for 93 per cent of the company's production.⁸ Dubarry Shoemakers was in difficulties around 1970 when its associate company, Norvic Ltd, went out of business, but it was able to retain the use of the Norvic name in Ireland while gradually switching over to own-brand production. While Padmore & Barnes did well abroad, Dubarry was able to prove that there existed a lucrative market for moccasin-type footwear in Ireland. In 1976 a need for extra capacity led it to acquire the Westport factory of the Reliable Shoe Co. which had gone into liquidation.⁹ Woodingtons did poorly in the early 1970s, making losses in 1969-72 and 1974, but thereafter the company made steady progress until the end of the decade. The Edenderry Shoe Co. generally did well, even during periods when trading conditions were bad, although it too went through a sticky patch with short time working and some redundancies in 1974-5.¹⁰

After 1975 there was something of a respite for the footwear manufacturers, based upon the general recovery in world markets. Government grants, backed by tax concessions upon export sales, also did something to encourage foreign companies to set up in Ireland; U.S.-owned companies like the New Balance Athletic Shoe Co. of Boston, which commenced production in Tralee in 1978, viewed the Irish Republic as a cheap manufacturing base from which to develop European sales. Ireland's nearness to Europe meant a 15 per cent saving on transportation costs, and footwear made in Ireland was exempt from the 9-14 per cent EEC duty payable on U.S.-made footwear.¹¹

Around the end of the 1970s, however, the Irish footwear industry entered another, and more serious, period of decline. The government had arranged with the EEC that tariffs should be wound down gradually, but now Ireland had finally become an 'open economy'. In addition, Ireland was seriously affected by the second upswing in oil prices towards the end of the decade, and the next few years were characterised by rapid inflation.¹² High inflation rates led to Ireland's joining the European Monetary System in 1979 and abandoning parity with sterling, but this did not have the desired effect. Price and wage inflation was persistently higher than in other European countries in the late 1970s and early 1980s; in 1981, for example, the inflation rate was 21 per cent per year.¹³ Rapid wage inflation was particularly worrying, because labour productivity was rising more slowly than in Britain or Europe. As a result, the cost of manufacturing in Ireland rose sharply. Inflation rates slowed considerably after about 1982, but because other countries experienced a similar trend Ireland's relative position — in terms of price levels — did not improve.¹⁴

As a result of these pressures, footwear production in Ireland declined continuously in the 1970s and the 1980s. Exports remained fairly static, but home sales fell sharply. Employment in the Irish footwear industry almost halved between 1973 and 1983 (Table 29). This was ironic, because the home market was at last beginning to expand. In the same period, the population was growing at an annual average of 1.25 per cent, and per capita consumption rose from 2.8 pairs to 3.9 pairs per year.[15] Importers reaped the benefit; imports more than trebled between 1973 and 1983, and their share of the home market rose from just under 50 per cent to over 90 per cent.

TABLE 29

Performance of the Irish footwear industry, 1973-83
(all types of footwear)

	Imports	Home production	Exports	Total Production for the Irish market	Imports' share of the Irish market	Index of volume of home production	Average employment	Index of average employment
	000 pairs	000 pairs	000 pairs	000 pairs	%	1973 = 100	No.	1973 = 100
1973	4,200	7,590	3,100	8,710	48.5	100.0	4,891	100.0
1974	5,200	7,460	3,600	9,060	57.4	98.3	4,635	94.8
1975	5,120	5,470	2,820	7,770	65.9	72.1	3,388	69.3
1976	7,250	5,070	2,340	9,980	72.6	66.8	3,512	71.8
1977	7,160	5,040	2,570	9,630	74.4	66.4	3,635	74.3
1978	9,390	5,000	2,600	11,790	79.6	65.9	3,544	72.5
1979	10,300	4,860	2,800	12,360	83.3	64.0	3,636	74.3
1980	10,400	4,260	2,530	12,130	85.7	56.1	3,298	67.4
1981	12,300	4,700	2,750	14,250	86.3	61.9	3,112	63.6
1982	12,200	4,240	2,800	13,640	89.4	55.9	2,810	57.5
1983	13,000	4,110	2,850	14,260	91.2	54.2	2,725	55.7

Sources: *Statistical Abstracts*; C. & J. Clark Ltd, internal reports.

In the early 1980s, roughly two-thirds of all imports came from Britain and Italy; these were mostly good quality lines, but they were very competitive in terms of price because footwear companies in these countries had achieved substantial improvements in productivity in recent years. In addition, pressure from low cost producers in Eastern Europe and Asia, which had been increasing since the late 1960s, grew sharply in the 1970s and 1980s. Footwear manufacturing was still a labour-intensive activity, and the availability of cheap labour conferred significant advantages.[16] Another factor behind the massive influx of imports was the growth of multiple trading. Irish-owned concerns were still important — Connollys the Shoe People was the largest chain in 1986, with 26 shops, and Boylan Shoes had 18 — but the British Shoe Corporation had established a strong presence, with 20 shops and concessions. Another British-owned company, John Tyler

Conclusion: Ireland and the EEC

& Sons Ltd, had become the second largest multiple with 25 shops in Dublin, Cork, Galway, Limerick and Waterford.[17] The problem for Irish manufacturers was that these foreign-owned multiples tended to meet their needs from overseas suppliers.

One by one, many of the well-known names in the Irish footwear industry have closed down. James Winstanley closed early in 1986,[18] and Tuf Shoes of Killarney — the old Hilliard & Palmer factory which had become a subsidiary of G.B. Britton of Kingswood, Bristol — made its last 96 workers redundant in July 1985.[19] In the recent past, exports have also begun to contract sharply. In 1984, Clarks and its subsidiaries accounted for 48 per cent of footwear exports from the Republic. However, the Dundalk factory closed in February 1985, and rapid inflation, coupled with a weakening dollar, meant that Padmore & Barnes was being priced out of its North American markets. Padmore & Barnes' high quality casuals rose from $89 to $130-140 a pair by late 1986 and became quite unsaleable. The Kilkenny factory was the subject of a management buyout in early 1987, and Clarks now supplies its Irish and overseas customers from its factories in the United Kingdom.[20]

Other companies have survived, but with reduced turnovers and falling profits. Dubarry closed its Westport factory in 1981 due to falling sales, and concentrated production in Ballinasloe. The company was sold to the management in 1983, and continued to operate with a reduced labour force of about 150 workers.[21] J.H. Woodington, which had been one of the most successful footwear manufacturers in the late 1970s, underwent a major decline. In 1979 the company made a pretax profit of IR£154,124 on turnover of IR£1,033,045. In the following year, however, the profit was cut to IR£30,413 on a turnover of IR£937,858. By 1984, turnover had fallen to IR£798,534 and Woodingtons made a net loss of IR£180,692. The company is still trading, although redundancies have recently cut the workforce to about 40.[22]

By May 1986, when there were 24 footwear factories in operation in the Irish Republic, employment in the industry had slumped to just 1,675 workers — a 39 per cent reduction on the 1983 figure — and there were just four manufacturers employing more than 150 workers.[23] The most successful of them in recent years had been the Edenderry Shoe Co., which employs between 250 and 300 people. The company has been consistently profitable, although trading profits were down in the early 1980s. In addition to manufacturing, there has also been a successful venture into importing — Edenderry Distributors Ltd was set up in October 1984 — and cautious policies have led to the acquisition of substantial investments which now make a major contribution to profits.[24]

Most of the surviving factories, however, are very small. A particular feature of the last few years has been the emergence of co-operatives, which have often appeared as a result of redundancies or the closure of more long-established firms. The Westport Shoe Co-operative Society, for example, was set up in 1982 by 37 of the 60 employees made redundant by Dubarry, and Setanta Shoes and C-Step were set up in Dundalk by ex-Hallidays managers following Clarks' withdrawal from Ireland.[25] It is uncertain whether companies such as these will stand the test of time and survive in what had become a highly competitive market. One suspects that their survival will depend upon the personal commitment of their members, and upon their ability to find and exploit a suitable niche in the market.

How, then, are we to assess the performance of the Irish footwear industry between 1922 and 1973? Initially an industry with little growth potential, it owed its 'spurt' during the 1930s to Fianna Fáil's decision to industrialise on the basis of small consumer goods industries, producing items for which a demand already existed in Ireland. As very few industries possessed a comparative advantage over their foreign competitors, export opportunities would be limited and protection would be essential to safeguard the home market. Foreign competition was regulated by way of tariffs, quotas and the Control of Manufactures legislation, and the government offered financial assistance to new industries through the Industrial Credit Co. and (later in the period) an increasingly wide-ranging grants programme. The banks also played a vital role because of the scarcity of long-term investment capital and the need for substantial short-loan and overdraft facilities. We can see peaks in banking activity associated with the outbreak of the Korean War and the financing of the British import deposit scheme in 1968, but throughout the period the most substantial creditor of every Irish footwear manufacturer was its bank.

Economic development presented a major dilemma for the Fianna Fáil government. British concerns were already dominating many sectors of Irish industry, and the prospect was one of an Ireland which, although politically independent, would remain economically dependent. Business interests were also strongly opposed to economic penetration by foreign firms. Throughout the 1930s, Fianna Fáil was under pressure from organisations like the Federation of Irish Industry and the National Agricultural and Industrial Development Association to prohibit foreign-owned firms from operating in Ireland.[26] Yet foreign capital, entrepreneurial skills and technical expertise were badly needed if the government was to generate rapid industrial growth and tackle the chronic unemployment problem. In addition, there is some evidence to suggest that British-owned companies were seen as providing healthy competition for Irish firms, thus leading to greater efficiency and improvements in product quality.[27] In practice, ideological commitment to self-sufficiency did not lead the government to reject British assistance out of hand; foreign involvement was to be permitted, but would be subject to scrutiny and regulation by the Department of Industry and Commerce. If Irish economic growth did not always take place under Irish ownership, it was at least achieved under Irish supervision. Although this compromise was ideologically unsatisfactory, it did make a vital contribution to industrial expansion, and in economic terms was distinctly preferable to the exclusion of foreign capital, entrepreneurs and technical experts.

Nevertheless, the policies adopted by Fianna Fáil leaders did create difficulties for manufacturers. Clearly, tariffs and quotas were a somewhat unsophisticated means of generating industrial growth, and the experience of the footwear industry demonstrated the problems as well as the benefits associated with protection and self-sufficiency in a small country. Rapid growth could not be maintained once import substitution had taken place, and there were often contradictions between the planners' overall objectives and the interests of individual industries. This was demonstrated by the establishment of an unnecessarily large number of footwear factories — about which the Department of Industry and Commerce could do little — and by the problems experienced with intermediate industries like leather production. The existence of surplus production capacity continued to bedevil footwear manufacturers until the 1960s and manufacturing costs in the industry were always high compared to those of its British and European rivals.[28] Such problems initially came to a head in the crisis of 1937-8, when production exceeded consumption for the first time and most companies were faced with the need for prolonged periods of short-time working. Of the Irish companies, only John Halliday & Son Ltd was able to take decisive action to remedy the difficulties which they were facing, and the agreement with C. & J. Clark Ltd and subsequent switch to better quality ladies' and children's footwear led to Hallidays' gradual emergence as a market leader.

The problems of the late 1930s were eased and obscured during the Emergency, although wartime conditions did impose other restraints upon growth — notably the unavailability of many essential supplies and the controls upon prices, profits and industrial relations. The Irish footwear companies all survived the war, and the government was largely successful in preventing a sharp increase in unemployment as output fell, but few companies were in a position to do very much to prepare for the return to peacetime conditions. The end of the Emergency offered the prospect of a new period of expansion, for the Irish public was tired of shortages and 'ersatz' footwear. There were also opportunities for the development of export business, and this offered the prospect of an alternative to the fierce competition for the home market which had characterised the pre-war industry. Foreign competition had been dislocated or destroyed and the dollar reserves which had been built up during the war enabled Irish manufacturers to tap supplies which were inaccessible to their British counterparts. Yet it must be concluded that the Irish footwear industry was unable to make the maximum use of post-war opportunities. There was indeed an immediate boom in home demand but the wartime restrictions meant that most companies lacked the capital needed for expansion projects. The rate of growth between 1945 and 1947, although very rapid, was not fast enough to suit the government and, for political reasons, it was decided that import quotas should be increased. The subsequent flood of imports in 1947 quickly brought the period of expansion to an end. As far as exports were concerned, the Irish government did not initate an export drive like that which was taking place in Britain at this time and, in the event, Irish manufacturers were unable to make substantial inroads into foreign markets.

Part of the trouble was that improvements in productive efficiency and quality were needed. The market for footwear, in Ireland and abroad, was becoming more sophisticated and now that the war was over manufacturers were no longer able to sell every pair they made regardless of quality. Coupled with this trend was the need to move away from the fast-declining heavy boot sector towards the lighter footwear which the general public wanted. Although some progress had been made in these directions during the late 1940s, sales had only just begun to recover from the downturn of 1947-8 when demand was again depressed by Ireland's worsening balance of payments deficit and the government's attempts to remedy the situation. Nevertheless, while the early 1950s was a very difficult time for the footwear companies, this was also a time of intense activity as most manufacturers made some efforts to improve the saleability of their footwear. As in the 1930s, the use of agreements was crucial to this process, and it has been argued that the peculiar advantages of Hallidays' agreement with Clarks made it a key factor in its record of steady progress towards market leadership. The pace of technological change was beginning to quicken too, with the advent of new construction methods and soling materials.

When trading conditions began to improve towards the end of the 1950s, the footwear industry was able to benefit from the improvements which had been put in hand. Production and marketing techniques were becoming more sophisticated, the size of the home market was beginning to expand, and some manufacturers were beginning to show that Irish-made footwear could be exported in substantial quantities. There began a period of unusually rapid and sustained growth and, despite the demise of John Rawson & Son Ltd, the industry generally was in a healthier financial condition than at any time in its history. Yet the Committee on Industrial Organisation and the Committee on Industrial Progress were able to identify a number of continuing weaknesses, and the industry's experience in the 1970s and 1980s

Conclusion: Ireland and the EEC

suggested that it was still not ready for the arrival of freer trading conditions — despite the fact that the projected move towards free trade had been part of government policy since the late 1950s and the ending of quotas had been envisaged since 1965.

The overall impression, therefore, is one of an industry labouring under a series of difficulties, and it has been necessary to consider the nature of these problems in some detail. Nevertheless, the performance of the Irish footwear manufacturers should not be under-estimated. Most companies proved surprisingly resilient and, until recent years, the industry's failure rate has not been high by Irish standards. The improvements made over the period did not succeed in closing the gap with Britain in terms of output per employee, production costs or profitability. But, on the other hand, the Irish did not fall much further behind. This, in view of the considerable handicaps under which the Irish manufacturers operated, was itself a considerable achievement. Once comparisons began to be made with EEC countries, however, the weakness of the Irish industry became fully apparent. Free trade combined with rapid price and wage inflation has had a disastrous impact upon footwear manufacturing in Ireland in recent years.

APPENDICES

APPENDIX I

Footwear production and foreign trade, 1926-73[1]

1. Footwear wholly or mainly of leather

	Quantity (000 pairs)				Value (£000) (current prices)			
	Imports	Home production	Exports	Total production for sale in Ireland[2]	Imports[3]	Home production[4]	Exports[5]	Total production for sale in Ireland[2]
1926	n.a.	502	n.a.	n.a.	n.a.	319	n.a.	n.a.
1929	n.a.	521	n.a.	n.a.	n.a.	339	n.a.	n.a.
1930	4,155	n.a.	7	n.a.	1,600	n.a.	5	n.a.
1931	3,905	660	5	4,559	1,459	401	4	1,856
1932	2,879	841	4	3,715	1,032	460	1	1,490
1933	2,770	1,589	1	4,358	781	756	—	1,536
1934	2,364	1,965	1	4,328	643	832	—	1,475
1935	1,348	3,044	3	4,389	423	1,252	—	1,675
1936	784	4,407	—	5,190	291	1,752	—	2,043
1937	399	4,007	—	4,406	157	1,681	—	1,838
1938	216	3,797	—	4,014	101	1,625	—	1,727
1939	206	4,188	—	4,394	106	1,884	—	1,990
1940	162	3,982	30	4,114	103	2,033	17	2,119
1941	226	4,140	8	4,358	162	2,244	5	2,402
1942	358	3,749	—	4,106	243	2,303	—	2,546
1943	42	3,706	—	3,749	48	2,579	—	2,627
1944	46	3,670	—	3,716	44	2,732	—	2,776

1. Until 1973, the Central Statistics Office in Dublin used the United Nations' International Standard Industrial Classification (ISIC). With Ireland's entry into the E.E.C. a gradual change was made to the NACE classification (Nomenclature Générale des Activités Economiques dans les Communautés Européens). Post-1973 figures, therefore, are not compatible with the earlier series, and are omitted.
2. 'Total production for sale in Ireland' is defined as imports *plus* home production *minus* exports. Figures relating to retail sales would obviously be a more satisfactory measure, but are not available until 1966.
3. Carriage, insurance and freight (c.i.f.).
4. Wholesale prices.
5. Free on board (f.o.b.).

	Quantity (000 pairs)				Value (£000) (current prices)			
	Imports	Home production	Exports	Total production for sale in Ireland[2]	Imports[3]	Home production[4]	Exports[5]	Total production for sale in Ireland[2]
1945	62	4,021	—	4,082	60	3,047	—	3,107
1946	739	4,615	—	5,355	695	3,585	—	4,280
1947	1,211	5,109	5	6,315	1,110	4,502	6	5,606
1948	679	4,273	17	4,936	878	4,424	25	5,277
1949	133	4,341	121	4,352	219	4,421	115	4,525
1950	19	4,591	172	4,438	35	5,118	181	4,973
1951	26	3,937	483	3,480	39	5,320	581	4,777
1952	21	3,716	278	3,460	39	4,869	436	4,472
1953	22	4,295	395	3,933	44	5,600	592	5,051
1954	17	3,820	414	3,423	42	5,111	629	4,524
1955	23	3,984	432	3,575	52	5,417	682	4,787
1956	37	3,955	501	3,491	84	5,381	788	4,677
1957	61	3,921	563	3,420	135	5,465	910	4,690
1958	84	4,055	592	3,547	212	5,707	941	4,978
1959	98	4,440	828	3,710	219	6,365	1,348	5,236
1960	121	4,785	1,086	3,819	284	6,860	1,707	5,437
1961	146	5,278	1,302	4,122	334	7,709	2,050	5,992
1962	170	5,157	118	5,209	385	7,675	1,818	6,242
1963	181	5,783	1,259	4,705	357	8,278	1,968	6,667
1964	224	6,643	1,764	5,103	435	9,768	2,702	7,501
1965	258	6,467	1,604	5,121	429	9,279	2,344	7,379
1966	224	6,308	1,640	4,892	449	9,364	2,434	7,379
1967	322	5,963	1,613	4,672	523	9,402	2,402	7,523
1968	244	6,285	1,859	4,671	572	10,009	2,808	7,773
1969	358	6,585	1,998	4,945	808	12,267	3,611	9,464
1970	682	6,032	1,799	4,906	1,351	12,318	3,812	9,857
1971	1,442	n.a.[6]	2,163	n.a.[6]	2,185	13,004	4,843	10,346
1972	1,870	n.a.	2,269	n.a.	3,180	14,987	5,590	12,577
1973	2,327	n.a.	3,103	n.a.	4,784	16,968	8,151	13,601

Sources: *Census of Industrial Production; Trade and Shipping Statistics.*

6. Figures not given due to classification changes.

Appendix I

2. Footwear wholly or mainly of other materials
(excluding footwear wholly of rubber)

	Quantity (000 pairs)				Value (£000) (current prices)			
	Imports	Home production	Exports	Total production for sale in Ireland[1]	Imports[2]	Home production[3]	exports[4]	Total production for sale in Ireland[1]
1926	n.a.	n.a.	n.a.	n.a.	n.a.	n.a.	n.a.	n.a.
1929	n.a.	n.a.	n.a.	n.a.	n.a.	n.a.	n.a.	n.a.
1930	241	n.a.	—	n.a.	31	n.a.	—	n.a.
1931	231	n.a.	—	n.a.	27	2	—	30
1932	336	n.a.	—	n.a.	40	2	—	42
1933	1,448	n.a.	—	n.a.	104	4	—	108
1934	1,076	n.a.	—	n.a.	77	13	—	91
1935	700	n.a.	—	n.a.	40	20	—	60
1936	374	404	—	751	24	54	—	78
1937	62	604	—	666	7	85	—	91
1938	39	645	—	684	5	93	—	98
1939	47	613	—	660	7	94	—	101
1940	35	676	—	711	3	118	—	122
1941	65	424	—	489	12	85	—	97
1942	107	377	—	484	15	115	—	129
1943	—	201	—	201	—	88	—	88
1944	—	469	—	469	—	236	—	236
1945	122	634	—	755	38	279	—	317
1946	329	648	—	977	74	277	—	351
1947	321	479	—	800	166	262	—	428
1948	449	518	—	967	122	346	—	468
1949	18	685	—	703	13	419	—	432
1950	17	828	—	846	8	521	—	529
1951	18	886	—	904	9	585	—	595
1952	37	775	—	811	5	531	—	536
1953	46	1,131	—	1,177	11	754	—	766
1954	43	1,132	n.a.	n.a.	12	756	29	739

1. 'Total production for sale in Ireland' is defined as imports *plus* home production *minus* exports. Figures relating to retail sales would obviously be a more satisfactory measure, but are not available until 1966.
2. Carriage, insurance and freight (c.i.f.).
3. Wholesale prices.
4. Free on board (f.o.b.).

	Quantity (000 pairs)				Value (£000) (current prices)			
	Imports	Home production	Exports	Total production for sale in Ireland[1]	Imports[2]	Home production[3]	exports[4]	Total production for sale in Ireland[1]
1955	63	1,027	n.a.	n.a	15	655	18	651
1956	98	1,086	n.a.	n.a.	30	701	22	709
1957	72	1,235	n.a.	n.a.	22	817	8	831
1958	70	1,246	n.a.	n.a.	26	710	1	735
1959	24	1,054	n.a.	n.a.	5	598	3	599
1960	36	1,574	n.a.	n.a.	8	929	6	931
1961	44	1,694	n.a.	n.a.	9	885	3	890
1962	31	1,479	n.a.	n.a.	8	653	6	654
1963	53	1,474	n.a.	n.a.	18	709	35	692
1964	54	1,568	n.a.	n.a.	26	815	79	762
1965	56	1,489	n.a.	n.a.	21	859	110	771
1966	30	1,635	n.a.	n.a.	17	976	126	867
1967	59	1,722	n.a.	n.a.	31	1,076	203	905
1968	248	1,815	348	1,715	122	1,253	203	1,172
1969	592	2,153	233	2,511	463	1,681	153	1,991
1970	883	2,339	187	3,036	746	2,120	120	2,747
1971	1,059	n.a.	n.a.	n.a.	1,094	n.a.	104	n.a.
1972	1,396	n.a.	n.a.	n.a.	1,548	n.a.	154	n.a.
1973	1,896	n.a.	n.a.	n.a.[5]	2,501	n.a.	n.a.	n.a.[5]

Sources: *Census of Industrial Production; Trade and Shipping Statistics.*

5. Figures for 1970s are unavailable due to classification changes.

APPENDIX II

Average price per pair of imported and Irish-made footwear, 1926-70

(current prices)

	Footwear wholly or mainly of leather		Footwear wholly or mainly of other materials (excluding rubber)	
	Imports (new pence)	Home production (new pence)	Imports (new pence)	Home production (new pence)
1926	n.a.	63.6	n.a.	n.a.
1929	n.a.	65.1	n.a.	n.a.
1930	38.5	n.a.	12.7	n.a.
1931	37.4	60.7	12.1	n.a.
1932	35.9	54.7	11.9	n.a.
1933	28.2	47.5	7.2	n.a.
1934	27.2	42.3	7.2	n.a.
1935	31.3	41.1	5.1	n.a.
1936	37.1	39.8	6.8	13.4
1937	39.4	41.9	10.9	14.0
1938	46.9	42.8	12.3	14.4
1939	51.3	45.0	15.3	15.3
1940	63.5	51.1	11.1	17.5
1941	71.8	54.2	19.1	19.9
1942	67.9	61.4	13.7	30.5
1943	112.1	69.6	20.0	43.8
1944	96.3	74.4	12.5	50.3
1945	97.5	75.8	31.3	44.0
1946	94.0	77.7	22.6	42.7
1947	91.6	88.1	51.7	54.8
1948	129.3	103.5	57.2	66.8
1949	165.4	101.8	69.8	61.2
1950	184.1	111.5	46.0	62.9
1951	151.8	135.1	50.9	66.1
1952	183.6	131.0	13.2	68.6
1953	197.1	130.4	25.1	66.8
1954	239.4	133.8	28.2	66.8
1955	222.4	136.0	23.9	63.7
1956	231.2	136.1	30.4	64.6
1957	219.0	139.4	30.6	66.2
1958	252.7	140.7	37.7	56.9
1959	222.0	143.4	20.7	56.7

(current prices)

| | Footwear wholly or mainly of leather | | Footwear wholly or mainly of other materials (excluding rubber) | |
	Imports (new pence)	Home production (new pence)	Imports (new pence)	Home production (new pence)
1960	234.8	143.8	22.7	59.0
1961	228.9	146.1	20.0	52.2
1962	226.4	148.8	25.2	44.1
1963	197.4	143.1	34.3	48.1
1964	194.2	147.0	47.4	51.9
1965	166.3	143.5	37.5	57.7
1966	174.3	148.9	54.6	59.7
1967	162.3	157.7	53.1	62.5
1968	234.8	159.2	49.3	69.1
1969	226.0	186.3	78.2	78.1
1970	198.2	204.5	84.5	90.7
1971	151.5	n.a.[3]	102.3	n.a.[3]
1972	170.1	n.a.	110.9	n.a.
1973	182.1	n.a.	131.9	n.a.

Sources: *Census of Industrial Production; Trade and Shipping Statistics.*

1. C.i.f. prices.
2. Wholesale prices.
3. Figures not given due to classification changes.

APPENDIX III

Imports of footwear wholly made of rubber, 1930-1970: pairage, value and average price per pair

(current prices)

	Pairage	Value (£)	Average wholesale price per pair (new pence)
1930	897,156	90,679	10.1
1931	1,022,040	100,959	9.9
1932	1,061,940	97,817	9.2
1933	1,126,716	85,582	7.6
1934	658,740	40,747	6.2
1935	32,028	9,577	29.9
1936	28,596	10,086	35.3
1937	10,608	4,606	43.4
1938	9,996	3,610	36.1
1939	9,000	3,323	36.9
1940	7,800	3,127	40.1
1941	15,588	4,789	30.7
1942	2,652	1,384	52.2
1943	72	71	98.6
1944	26,052	26,663	102.3
1945	66,828	91,322	136.6
1946	254,304	192,530	75.7
1947	609,300	297,947	48.9
1948	457,440	296,637	64.9
1949	255,600	133,160	52.1
1950	435,348	227,440	56.5
1951	402,672	342,679	85.1
1952	63,288	65,564	103.6
1953	39,360	38,014	96.6
1954	42,852	38,974	91.0
1955	53,880	49,838	92.5
1956	45,600	46,908	102.9
1957	56,640	56,259	99.3
1958	69,192	72,256	104.4
1959	47,976	50,860	106.0

Appendix III

(current prices)

	Pairage	Value (£)	Average wholesale price per pair (new pence)
1960	45,912	51,854	112.9
1961	44,352	49,965	112.7
1962	53,940	58,005	107.5
1963	128,952	143,491	111.6
1964	187,728	177,162	94.4
1965	158,304	135,149	85.4
1966	76,116	66,717	87.7
1967	79,380	77,807	98.0
1968	172,692	111,441	64.5
1969	196,152	179,102	91.3
1970	307,872	243,371	79.0

Sources: *Trade and Shipping Statistics.*

APPENDIX IV

Import quota restrictions on footwear wholly or mainly of leather, 1934-62

		Pairs
1934	October to December	540,000
1935	Quarter to March	1,000,000
	Half-year to September	640,000
1936	Half-year to March	1,400,000
	Half-year to September	640,000
1937	Half-year to March	882,750
	Half-year to September	147,000
1938	Half-year to March	200,000
	Half-year to September	135,500
1939	Each half-year	150,000
1940	Each half-year	150,000
1941	Half-year to March	150,000
	Half-year to September	150,000
	Quarter to December	250,000
1942	Half-year to June	500,000
	Half-year to December	625,000
1943	Each half-year	625,000
1944	Each half-year	625,000
1945	Half-year to June	625,000
	Half-year to December	300,000
1946	Half-year to June	300,000
	Half-year to December	625,000
1947	Each half-year	625,000
1948	Half-year to June	625,000
	Half-year to December	150,000
1949	Year	200,000
	(subsequently reduced to 108,000)	

Appendix IV

Year		Pairs
1950	Year	20,000
1951	Year	20,000
1952	Year	20,000
1953	Year	20,000
1954	Year	20,000
1955	Year	40,000
1956	Year	60,000
1957	Year	80,000
1958	Year	100,000
1959	Year	100,000
1960	Year	125,000
1961	Year	150,000
1962	Year	150,000

Source: *Report on the Leather Footwear Industry* (Committee on Industrial Progress, Dublin, 1962), 295-6.

APPENDIX V

Estimated size of the Irish market, 1926-73[1]

	Total production for sale in Ireland (all types of footwear) (000 pairs)	Total population (000)	Implied 'consumption' per capita (pairs p.a.)
1926	n.a.	2,970	n.a.
1929	n.a.	2,937	n.a.
1931	5,813	2,935	1.98
1932	5,113	n.a.	n.a.
1933	6,933	2,962	2.35
1934	6,063	n.a.	n.a.
1935	5,350	n.a.	n.a.
1936	6,164	2,968	2.08
1937	5,084	2,948	1.82
1938	4,708	2,937	1.60
1939	5,063	n.a.	n.a.
1940	4,833	n.a.	n.a.
1941	4,861	n.a.	n.a.
1942	4,593	n.a.	n.a.
1943	3,950	n.a.	n.a.
1944	4,211	n.a.	n.a.
1945	4,904	n.a.	n.a.
1946	6,586	2,955	2.23
1947	7,724	2,974	2.60
1948	6,337	2,985	2.13
1949	5,311	2,981	1.78
1950	5,719	2,969	1.93
1951	4,787	2,961	1.62
1952	4,334	2,953	1.47
1953	5,138	2,949	1.74
1954	4,688	2,941	1.58

1. 'Total production for sale in Ireland' is defined as imports *plus* home production *minus* exports. Figures relating to retail sales would obviously be a more satisfactory measure, but are not available until 1966.

Appendix V

	Total production for sale in Ireland (all types of footwear)	Total population	Implied 'consumption per capita
	(000 pairs)	(000)	(pairs p.a.)
1955	4,719	2,921	1.50
1956	4,729	2,893	1.63
1957	4,784	2,885	1.66
1958	4,932	2,853	1.73
1959	4,837	2,846	1.70
1960	5,476	2,832	1.93
1961	5,905	2,818	2.10
1962	5,772	2,830	2.04
1963	6,360	2,850	2.23
1964	,.913	2,864	2.41
1965	6,824	2,876	2.37
1966	6,634	2,884	2.30
1967	6,533	2,899	2.25
1968	6,558	2,910	2.60
1969	7,652	2,933	2.61
1970	7,993	2,955	2.70
1971	8,277	3,032	2.73
1972	8,529	3,068	2.78
1973	8,710	3,078	2.83

Sources: *Census of Industrial Production; Census of Population.*
Estimates of the inter-censal population are based upon
K.A. Kennedy, *Productivity and Industrial Growth:
The Irish Experience* (Oxford, 1971), 3.

APPENDIX VI

Number of employees in the Irish footwear industry, and output per employee (by volume and value), 1926-73

	Number of employees	Annual output per employee (pairs)	$(£)^1$
1926	967	519	330
1929	1,056	494	321
1930	n.a.	n.a.	n.a.
1931	1,195	522	338
1932	1,714	491	270
1933	2,524	630	302
1934	2,976	660	285
1935	4,195	726	309
1936	5,617	856	324
1937	5,715	807	314
1938	5,358	829	325
1939	5,428	885	373
1940	5,202	895	425
1941	5,337	855	451
1942	5,173	798	480
1943	5,121	763	535
1944	5,307	778	573
1945	5,587	833	626
1946	5,928	888	692
1947	6,351	880	797
1948	6,199	773	810
1949	6,233	806	793
1950	6,547	828	909
1951	6,404	753	974
1952	5,778	777	991
1953	6,426	844	1,055
1954	6,290	793	997
1955	6,068	775	1,064
1956	5,913	852	1,102
1957	5,522	934	1,207
1958	5,349	991	1,265
1959	5,423	1,013	1,345

1   Wholesale prices.

Appendix VI

	Number of employees	Annual output per employee (pairs)	(£)[1]
1960	5,661	1,119	1,450
1961	5,964	1,169	1,511
1962	5,773	1,150	1,507
1963	5,967	1,216	1,579
1964	6,222	1,320	1,785
1965	6,149	1,294	1,745
1966	6,134	1,295	1,809
1967	5,821	1,320	1,952
1968	5,542	1,462	2,200
1969	6,150	1,421	2,460
1970	5,890	1,398	2,645
1971	5,430	n.a.[2]	n.a.[2]
1972	5,180	n.a.	n.a.
1973	4,891	n.a.	n.a.

Source: *Irish Trade Journal and Statistical Bulletin.*

1 Wholesale prices.
2 Figures omitted due to classification changes.

NOTES

Notes to Chapter One

1. J. Meenan, *The Irish Economy since 1922* (Liverpool, 1970), 30.
2. R.C. Geary, 'Irish Economic Development since the Treaty', *Studies* xl (1951), 404.
3. Meenan, *op. cit.*, 139.
4. G. Fitzgerald, *Planning in Ireland* (Dublin, 1968), reprinted in J.W. O'Hagan (ed.), *The Economy of Ireland; Policy and Performance* (Dublin, 1975), 3.
5. K.A. Kennedy, *Productivity and Industrial Growth: the Irish Experience* (Oxford, 1971), 3.
6. *Census of Ireland*, 1901, *General Report*, 4.
7. Kennedy, *loc. cit.*
8. Winstanley was a well-known figure in Dublin; he had interests in several shops and was a member of the city council, later becoming High Sheriff of Dublin. *The Industries of Dublin* (Dublin, *c.* 1888), 67.
9. Interview with Denis O'Neill.
10. *The Irish Insurance, Banking and Finance Journal* (November 1881).
11. *Report of the Select Committee on Industries (Ireland)*, Brit. Parl. Papers, 1884-85, ix, 740.
12. *Ibid.*
13. *Ibid.*
14. *Ibid.* This may have been Williamson Brothers Ltd, listed in 1921 as a manufacturer of heavy boots and men's welted footwear. *Yearbook of the Boot Manufacturers' Federation of Great Britain and Ireland* (1920-21), 423-4.
15. *Freeman's Journal* (1 September 1881); *Limerick Reporter and Tipperary Vindicator* (22 August 1882); *Industries of Dublin, op. cit.*, 67.
16. R.A. Church, 'The Effect of the American Report Invasion on the British Boot and Shoe Industry', *Journal of Economic History* xviii (1968), 237.
17. Reprinted in *Report of the Select Committee on Industries (Ireland)*, 740. Sexton was M.P. for Sligo County and a member of the Committee.
18. *Ibid.* Also see *Freeman's Journal* (1 September 1881).
19. L.M. Cullen, *An Economic History of Ireland since 1660* (1972), 163.
20. Thomas Murphy's factory manufactured heavy boots and employed about fifty people, some of whom had been recruited from Northampton and Leicester. The company was relatively short-lived, however, and production ceased around 1910; *Tempest's Annual* (Dundalk, 1965), 31.

21. *Irish Trade Journal* (August 1927), 171.
22. Cullen, *op. cit.*, 163.
23. *Report of the Leather Footwear Industry* (Committee on Industrial Organisation, Dublin 1962), 57.
24. Lasts were usually made of beech or iron. For ready-made footwear the last conformed to the patterns provided by the designer, and a different last was required for each size and fitting. In bespoke shoemaking, of course, a last would be made or modified to fit the foot of the individual customer.
25. R.A. Church, 'Labour Supply and Innovation, 1800-1860; the Boot and Shoe Industry', *Business History* xxii (1970), 26-8, 30.
26. *Ibid.*, 30-1. Also see H. Bradley, *The Technical Growth of the Footwear Industry* (British Boot, Shoe and Allied Trades Research Association, paper no. 35, September 1930).
27. Church, 'Labour Supply', *art. cit.*, 30-1.
28. Church, 'American Export Invasion', *art. cit.*, 229.
29. *Ibid.*, 234.
30. Riveting was originally introduced early in the nineteenth century. The sole was fastened to the insole and upper by brass or iron rivets, and a metal last was used to clench the rivets on the inside. It was suitable for cheap work boots where flexibility and appearance were not of primary importance.
31. Church, 'American Export Invasion, *art. cit.*, 234.
32. *Ibid.*, 232.
33. However, it should be noted that while the extension of mechanisation and the development of the team system permitted an increase in scale and lengthened the train of processes, the essential stages in the making of shoes remained more or less unaltered. Factory organisation followed the traditional division into clicking, press-cutting (of soles), closing, lasting and finishing. This departmentalisation was further emphasised by the fact that men and women were rarely employed upon the same process. Clicking, press-cutting and lasting were almost exclusively carried out by male labour, while closing, finishing and packing was performed by female operatives. H.A. Silverman (ed.), *Studies in Industrial Organisation* (1946), 201-2; *Report on the Leather Footwear Industry* (1962), 14.
34. Church, 'American Export Invasion', *art. cit.*, 239.
35. Silverman, *op. cit.*, 218-20; A. Fox, *History of the National Union of Boot and Shoe Operatives, 1874-1957* (Oxford, 1958), 422-3; H.C. Hillman, 'Size of Firms in the Boot and Shoe Industry', *Economic Journal* (June 1939), 279-83.
36. *Final Report of the Fiscal Inquiry Committee* (Dublin, 1923), *passim.*
37. Dublin Industrial Development Association (hereafter DIDA), *Council Minutes*, 18 February 1924 (National Library of Ireland, MS 16243).
38. *Yearbook of the Boot Manufacturers' Federation of Great Britain and Ireland* (1920-1), 432-4; (1924), 333-4; *Irish Trade Journal* (August 1927), 171; (June 1933), 39.
39. *Tempest's Annual* (Dundalk, 1965), 31-2.
40. *Irish Trade Journal* (August 1927), 172; *Report on the Leather Footwear Industry* (1962), 58.

Notes to pages 27-31

41. *Census of Industrial Production; Irish Trade Journal* (November 1928), 30; (February 1931), 60. Initially, the 1926 Census included all footwear manufacturing establishments with a gross output of over £300 — a total of 105 concerns. It was inaccurate, particularly in the case of the small concerns, and in 1929 it was decided to confine the Census to the nine comparatively large factories then in operation. The 1926 results were then adjusted to permit comparisons to be made with subsequent years. The adjusted figures are used throughout this book.
42. Cullen, *op. cit.*, 172-6.
43. McGilligan Papers, P35b/14, October 1928 (University College, Dublin, Department of Archives).
44. DIDA, *Council Minutes*, 2 November 1925 ff.
45. *Irish Trade Journal* (September 1935), 99.
46. *Report on the Leather Industry* (Committee on Industrial Progress, Dublin, 1964) 4-5. D.J. Dwyer, 'The Leather Industries of the Irish Republic, 1922-55', *Irish Geography* iv (1961), 175-89. In 1923, imports met 95 per cent of total demand in Ireland.
47. Fanning, *op. cit.*, 204.
48. M. Daly, 'An Irish Ireland for Business? The Control of Manufactures Acts, 1932 and 1934', *Irish Historical Studies* xxvi (1984), 246-8.
49. *Ibid.*, 248. Department of Industry and Commerce, Overseas Industries Branch, File 1207, 18 June 1932.
50. McGilligan Papers, P35b/14.

Notes to Chapter Two

1. *The Economist* (1938), 433; J. Press, 'Protectionism and the Irish Footwear Industry, 1932-39', *Irish Economic and Social History* xiii (1986), 74-89. I am grateful to the editors for permission to reproduce sections of this article.
2. Kennedy, *Productivity and Industrial Growth, op. cit.* 28.
3. See, for example, A. Griffith, *The Sinn Féin Policy* (Dublin, 1905).
4. J.M. Keynes, 'National Self-Sufficiency', *Studies* (1933), 177.
5. *Dáil Éireann Debates*, xliv, cols 138-42, 19 Oct 1932. The Earl of Longford and T.P. O'Neill, *Eamon de Valera* (London, 1970), 281.
6. Fanning, *op. cit.*, 257-8.
7. *Irish Trade Journal* (June 1933), 39; *Journal of the Incorporated Federated Associations of Boot and Shoe Manufacturers of Great Britain and Ireland* (hereafter *Federation Journal*), 12 (1931/2), 235-6.
8. Cullen, *op. cit.*, 179.
9. Irish Free State Special Duties Act.
10. Cullen, *op. cit.*, 178; O'Hagan, *op. cit.*, 7-8.
11. *Irish Trade Journal* (June 1933), 39.
12. *Ibid.*
13. *Federation Journal*, xv (1933-34), 2-3.

14. Excluding infants' foortwear, which was exempted until an Amendment Order was made on 22 January 1935. *Irish Trade Journal* (September 1935), p. 99.

15. G. Rimmer, 'The Leeds Boot and Shoe Industry in the 19th Century', *British Boot and Shoe Institution Journal* (hereafter *BBSI Journal*), xii (1965), 420. Fred Halliday was John Halliday's son and had run the business since his father's death, although financial difficulties had compelled him to relinquish ownership between 1902 and 1912. Hallidays, H 1/3; H 17/7.

16. *The Democrat* (20 August 1932); *The Independent* (24 November 1932).

17. *Ibid*. The average output of an Irish footwear factory at this time was about 3,000 pairs per week. *Census of Industrial Production*.

18. *The Examiner* (11 June 1933).

19. This system was made necessary by the advent of multiple fittings. Padmore & Barnes' retail customers had to stock at least one pair in each size and fitting, and when a pair was sold a postcard to the factory would secure an immediate replacement. At that time it was the only company prepared to supply a single pair of shoes to a retailer.

20. Padmore & Barnes archives; *Clarks' Courier* (14 January 1966), 6.

21. S.J. Davis to J.P. Hawe, 26 July 1933; *Minutes of the Kilkenny Industrial Association*, 5 October 1933.

22. *Dáil Éireann Debates*, xlii, 1237 (14 June 1932).

23. For a detailed examination of the Acts, see Daly, *op. cit*.

24. See Chapter 3.

25. Department of Industry and Commerce, New Manufacture Licence, 19 May 1933.

26. *Irish Times* (16 June 1932).

27. *The Examiner* (20 August 1932).

28. Meenan, *op. cit.*, p. 152.

29. *Dáil Éireann Debates*, xxi, 990 (7 November 1927).

30. *The Examiner* (11 June 1933).

31. This method of fastening soles became practicable during the 1920s with the appearance of cellulose cements, but it was not in widespread use in Ireland until after the Second World War.

32. See, for example, NUBSO, *Monthly Reports* (February 1934), 102.

33. Padmore & Barnes, *Annual Report* (year ending 31 January 1936); *Kilkenny People* (11 December 1937); *The Post* (8 December 1937).

34. Interview with Arthur Halliday.

35. On 1 June 1935, for example, a licence was obtained for the importation of 20,000 pairs of closed uppers. Padmore & Barnes, *Minutes* (4 May 1935); (1 June 1935).

36. In October 1936, Arthur Halliday commented that he was now compelled to buy virtually all his heavy leather from an Irish tannery.

37. Padmore & Barnes, for instance, paid 1.35p. per pair to Northampton for technical and other services.

38. It should be noted, of course, that the advantages were not entirely one sided. Licensing was profitable to British manufacturers, and enabled them to keep their brands in

Notes to pages 41-6

existence in Ireland despite the prohibitive import restrictions.
39. C. & J. Clark, *Minutes* (15 October 1934).
40. *Ibid.* (15/22 October 1934).
41. *Ibid.* (25 October 1934). In fact, the suggestion was that C. & J. Clark should invest only £5,000 in ordinary shares, but a large temporary loan would also be required.
42. *Ibid.* (5/12 November 1934).
43. Matters were complicated early in 1935 by an approach from H.J. Bostock of Lotus Shoes, who enquired whether Clarks would be interested in joining with Lotus and K Shoes to establish a factory in Ireland. Eventually, it was decided that negotiations with Padmore & Barnes had gone too far to permit this. *Ibid.* (4 March 1935).
44. *Ibid.*
45. Interview with Bancroft Clark.
46. *Census of Industrial Production.*
47. Padmore & Barnes' boots were considered suitable for parish priests and farmers' Sunday wear.
48. Appendix I.
49. NUBSO, *Monthly Reports* (May 1934), 271. Japan and Czechoslovakia both supplied about 4 per cent of non-leather imports (and about 2 per cent of total imports) in 1934. Although their share of the market was quite insignificant in comparison with Britain's, it was growing rapidly and they were an obvious target for the protectionist lobby.
50. See Appendix II.
51. Sewing machines for stitching uppers, however, were usually obtained from American manufacturers.
52. The duty on components was raised in September 1936 and April 1937. By the latter date duties on components made of leather varied from 30 to 60 per cent and those on components of other materials were 20 to 40 per cent. *Federation Journal* xvii (1935-6), 387.
53. *Statistical Abstract.*
54. 1933 Finance Act, s. 4.
55. *Federation Journal*, xvii (1935-6), 3; *Report on the Leather Industry* (1964), 6.
56. *Report on the Leather Industry* (1964), 7.
57. Interview with Stephen Lowry.
58. Another small sole industry tannery began production at Portarlington, Co. Offaly, in 1940, just before wartime shortages brought the period of expansion to a close. Dwyer, *op. cit.*, pp. 178-9.
59. *Shoe and Leather News* (16 November 1944).
60. NUBSO, *Official Report of the Irish Union Delegate Conference* (1-2 December 1952), 2.
61. NUBSO, *Monthly Reports* (July 1935), 293.
62. NUBSO, *Monthly Reports* (July 1935), 293; (December 1935), 527. *Shoe and Leather News* (16 November 1944).

63. NUBSO, *Monthly Reports* (April 1934), 212-6.
64. *Ibid.* (March 1936), 175.
65. For a more detailed description, see K.G.J.C. Knowles & M. Verry, 'Earnings in the Boot and Shoe Industry', *Bulletin of the Oxford University Institute of Statistics* (February/March 1954), 32ff.
66. *Ibid.*, 32.
67. NUBSO, *Monthly Reports*.
68. *Statistical Abstract*.
69. *Ibid.*
70. *Irish Trade Journal, passim; Census of Industrial Production*.
71. *Ibid.* This calculation excludes concerns producing boot uppers only and clog manufacturers.
72. *Final Report of the Fifth Census of Production* (1935), Part I, p. 445. Also see Silverman, *op. cit.*, 201.
73. *Ibid.*

Notes to Chapter Three

1. Saorstát Éireann, *Census of Population 1936, Preliminary Report*, p. 21.
2. Appendix I.
3. Silverman, *op. cit.*, 204-5, 266.
4. *Trade and Shipping Statistics*.
5. Appendix I.
6. In fact, the figure was just over 183,000 pairs.
7. Hallidays, H 2/21.
8. NUBSO, *Monthly Reports* (February 1937), 85.
9. *Census of Industrial Production*.
10. Interview with Philip McLoughlin. Payments did not commence until the third day off work.
11. NUBSO, *Monthly Reports* (June 1936), 303-5.
12. *Ibid.* (February 1937), 84-5.
13. *Ibid.*
14. *Ibid.* (December 1937), 630.
15. *Ibid.* (January 1938), 68.
16. *Census of Industrial Production*.
17. Interview with Stephen Lowry.
18. Interview with E.J. Connolly.
19. NUBSO, *Monthly Reports* (March 1938), 124.
20. Densons was owned by the O'Neill family, who also had a controlling interest in James

Winstanley. Tylers was a subsidiary of John Tyler & Sons Ltd of Leicester. E.J. Connolly, the nephew of Matthew Connolly, also began to acquire a chain of retail shops after 1939.
21. Interview with Arthur Halliday.
22. J.M. Keynes, 'Self-Sufficiency', *Studies* (1933), 177.
23. D.S. Johnson, 'The Economic History of Ireland between the Wars', *Irish Economic and Social History* i (1974), 57. Also see G. Fitzgerald, *Planning in Ireland* (Dublin, 1968), 7.
24. K.A. Kennedy, *Productivity and Industrial Growth: The Irish Experience* (Oxford, 1971), 53-55.
25. H.C. Hillman, 'Size of Firms in the Boot and Shoe Industry', *Economic Journal* xlix (June 1939), 293.
26. NUBSO, *Monthly Reports* (February 1937), 84-5; (April 1937), 270; *Report of the Proceedings of the 1939 Union Conference*, 199-200.
27. See, for example, *Report on the Leather Footwear Industry* (1962), 68.
28. *Ibid.*
29. *Ibid.*
30. *Ibid.*
31. *Ibid.*
32. Its principal industry was the locomotive and carriage works of the Great Northern Railway.
33. *Report on the Footwear Industry* (Committee on Industrial Progress, Dublin, 1971), 19, 43.
34. Dwyer, *op. cit.*, 178-9; *Report on the Leather Industry* (1964), 7; *Leather* (September 1975), 71.
35. *Federation Journal*, 17 (1935-6), 3. From 5 October 1935 imported leather was subject to an *ad valorem* duty of 37.5 per cent (full) and 22.5 per cent (preferential).
36. *Report on the Leather Industry* (1964), 178.
37. *Ibid.*
38. *Trade and Shipping Statistics; Statistical Abstracts.*
39. This point had been made by the Irish Free State Boot Manufacturers' Federation as early as 1931, when the Tariff Commission was considering the Tanners' Federation's application for protection: SPO, Department of the Taoiseach, S.11987A; *Report on Application for a Tariff on Leather* (Tariff Commission Report No. 11, Dublin, 1931), p. 23. By October 1937, 5,691 persons were employed in footwear factories and 1,178 in tanneries: *Irish Trade Journal and Statistical Bulletin* (June 1938), 119; (September 1939), 177.
40. Fitzgerald, *op. cit.*, 7.
41. For example, see O'Mahony, *op. cit.*, 324.
42. See, for example, NUBSO, *Monthly Reports* (August 1937), 419; (March 1939), 135.
43. *Ibid.* (January 1940), 4; K.G.J.C. Knowles & M. Verry, 'Earnings in the Boot and Shoe Industry', *Bulletin of the University Institute of Statistics* (February/March 1954), 34.

44. Conditions of Employment Act; NUBSO, *Monthly Reports* (April 1936), 307; (June 1936), 301; *Report of the Proceedings of the 1939 Union Conference*, 198.
45. Knowles & Verry, *op. cit.*, 40.
46. Appendix IV; Silverman, *op. cit.*, 205-10.
47. Marshall, *op. cit.*, 745.
48. Later Munster Shoes Ltd.
49. See, for example, Hallidays, H 2/21.
50. NUBSO, *Monthly Reports* (January 1939), 14.
51. Hillman, *op. cit., passim.*
52. Silverman, *op. cit.*, 215.
53. By 1937, total heavy book production in Ireland was only 10,000 pairs per week: *Census of Industrial Production*.
54. Interview with F.J. Scott; also see NUBSO, *Monthly Reports* (July 1937), 369; (September 1937), 469.
55. NUBSO, *Monthly Reports* (October 1937), 516.
56. Woodington, *Minutes* (20 July 1936); (23 February 1937); (3 April 1939).
57. In 1940, for example, Woodington was to set up a sandal manufacturing unit, because the annual pattern of demand for sandals peaked at times when heavy book sales were lowest. This, however, did not lead to a more efficient use of existing capacity, because the equipment required was quite different. Interviews with Philip McLoughlin and Stephen Lowry.
58. See, for example, NUBSO, *Monthly Reports* (May 1939), 235.
59. Woodington, *Minutes* (2 February 1938); (28 November 1938).
60. Hallidays, *Minutes* (28 October 1936).
61. *Ibid.* (11 January 1937).
62. Hallidays, H 1/5.
63. Interview with Arthur Halliday.
64. Hallidays, H 2/25; interview with Bancroft Clark.
65. *Ibid.*
66. C. & J. Clark, *Minutes* (19 July 1937).
67. This agreement followed the lines of an agreement which Clarks was itself negotiating — unsuccessfully, as it turned out — with the Selby Shoe Co. of Portsmouth, Ohio for the use of Selby's 'Trupoise' brand.
68. Hallidays, H 2/25; C. & J. Clark, *Minutes* (19 July 1937); (9 November 1937).
69. 1.25p. per pair on children's shoes.
70. Hallidays, H 2/25.
71. *Ibid.*
72. Interview with Bancroft Clark.
73. C. & J. Clark, *Minutes* (November 1938 - March 1939).
74. Hallidays, H 2/25.

Notes to pages 70-6 203

75. By October 1938, he could report to Clarks that 'the lasting is as good as our own; and that all processes were satisfactory except for finishing, which needed more attention'. C. & J. Clark, *Minutes* (24 October 1938).
76. Hallidays, H 10/6.
77. NUBSO, *Monthly Reports* (May 1939), 237.
78. See Tables 7 and 8.
79. NUBSO, *Monthly Reports* (May 1939), 237; (June 1939), 287.
80. *Census of Industrial Production.*
81. *Federation Journal*, xix (1937-8), 196-7, 247; xx (1938-9), 155.
82. NUBSO, *Monthly Reports* (May 1938), 222ff. The Dundalk branch reported that many orders were cancelled, especially for heavy boots.
83. NUBSO, *Report of the Proceedings of the 1939 Union Conference*, 198-201.
84. The question was quietly forgotten during the Second World War.

Notes to Chapter Four

1. B.R. Mitchell, *European Historical Statistics, 1750- 1970* (1975), 495; Cullen, *op. cit.*, 180.
2. F. Forde, *The Long Watch: the History of the Irish Mercantile Marine in World War Two* (Dublin, 1981), 2.
3. Fanning, *op. cit.* 311.
4. *Ibid.*, 312. MacEntee had been Minister for Finance since 1932.
5. It was kept going after the war and was permanently established by the Irish Shipping Act 1947. *Ibid*, 350-1.
6. *Ibid.*, 344.
7. Emergency Powers (No. 83) Order, 1941; Woodingtons, *Minutes* (7 April 1943); Hallidays, *Minutes* (12 July 1944); (5 January 1945).
8. The deposit varied from £1,000 to £10,000 according to the size of the membership.
9. NUBSO, *Report of the Proceedings of the 1943 Union Conference*, 89; *Monthly Reports* (June 1941), 71; Fox, *op. cit.*, 566.
10. Hallidays, *Minutes* (10 July 1941).
11. O'Hagan, *op. cit.*, 8.
12. Hallidays, H 1/24.
13. It should be noted, however, that these figures include work in progress and stocks of finished goods.
14. Interview with F.J. Scott.
15. NUBSO, *Monthly Reports* (June 1941), 298.
16. NUBSO, *Monthly Reports* (October 1939), 484. Woodingtons, *Minutes* (31 October 1939).
17. NUBSO, *Monthly Reports* (February 1940), 56, 58; (August 1940), 339; Hallidays, *Minutes* (26 June 1940).

18. *Report of the Leather Footwear Industry* (1962), 60.
19. Emergency Powers (Control of Export) Order (No. 149), 12 June 1940; *Report on the Leather Industry (1964)*, 7-8.
20. Hallidays, Chairman's Report, 30 November 1940.
21. J.E. Harris, 'Ireland since the Leprechauns: a Report on the Irish Footwear Industry', *Creative Footwear* (December 1947), 29.
22. Hallidays, Chairman's Report, 30 November 1940.
23. Hallidays, H 1/24. Toe puffs are stiffeners inserted between the upper and the lining of the toe before lasting.
24. Hallidays, Chairman's Speech, 30 November 1940; NUBSO, *Monthly Reports* (November 1940), 470.
25. *Ibid.*
26. Export of Goods (Control) (No. 39) Order, 4 November 1940; Hallidays, H 1/24. As a result of this Order, imports of undressed sole leather from Britain fell to about 20 per cent of the 1939 level. Imports of dressed upper leather roughly halved over the same period.
27. NUBSO, *Monthly Reports* (May 1944), 91.
28. Hallidays, H 2/6.
29. In the late summer of 1941, for example, Kilkenny and Waterford were working an average of 20-24 hours per week, while J.H. Woodington was down to 34 hours per week and had closed down its sandal plant because suitable leather was unobtainable. NUBSO, *Monthly Reports* (June 1941), 258; (September, 1941), 360, 362.
30. Hallidays, H 6/19; H 16/6; NUBSO, *Monthly Reports* (September, 1940), 372; (October 1941), 395.
31. Interview with E.J. Connolly.
32. Interview with Arthur Halliday.
33. Interview with E.J. Connolly.
34. Clarks Ireland Ltd to customers (14 December 1943): Hallidays, H 2/11.
35. Hallidays, H 10/20.
36. Clarks Ireland Ltd to customers, 14 December 1943: Hallidays, H 2/11.
37. Woodingtons, *Minutes* (19 October 1943); interview with Denis O'Neill.
38. In September 1941, for example, it was reported that the Gorey Leather Co. was experimenting with locally obtained oak bark. The leather was then retanned with chrome to 'draw the hide together', but it was being produced far too quickly and the tanning agents were not fully penetrating the hides: Hallidays, H 1/24.
39. Interviews with E.J. Connolly and Stephen Lowry. Incidentally, this led to consumer resistance to this type of finish long after the war was over.
40. Hallidays, H 6/19; H 16/6.
41. Interview with Arthur Halliday.
42. Hallidays, H 6/5. Most of the problems encountered were caused by a lack of flexibility in the board.

43. Interview with Philip McLoughlin: Hallidays, H 2/16.
44. Hallidays, H 1/9.
45. Hallidays was also able to make a useful profit after the war by selling rubber solutions to C. & J. Clark. Rubber solutions were not available in Britain because of the shortage of dollars and exports from Dundalk realised £1.25 per gallon, compared with a manufacturing cost of about 25p. Interview with Arthur Halliday.
46. Interview with F.J. Scott.
47. Woodingtons, *Minutes* (19 October 1943).
48. NUBSO, *Monthly Reports* (July 1941), 298.
49. In September 1941, for example, the Gorey Leather Co. was operating at less than half its full capacity: Hallidays, H 1/24.
50. NUBSO, *Monthly Reports* (July 1941), 298.
51. The previous peak was in 1937, when industrial unrest resulting from the recession led to eight disputes involving just over 1,000 people. Most of these, however, were of fairly short duration and only 4,381 working days were lost. In 1942, there were seven strikes which involved 1,124 employees and lost 30,756 working days — a total which has never been exceeded in more recent years: *Irish Trade Journal and Statistical Bulletin.*
52. Mitchell, *op. cit.*, 745.
53. It varied slightly according to sex and age group.
54. NUBSO, *Monthly Reports* (September 1941), 360; (November 1941), 430.
55. *Ibid.* (June 1942), 158; (July 1942), 189-90; (November 1942), 271.
56. Fox, *op. cit.*, 566; C. McCarthy, *Trade Unions in Ireland, 1894-1960* (Dublin 1977), 405; *Report of the Proceedings of the 1943 Union Conference, passim.*
57. In 1945, when Paul Alexander made a plea for continuing unity at the Union Conference, he stated that maintenance of these connections had been a major factor behind the Irish branches' success in weathering the storm: Fox, *loc. cit.*
58. NUBSO, *Monthly Reports* (June 1942), 158.
59. Hallidays, H 14/18; NUBSO, *Monthly Reports* (October 1944), 202.
60. Hallidays, H 14/17.
61. Hallidays, H 1/3, H 15/16.
62. Hallidays, H 2/16; H 6/19.
63. Hallidays, *Minutes* (9 October 1942).
64. Hallidays, H 13/7.
65. Interview with Arthur Halliday.
66. Woodingtons, n.d.
67. Department of Supplies to J.H. Woodington, 12 May 1943.
68. Interview with E.J. Connolly.
69. Hallidays was obliged, however, to defer the commission and service charges due to C. & J. Clark Ltd. By 30 April 1943, the total sum due had reached £17,000 and Clarks agreed to accept ordinary shares in settlement of the debt. Apart from the fact that the transfer of money was hindered by wartime controls, C. & J. Clark was prepared to

accept shares because this was a relatively small investment which promised useful returns after the war. For instance, it was already evident that Britain would suffer from a shortage of dollars, which would hinder buying in world materials markets. Hallidays, however, could obtain dollars and hence there was the possibility that Ireland would recover more quickly from wartime conditions.

70. *Irish Trade Journal and Statistical Bulletin* (September 1942), 116.
71. Hallidays, H 15/22.
72. It was reported that 'The bottoms appears to have been cut out by a hacksaw and edges trimmed on a grindstone, and any attempt at finishing appears to have been eliminated as an obstacle to production': NUBSO, *Monthly Reports* (August 1944), 156.

Notes to Chapter 5

1. See, for example, P. Lynch, 'The Irish Economy since the War, 1946-51', in K.B. Nowlan & T.D Williams (eds.), *Ireland in the War Years and After* (Dublin, 1969), 191-5.
2. O'Hagan, *op. cit.* 9-10.
3. *Irish Trade Journal and Statistical Bulletin* (September 1946), 103-4.
4. O'Hagan, *op. cit.*, 9-10.
5. *Ibid.*
6. K.A. Kennedy, 'Growth of Labour Productivity in Irish Manufacturing Industry, 1953-67', *Journal of the Statistical and Social Inquiry Society of Ireland* xxii (1968-9), 114.
7. Fanning, *op. cit.* 465.
8. O'Hagan (ed.), *op. cit.*, 13-14. Sean Lemass, however, seems to have been more aware of the nature of Ireland's problems and devoted more time to their solution than some of his government colleagues. See below, chapter 6.
9. Fanning, *op. cit.*, 496.
10. Underdeveloped Areas Act, 1952. In the specified areas, new and existing concerns were eligible for grants equivalent to the full cost of plant and half the cost of equipment and training for approved projects.
11. The agreement permitted free entry into the UK for a wide range of Irish goods in return for preferential treatment of British exports. See O'Mahony, *op. cit.*, 47.
12. O'Hagan, *op. cit.*, 13.
13. Irish balance of payments problems were exacerbated by the devaluation of the pound in 1949 because imports of raw materials from America and Europe were growing rapidly in the late 1940s. In the footwear industry, for example, one can cite the growing use of American and French leather. However, this was mitigated by the fact that Britain was still by far the largest supplier of raw materials and finished goods; the cost of imports from Britain did not alter because the Irish pound was tied to the fortunes of sterling.
14. Fanning, *op. cit.*, 464ff.
15. Woodingtons, *Minutes* (31 July 1945); (4 October 1945); (15 October 1945).

16. Hallidays, *Minutes* (20 June 1945).
17. Hallidays, H 6/19.
18. Hallidays, H 6/11.
19. J.E. Harris, 'Since the Leprechauns; A Report on the Irish Footwear Industry', *Creative Footwear* (December 1947), 41.
20. See, for example, Hallidays, *Minutes* (31 July 1946); (22 August 1946); (10 October 1946).
21. *Irish Trade Journal and Statistical Bulletin* (December 1947), 184.
22. This figure was not reached again until 1964: *Trade and Shipping Statistics*.
23. NUBSO, *Monthly Reports* (December 1948), 368.
24. *Ibid.* (March 1949), 101.
25. *Ibid.* (June 1949), 202.
26. Hallidays, H 6/19.
27. NUBSO, *Report of the Proceedings of the 1949 Union Conference*, 226.
28. *Ibid.*
29. Woodingtons, chairman's speech (31 December 1950).
30. Woodingtons, *Minutes* (12 May 1950); chairman's speech (31 December 1951). This increase in working capital, however, was also partly due to the company's entry into the ladies' fashion market. See below.
31. Hallidays, H 15/19; H 19/1.
32. Dwyer, *op. cit.*, p. 179. *Report on the Leather Industry* (1964), 9.
33. *Ibid.*
34. *Irish Trade Journal and Statistical Bulletin* (September 1946), 103-4. NUBSO, *Monthly Reports* (November 1946), 317-8.
35. NUBSO, *Report of the Proceedings of the 1949 Union Conference*, 225.
36. NUBSO, *Report of the Proceedings of the 1951 Union Conference*, 337-9. Some of the Dundalk shop stewards, for example, had proposed an *en bloc* transfer to the Irish Transport and General Workers' Union. Although some discussions took place, the proposal was not followed up, largely because of widespread hostility to the ambitions of the ITGWU: McCarthy, *op. cit.*, 405-6.
37. NUBSO, *Report of the Proceedings of the 1951 Union Conference*, 342.
38. *Ibid.*, 344. This represented a 63 per cent poll which was quite high in view of the usual level of NUBSO voting in the United Kingdom.
39. McCarthy, *op. cit.*, 405-6; Fox, *op. cit.*, 622.
40. NUBSO, *Report of the Proceedings of the 1951 Union Conference*, 342.
41. *Ibid.*, 130.
42. Hallidays, H 19/1.
43. *Ibid.*
44. Winstanleys, company accounts.
45. However, some manufacturers did express the fear that falling real incomes would

encourage the public to buy cheap non-leather shoes in preference to home-produced leather footwear and, of course, the importation of rubber boots continued to depress demand for heavy boots.

46. An American team of experts which was brought over to Ireland in 1952 found that all the factories which they visited were working below full capacity and estimated that the industry's total capacity was about 8,000 pairs per week in excess of home market requirements: *American Team Report on Leather Shoes* (Coras Trachtála, Dublin, 1952).

47. Between 1951 and 1956, the average ex-factory price of home-produced leather footwear fell from 135p to 130p per pair and then recovered to 136p. The average c.i.f. price of imported leather shoes, however, rose fairly steadily from 152p to 231p. See Appendix II.

48. In 1957, multiple retailers owned 43 per cent of Britain's 13,800 footwear shops and accounted for 64 per cent of their total turnover of £170 million: *Report on the Leather Footwear Industry* (1962), p. 38.

49. These links with manufacturing interests were usually indirect and, in most cases, shop managers were expected to maximise their profits even if this meant buying a competitor's products. Moreover, it was unusual for manufacturers to offer footwear on preferential terms to retailers with whom they were linked by common ownership. But such a connection was not entirely without significance to the growing success of these multiples. In particular, it potentially offered access to the kind of capital resources which most retailers lacked.

50. Silverman, *op. cit.*, 222; also see Hillman, *op. cit.*, 290-1.

51. Hallidays, H 1/8; H 11/1; H 16/15.

52. Irish manufacturers could gain access to new technology via their agreements with BUSMC. BUSMC had acquired much of the responsibility for research and development work in the British footwear industry, and in addition to supplying up-to-date machinery it now made a wide range of technical services available to its lessees. Some Irish manufacturers, as we have seen, also obtained technical support from associated companies in the United Kingdom.

53. *Report on the Leather Industry* (1964), 144.

54. The time spent in the mould.

55. Initially, carbon black was used but it fell out of favour because of its propensity for marking floors. More recent (and more expensive) alternatives include aluminium silicate and calcium silicate.

56. Solid rubber was used for direct vulcanisation; micro-cellular soles were usually pre-moulded and stuck on, because the expansion process was too unreliable.

57. *Trade and Shipping Statistics.*

58. SATRA Research Report No. 16, quoted in *A Review of Productivity in the Footwear Industry* (British Productivity Council, 1953), 13. Also see SATRA *Monthly Report* (October 1950).

59. *Report on the Leather Footwear Industry* (1962), 96. In comparison, more than half the British operatives were on piece work by 1953. K.G.J.C. Knowles and M. Verry, 'Earnings in the Boot and Shoe Industry', *Bulletin of the Oxford University Institute of Statistics* xvi (February/March 1954), 33.

60. Hallidays, *Minutes* (18 January 1944); (7 March 1944).

Notes to pages 109-14

61. This is interesting as another indication of the compartmentalisation of the footwear industry; ability and experience in one type of footwear counted for little in other sectors of the market.
62. Harris, *op. cit.*, 41.
63. Hallidays, H 1/13.
64. *Ibid.*, H 29/8; H 36/21.
65. *Ibid.*, H 15/18.
66. *Ibid.*, H 13/2.
67. Hallidays, *Minutes* (7 March 1946); (4 April 1946); (7 November 1946); (20 February 1947); (28 January 1948); (24 March 1948).
68. *Ibid.*, (7 March 1946); (23 December 1947).
69. *Ibid.*, (10 October 1946); (22 April 1948). Inevitably, this increase had a noticeable effect on return on capital. Pre-tax net profit as a percentage of total assets fell from about 9 per cent in 1944-5 to 6.3 per cent in 1948 and 5.3 per cent in 1949.
70. Munster Shoes Ltd, *Memo in support of Adaptation Grant to cover expenditure on plant and machinery* (3 June 1964).
71. Interview with F.J. Scott.
72. This is somewhat analogous to the situation in the tobacco industry; see B.W.E. Alford, *W.D. & H.O. Wills and the Development of the UK Tobacco Industry* (1973), 429.
73. Appendix II.
74. These remarks refers to all-rubber footwear; there was, however, a growing use of rubber and rubber-based soles in the 1950s. This development will be discussed later.
75. It would have been possible to produce rubber boots using the calendered process, which was not patented. (Calendered rubber is produced by rolling the material to the required thickness in a device like an old-fashioned mangle. The calendered rubber is then laid over fabric on a metal last and vulcanised in a steam chamber.) Calendered rubber boots, however, were less flexible and less comfortable than those produced by the latex-dipped process. They were also considerably more expensive to make.
76. Hallidays, H 16/3.
77. The Kells factory was originally owned by Toone & Sons Ltd, which was an offshoot of a Leicester company. Its output consisted mainly of children's shoes and it was not very successful. It was later taken over by Hilliards as a potential cutting/closing unit and was acquired by F.J. Scott and Benjamin Rawson in 1953/4 when the Norvic agreement was being negotiated.
78. Interview with F.J. Scott.
79. Woodingtons, *Minutes* (7 January 1952). Since the company was now owned by Irish nationals, it was no longer subject to the Control of Manufactures Acts. Accordingly, its New Manufactures Licence, which had imposed restrictions on the type and quantity of footwear which could be produced, was revoked by the Department of Industry and Commerce in November 1951.
80. *Ibid.* (12 May 1950).
81. P. McLoughlin to James F. Bostock, 6 September 1955.
82. Interview with Philip McLoughlin.

83. Edwards & Holmes was initially opposed to any agreement between Woodingtons and another English firm which might prejudice its Irish interests and might enable a British competitor to benefit from their technical and design expertise. Moreover, the company had put a lot of work into the improvements of Woodingtons' ladies shoes over the past three or four years and considered that Lotus would be getting something for nothing. Eventually, it was agreed that Woodingtons would pay Edward & Holmes half a per cent royalty per pair sold under the Lotus brand for the first three years of the agreement, and that the revenue would be used to advertise Holmes of Norwich footwear in the Irish Republic. In consideration of this, Lotus agreed to remit one quarter per cent of the service charge due. cf. *Report of interview with Directors of Messrs. Edwards and Holmes of Norwich re their attitude to Lotus Ageement* (October 1955); also see Woodingtons, *Minutes* (17 October 1955).
84. Woodingtons, *Minutes* (18 December 1950 - 10 July 1953).
85. *Ibid.* (13 December 1954).
86. Hallidays, H 6/13.
87. Hallidays, *Minutes* (16 September 1949); (25 October 1949).
88. *Ibid.* (12 September 1950).
89. Hallidays, H 14/8.
90. *Ibid.*, H 11/1.
91. *Ibid.*, H 16/2.
92. *Ibid.*, H 15/19; H 16/3.
93. *Ibid.*, H 16/2. Connolly Shoes was eventually liquidated in November 1953 and its assets transferred to Hallidays: Hallidays, *Minutes* (13 January 1954).
94. Hallidays, H 2/20.
95. *Ibid.*
96. *Ibid.*
97. *Ibid.*, H 11/1.
98. Sales to wholesalers averaged around 40 per cent of turnover in 1949-51.
99. In fact there was a general move away from wholesale business, and the wholesalers' share of the market declined slowly but steadily, from 35.4 per cent in 1951 to about 30 per cent in 1960: *Census of Distribution, 1951; Report of the Leather Footwear Industry* (1962), 165.
100. Clarks Ireland Ltd to customers (24 May 1949); Hallidays, H 15/18.
101. *Ibid.*
102. *Ibid.*
103. *Ibid.*, H 1/11.
104. *Ibid.*, H 19/1.
105. *Ibid.*, H 11/4.
106. *Ibid.*, H 2/16; H 11/4.
107. *Ibid.*
108. *Ibid.*, H 15/18.

109. *Ibid.*, H 10/9; H 12/4.
110. *Ibid.*
111. See, for example, Hallidays, H 15/8.
112. *Ibid.*, H 10/21; H 12/4.
113. *Ibid.*, H 11/1.
114. Winstanleys' welted production, however, was a relatively small operation at this date; according to Hallidays' information, it averaged around 300 pairs per week. *Ibid.*
115. See, for example, Woodingtons, *Minutes* (8 July 1951).
116. *Report of the Leather Footwear Industry* (1962), 177-80.
117. *Ibid.*, 168-70.
118. CTT Report, 10 January 1953; Hallidays, H 3/4.
119. See O'Mahony, *op. cit.*, 12.
120. Hallidays, H 14/1.
121. These were the Arcola Shoe Works Ltd, Meteor Shoes Ltd, Selward Shoes Ltd and Whispies Shoes Ltd. They were each run by a brother of Norman H. Wachman, the managing director of Edenderry.
122. Edenderry became a public company in May 1965 with an issued capital of £100,000.
123. Hallidays, H 17/1.

Notes to Chapter Six

1. Kennedy, *Productivity and Industrial Growth, op. cit.*, 73; Kennedy, 'Growth of Labour Productivity in Irish Manufacturing', *art. cit.*, 114. Meenan, *op. cit.*, 58.
2. Industrial Grants Act, 1956.
3. *Report on the Leather Footwear Industry* (1962), 204-5.
4. O'Hagan, *op. cit.*, 103. Cullen, *op. cit.*, 183.
5. Cullen, *loc. cit.*
6. See Mitchell, *op. cit.* (1978 edition), 182.
7. Pr. 4796.
8. O'Mahony, *op. cit.*, 183.
9. O'Hagan, *op. cit.*, 103-4.
10. O'Mahony, *loc. cit.*
11. Meenan, *op. cit.*, 73.
12. *Ibid.*, 144.
13. *Ibid.* The failure of the EEC negotiations, however, led to further policy adjustments. See Chapter 7.
14. Appendix V.
15. See below.
16. *Report on the Leather Footwear Industry* (1962), 170.

17. *CTT Market Reports* (February and March 1956).
18. *Statistical Abstracts*, 1956-61.
19. Padmore & Barnes, *Minutes* (19 April 1956).
20. *Ibid.* (12 September 1956).
21. Hallidays, H 4/3.
22. *Ibid.*, H 16/5.
23. For the year ending 30 November 1957, rejects and returns had represented 15.5 per cent of total men's and youths' production, and this was far too high; a figure of 2.5 per cent was considered acceptable.
24. Hallidays, H 16/4.
25. The usual figure for Irish companies was around 45 per cent, and some distributed up to 75 per cent of net profits.
26. Hallidays, *Minutes* (30 December 1955); (6 March 1956). Also see H 1/8, H 17/5.
27. Hallidays, H 17/5.
28. *Clarks Courier Irish Special* (14 January 1966), 5.
29. Hallidays, H 17/5.
30. Munster Shoes Ltd, *Memo in Support of Adaptation Grant* (3 July 1964).
31. Woodingtons, *Minutes* (3 February 1960).
32. *Ibid.* (3 February 1960); (20 May 1960).
33. N.H. Wachman to Guinness & Mahon, 14 May 1965.
34. *Ibid.*
35. See *The Times* (23 February 1966), 3.
36. *Ibid.* Stekel and Kraft were fined £60,000 each, and Burden £8,000.
37. Padmore & Barnes, *Minutes* (17 May 1960).
38. Padmore & Barnes, *Circular to Customers*, 29 August 1960.
39. Padmore & Barnes, *Minutes* (18 August 1960).
40. *Ibid.* Also see *Kilkenny Journal* (3 September 1960).
41. Hallidays, H 15/21.
42. *Report on the Leather Footwear Industry* (1962), 165. Mail order business still made up an insignificant proportion of sales in Ireland.
43. Hallidays, F 26/4.
44. *Ibid.*, H 3/4.
45. It must be remembered that many Irish manufacturers had built up their business under brand names licensed from British manufacturers and these could not be used outside the home market.
46. Hallidays, H 2/17.
47. Hallidays, H 17/5.
48. NUBSO, *Report of the Proceedings of the 1963 Union Conference*, 127.

Notes to Chapter Seven

1. See, for example, E.J.L. Ruan, 'The Need for Structural Change in Irish Industry', *Irish Banking Review* (1961), 9-15.
2. Pr. 7239; Pr. 7670.
3. Fanning, *op. cit.*, 600.
4. *Second Programme for Economic Expansion*, Part I, ii, 34.
5. *Ibid.*, Part II, 142.
6. *Ibid.*, Part II, 156.
7. *Ibid.*, 150.
8. AFT was the body responsible for the underdeveloped areas under the Act of 1952.
9. *Second Programme for Economic Expansion*, Part II, 149; AFT, *Annual Report* (1965), 2-3.
10. Such loans could equal up to 75 per cent of the outlay on fixed assets; interest could be waived and capital repayments deferred for five years. *Ibid.*
11. Pr. 6727 and Pr. 7494.
12. K.A. Kennedy and B.R. Dowling, *Economic Growth in Ireland: The Experience since 1947* (Dublin, 1973), 24.
13. For example, Britain experienced a series of balance of payments crises in the 1960s. In October 1964, an attempt was made to curb imports into Britain by subjecting them to a 15 per cent levy. Although reduced to 10 per cent in April 1965, this was a major blow to Irish exporters who depended heavily upon the British market, and the Irish government tried to offset its effects by offering grants to cover half of the levy. The British government was again obliged to regulate imports in 1968. *Financial Times* (6 November 1964); AFT, *Annual Report* (1965), 2-3. The effects of British import restrictions on the Irish footwear industry are discussed below.
14. See, for example, S. Pollard, *The Wasting of the British Economy* (1982), *passim.*
15. *Report on the Leather Footwear Industry* (1962), 7.
16. Footwear Adaptation Association, *Second Annual Report* (1964), 1-14.
17. *Report on the Leather Footwear Industry* (1962), 8. The Committee, however, did expect some redundancies as a result of technological advances.
18. *Census of Population.*
19. Appendix V.
20. Between 1962 and 1970, the number of television licences rose fairly steadily from 127,448 to 438,489. *Statistical Abstracts.*
21. In 1964, purchases by Dublin retailers represented about 44 per cent of Hallidays' home sales. Hallidays, H 9/4.
22. This, incidentally, prevented footwear manufacturers from offering substantial quantity discounts to attract important customers.
23. Hallidays, *loc. cit.*
24. Appendix I.
25. This downturn led C.S. Leicester to postulate the existence of a four year cycle in the

footwear market, with periods of recession centred upon 1954 (actually reaching a low point at the beginning of 1955), 1958, and 1962. Leicester's analysis showed that, although there was a sizeable increase in the size of the footwear market as a whole, the quantity of footwear purchased by retailers moved in a markedly cyclical manner. The explanation given was that retailers, either through management weaknesses or a lack of capital, were unable to forecast demand trends accurately and maintain stocks at a suitable level. Consequently, the flow of orders to the manufacturer tended to be bunched around periods of peak demand. This is not the whole story, for the 1962 downturn was also due to bad weather, which depressed demand for the lighter spring/summer lines, and to the doubling of purchase tax, but it seems clear that in Britain, as in Ireland, retailers' budgeting and purchasing methods were capable of starting up cyclical fluctuations. Olsen has pointed out similar tendencies in the American footwear market. C.S. Leicester, 'The Causes of the Shoe Trade Cycle', *British Boot and Shoe Institution Journal* 11 (1963), 7; I. Olsen, 'How Cycles Work in Shoe Production', *Boot and Shoe Recorder* (November 1961).

26. Footwear Adaptation Association, *Second Annual Report* (1964), 14.
27. Hallidays, H 18/5; *Sunday Telegraph* (1 December 1968); *Irish Times* (26 November 1968).
28. *Trade and Shipping Statistics*.
29. *Ibid.*
30. *Ibid.*
31. *Report on the Footwear Industry* (1971), 36, 39; AFT, *Annual Reports, passim.*
32. *Clarks Courier* (14 January 1966), 5.
33. In 1947: *ibid.*, 6.
34. Hallidays, H 5/1; *Minutes* (21 August 1961).
35. *Ibid.*
36. Hallidays, *Minutes* (15 October 1963).
37. Hallidays, H, 6/10.
38. *Ibid.*, H 17/5.
39. *Ibid.*, H 18/1.
40. On Brittons, see J. Press, 'G.B. Britton and Footwear Manufacturing in Bristol and Kingswood', in C.E. Harvey and J. Press (eds.), *Studies in the Business History of Bristol* (Bristol, 1988).
41. Hallidays, H 9/4; H 11/2.
42. *Ibid.*, H 13/3.
43. *Ibid.*, H 5/1.
44. *Ibid.*, H 18/3; H 20/8.
45. *Ibid.*, H 9/4.
46. *Ibid.*, F 26/6.
47. *Irish Times* (3 November 1969). In this context, see P. Mathias, 'Conflicts of Function in the Rise of Big Business; The British Experience' in H.F. Williamson (ed.), *The Evolution of International Management* (Newark, Delaware, 1975). It is perhaps worth

noting that this was not a particularly successful investment and Densons was eventually sold back to the O'Neills in 1977.
48. Respectively the Lee Boot Manufacturing Co. and the Edenderry Shoe Co.
49. *Shoe and Leather News* (13 March 1969), 9.
50. *Ibid.*, also (28 March 1968), 126.
51. In 1965 and 1968 respectively.
52. John Tyler, *Annual Reports* (1966, 1967).
53. Although this Association was based in Britain, the Footwear Adaptation Association had arranged block membership for the Irish companies in 1964. Footwear Adaptation Association, *Second Annual Report* (1964), 9.
54. Hallidays, H 17/14.
55. *Shoe and Leather News* (26 July 1967), 3.
56. *Ibid.*, (8 February 1968), 9.
57. Hallidays, H 9/4.
58. Hallidays, H 20/8.
59. In the moccasin construction, the upper material passes under the foot and is stitched on top. As no insole is used, moccasins are very comfortable.
60. Clarks Ireland, *Minutes* (11 August 1967).
61. Whilst Padmore & Barnes owned the 'Moccasin' brand name, it had never utilised the moccasin construction.
62. *Shoe and Leather News* (17 April 1969), 29-32.
63. *Ibid.*, also see Hallidays, F 26/6.
64. Hallidays, F 26/6.
65. *Ibid.*; *Trade and Shipping Statistics*.
66. Stedfast was producing in the 59s. 11d. to 69s. 11d. retail price bracket (£2.99 to £3.49), whilst Fane concentrated upon the 49s. 11d. to 59s. 11d. (£2.49 to £2.99) bracket. Hallidays, F 26/6.
67. *Ibid.*
68. *Ibid.*, H 9/4.
69. *Report on the Footwear Industry* (1971), 47-8.
70. *Ibid.*, 241.
71. *Ibid.*, 16.
72. *Ibid.*, 105.
73. B. Lehane, *C. & J. Clark Ltd, 1825-1975* (Street, 1975), 38.
74. It had also been found that slip-lasted footwear was virtually impossible to repair.
75. *Shoe and Leather News* (30 November 1961), *passim.*; *Shoe Materials Progress* (August 1972), 246-7; *Report on the Footwear Industry* (1971), 241.
76. *Report on the Leather Footwear Industry* (1962), 16.
77. Appendix VI.

78. *Footwear on the Footwear Industry* (1971), 30-1.
79. *Ibid.*, 30-1, 138.
80. *Irish Statistical Bulletin*.
81. By size of capital employed.
82. *Irish Times* (3 November 1969).
83. Receiver's Report, 22 November 1966; *Shoe and Leather News* (9 June 1966), 54; (23 June 1966), 52.
84. *Shoe and Leather News* (28 September 1967), 150; (26 October 1967), 88; John Rawson, *Annual Report* (1966).
85. The surviving buildings were later acquired by Blackthorn Shoes Ltd. The closure of Rawsons' factory led to high unemployment in Dundalk. The government set up a special fund to contribute towards redundancy payments and declared County Louth an underdeveloped area for a year to attract new industries. The most significant result was the decision of the American Weyenberg Shoe Company to establish a factory in Dundalk, and the company eventually received IDA grant approval for a total of £1.38m. *Irish Times* (22 October 1966); *Shoe and Leather News* (4 September 1969), 3.
86. Footwear Adaptation Association, *Third Annual Report* (1965), 20; *Report on the Footwear Industry* (1971), 36.
87. *Report on the Footwear Industry* (1971), 133-4. In the late 1960s and early 1970s, wages in Ireland were tending to increase faster than in Britain. Average earnings, however, were still lower in Ireland.
88. *Ibid.*, 69. Duties eventually disappeared by 1978.
89. By this date it is more accurate to refer to this sector as 'footwear with leather uppers'.
90. See Appendix II. The average price of imported leather footwear had previously been considerably higher than that of home-produced leather footwear. By 1970-1, this position had been reversed.
91. Prl. 2153.

Notes to Chapter 8

1. J.W. O'Hagan and K.P. McStay, *The Evolution of Manufacturing Industry in Ireland* (1981), 35.
2. D. McAleese, 'The Foreign Sector', in N.J. Gibson and J.E. Spencer (eds.), *Economic Activity in Ireland: A Study of Two Open Economies* (1977), 143.
3. J.W. O'Hagan and H. Neary, 'EEC Entry and Ireland's Balance of Payments', *Central Bank Quarterly Review* (Autumn 1972), 117-8.
4. *Business and Finance* (26 June 1975), 213; *Shoe and Leather News* (18 April 1974), 29; (6 March 1975), 41; (5 June 1975), 29; (26 June 1975), 26.
5. *Shoe and Leather News* (15 May 1975), 30; (4 September 1975), 37; (29 April 1976), 33; *Irish Press* (11 June 1976); (14 July 1976).
6. *Irish Times* (7 January 1971), 12; *Footwear Weekly* (20 January 1971), 2; *Shoe and Leather News* (5 June 1975), 29.

Notes to pages 170-5

7. Hallidays, *Minutes* (12 November 1971); *Financial Times* (19 November 1971).
8. *Footwear Industry* (6 February 1975), 5.
9. *Irish Times* (6 March 1985).
10. *Irish Independent* (21 October 1976); *Business and Finance* (10 March 1983), 20-1.
11. *Footwear News* (11 November 1980), 24-5.
12. OECD, *Economic Surveys: Ireland* (1981), 6; (1982), 7.
13. *Financial Times* (27 March 1981), 2. On the factors which led Ireland to join the EMS, see D. McCormack, 'Policy Making in a Small Open Economy', *Central Bank Quarterly Review* (Winter 1979), 107-11.
14. OECD, *Economic Surveys: Ireland* (1985), 38-9.
15. C. & J. Clark Ltd, *Report on the Irish Footwear Market* (1984), 16.
16. *Ibid.*, p. 21; O'Hagan & McStay, *op. cit.*, 42.
17. Newman Books Ltd, *Retail Directory* (1984).
18. *Leather* (April 1986), 33; *Irish Times* (20 July 1985).
19. *Irish Times* (23 July 1985).
20. C. & J. Clark Ltd, *Report on the Irish Footwear Market* (1984), 18; *Irish Times* (14 October 1986); *Shoe and Leather News* (7 February 1985), 4; (14 May 1987), 3.
21. *Shoe and Leather News* (7 July 1983), 30; (14 February 1985), 21; (6 November 1986), 34.
22. *Irish Times* (5 March 1981); (3 August 1985).
23. *Shoe and Leather News* (29 May 1986), 3; *Leather* (April 1986), 33.
24. *Shoe and Leather News* (15 October 1981), 46; *Business and Finance* (10 March 1983), 20-1.
25. *Shoe and Leather News* (14 February 1985), 21; *Irish Times* (6 March 1985).
26. See, for example, National Agricultural and Industrial Development Association, *Council Minutes* (25 September 1933); (22 March 1937) (National Library of Ireland, Mss. 16244, 16245).
27. For a summary of the government position, see State Paper Office, Department of the Taoiseach, S.11987.
28. *Report on the Leather Footwear Industry* (1962), *passim*.

BIBLIOGRAPHY

a. *government records*

Census of Population (1926-).
Census of Industrial Production (1926-).
Census of Distribution (1933-).
Córas Trachtála (Exports Promotion Board), *Annual Reports* (1952-).
Industrial Development Authority, *Annual Reports* (1949-).
An Chuirt Oibrachais (Labour Court), *Annual Reports* (1946-).
Irish Trade Journal (1925-40) (becomes the *Irish Trade Journal and Statistical Bulletin* (1940-63) and the *Irish Statistical Bulletin* (1963-)).
Statistical Abstracts (1931-).
Trade and Shipping Statistics (1930-).
Final Report of the Fiscal Inquiry Committee (1923).
Saorstat Éireann Official Handbook (1932).
Industrial Directories (1935/40/55).
Programme for Economic Expansion (1958).
Committee on Industrial Organization, *Report on the Leather Footwear Industry* (1962).
Second Programme for Economic Expansion (1963/4).
Committee on Industrial Organization, *Report on the Leather Industry* (1964).
Survey of Grant-Aided Industry (1967).
Committee on Industrial Progress, *Report on the Footwear Industry* (1971).

b. *associations and institutions*

National Union of Boot and Shoe Operatives (NUBSO), *Monthly Reports*.
NUBSO, *Union Conference Reports*.

c. *newspapers and journals*

British Boot and Shoe Institution Journal.
Footwear.
Footwear Manufacturers' Journal.
Footwear Organiser.
Footwear Weekly.
Footwear World.
Journal of the Incorporated Federated Associations of Boot and Shoe Manufacturers of Great Britain and Ireland (the *Federation Journal*).
Leather.

Leather and Footwear Journal.
Shoe and Leather News.

d. books and articles
(all books published in Dublin unless otherwise stated)

J.C. Beckett, *The Making of Modern Ireland, 1603-1923* (London, 1966).
D.G. Joyce, 'From War to Neutrality: Anglo-Irish Relations, 1921-50', *British Journal of International Studies* 5 (1978).
H. Bradley, *The Technical Growth of the Footwear Industry* (London, 1930).
J.A. Bristow and A.A. Tait (eds.), *Ireland: Some Problems of a Developing Economy* (1972).
British Productivity Council, *A Review of Productivity in the Footwear Industry* (London, 1953).
J.F. Burke, *Outlines of the Industrial History of Ireland* (1928).
J.T. Carroll, *Ireland in the War Years, 1939-45* (Newton Abbot, 1975).
R.A. Church, 'Labour Supply and Innovation, 1800-60: The Boot and Shoe Industry', *Business History* xii (1970).
R.A. Church, 'The Effect of the American Export Invasion on the British Boot and Shoe Industry', *Journal of Economic History* xviii (1968).
L.M. Cullen, *An Economic History of Ireland since 1660* (London, 1972).
L.M. Cullen (ed.), *The Formation of the Irish Economy* (Cork, 1969).
M. Daly, 'An Irish Ireland for Business? The Control of Manufactures Acts, 1932 and 1934', *Irish Historical Studies* xxiv (1984).
T.K. Daniel, 'Griffith on his Noble Head: The Determinants of Cumann na nGaedhael Economic Policy, 1922-32', *Irish Economic and Social History* iii (1976).
B. Dowling and J. Durkan (eds.), *Irish Economic Policy: A Review of Major Issues* (1978).
D.J. Dwyer, 'The Leather Industries of the Irish Republic, 1922-55', *Irish Geography* iv (1961).
R. Fanning, *The Irish Department of Finance, 1922-58* (1978).
N.I.J. Farley, 'Capital Formation, Technical Change and Labour Productivity Improvement: An Analysis of a Cross-Section of Irish Manufacturing Industries, 1953-67', *Economic and Social Review* iii (1971).
B. Farrell, *Sean Lemass* (1981).
G. Fitzgerald, *Planning in Ireland* (1968).
F. Forde, *The Long Watch: The History of the Irish Mercantile Marine in World War Two* (1981).
A. Fox, *History of the National Union of Boot and Shoe Operatives, 1874-1957* (Oxford, 1958).
R.C. Geary, 'Irish Economic Development since the Treaty', *Studies* xl (1951).
W.C. Griffin, 'The Northampton Boot and Shoe Industry and its Significance for Social Change in the Borough from 1800 to 1914', (M.A. thesis, University of Wales (Cardiff) 1968-69).
P. Head, 'Boots and Shoes', in D.H. Aldcroft (ed.), *The Development of British Industry and Foreign Competition, 1870-1914* (London, 1968).
H.C. Hillman, 'Size of Firms in the Boot and Shoe Industry', *Economic Journal* xlix (1939).
V.P. Hogan, *The Neutrality of Ireland in World War Two* (Michigan, 1953).
K. Hudson, *Towards Precision Shoemaking: C. & J. Clark Ltd and the Development of the British Shoe Industry* (Newton Abbot, 1968).
J.B. Jeffreys, *Retail Trading in Britain, 1850-1950* (Cambridge, 1954).

Bibliography

D.S. Johnson, 'The Economic History of Ireland between the Wars', *Irish Economic and Social History* i (1974).
K.A. Kennedy, *Productivity and Industrial Growth: The Irish Experience* (Oxford, 1971).
K.A. Kennedy, 'Growth of Labour Productivity in Irish Manufacturing Industry, 1953-67', *Journal of the Statistical and Social Inquiry Society of Ireland* xxii (1968-9).
K.A. Kennedy and B.R. Dowling, 'Productivity, Earnings and the Composition of Labour: Irish Manufacturing Industries, 1953-66', *Economic and Social Review* i (1970).
K.A. Kennedy and B.R. Dowling, *Economic Growth in Ireland: The Experience since 1947* (1975).
M.J. Killeen, *Industrial Development and Full Employment* (1976).
K.G.J.C. Knowles and M. Verry, 'Earnings in the Boot and Shoe Industry', *Bulletin of the Oxford University Institute of Statistics* (1954).
J. Lee (ed.), *Ireland, 1945-1970* (1979).
B. Lehane, *C. & J. Clark, 1825-1975* (Street, 1975).
T.P. Linehan, 'The Structure of Irish Industry', *Journal of the Statistical and Social Inquiry of Ireland* xx (1961-2).
F. Long, 'Foreign Capital and Development Strategy in Irish Industrialisation, 1958-70', *American Journal of Economics and Sociology* 39 (1980).
The Earl of Longford and T.P. O'Neill, *Eamon de Valera* (1970).
F.S.L. Lyons, *Ireland since the Famine* (London, 1970).
D. McAleese, *A Profile of Grant-Aided Industry* (1977).
C. McCarthy, *The Decade of Upheaval: Irish Trade Unions in the Nineteen-Sixties* (1973).
C. McCarthy, 'From Division to Dissention: Irish Trade Unions in the 1930s', *Economic and Social Review* v (1973-4).
C. McCarthy, *Trade Unions in Ireland, 1894-1960* (1977).
J. McGilvray, *Irish Economic Statistics* (1966).
F. McManus (ed.), *The Years of the Great Test* (Cork, 1967).
J. Meenan, *The Irish Economy since 1922* (Liverpool, 1970).
B.R. Mitchell, *European Historical Statistics* (Cambridge, 1975).
R.J.P. Mortished, 'The Industrial Relations Act', *Journal of the Statistical and Social Inquiry Society of Ireland* v (1946-7).
P.R. Mounfield, 'The Location of Footwear Manufacture in England and Wales' (Ph.D. thesis, University of Nottingham, 1962-63).
E.T. Nevin, *The Irish Economy and the EEC* (1962).
K.B. Nowlan and T.D. Williams (eds.), *Ireland in the War Years and After* (1969).
G. O'Brien, 'The Economic Progress of Ireland', *Studies* 51 (1962).
G. O'Brien, 'The Impact of the War on the Irish Economy', *Studies* 35 (1946).
P. O'Farrell, *England and Ireland since 1800* (Oxford, 1975).
J.W. O'Hagan (ed.), *The Economy of Ireland: Policy and Performance* (1975).
J.W. O'Hagan and K.P. McStay, *The Evolution of Manufacturing Industry in Ireland* (1981).
C.H. Oldham, 'The Economics of Industrial Revival in Ireland', *Journal of the Statistical and Social Inquiry Society of Ireland* xii (1909).
D. O'Mahony, *The Irish Economy: An Introductory Description* (Cork, 1964).
E. O'Malley, 'The Decline of Irish Industry in the Nineteenth Century', *Economic and Social Review* xiii (1981).
P. O'Malley, *Irish Industry: Structure and Performance* (1971).
B. Peterson, *The Turn of the Tide* (1962).
J. Press, 'G.B. Britton and Footwear Manufacturing in Bristol and Kingswood, 1870-1973', in C.E. Harvey and J. Press (eds.), *Studies in the Business History of Bristol* (Bristol, 1988).

J. Press, 'Protectionism and the Irish Footwear Industry, 1932-39', *Irish Economic and Social History* xiii (1986).

E.J. Riordan, *Modern Irish Trade and Industry* (1920).

G. Rimmer, 'The Leeds Boot and Shoe Industry in the Nineteenth Century', *British Boot and Shoe Institution Journal* xii (1965).

W.J.L. Ryan, 'Measurement of Tariff Levels for Ireland for 1931, 1936, 1938', *Journal of the Statistical and Social Inquiry Society of Ireland* xviii (1958-9).

B. Share, *The Emergency: Neutral Ireland, 1939-45* (1978).

G.F. Stanlake, 'The Structure of the British Boot and Shoe Industry' (M.A. thesis, University of Leicester, 1961-62).

J.C. Steward, 'Foreign Direct Investment and the Emergence of a Dual Economy', *Economic and Social Review* vii (1976).

B. Sutton, 'The Marketing of Ready-Made Footwear in the Nineteenth Century', *Business History* vi (1964).

B. Sutton, 'Shoemakers of Somerset: A History of C. & J. Clark, 1833-1903' (M.A. thesis, University of Nottingham, 1959).

Tempest's Centenary Annual, 1859-1959 (Dundalk, 1959).

J.H. Thornton, *A Glossary of Shoe Terms* (London, 1973).

J.H. Thornton, *A Textbook of Footwear Manufacture* (London, 1953).

C.B. Tite, 'Piecework and Productivity in the Boot and Shoe Industry' (Ph.D. thesis, University of Birmingham, 1953-54).

J.J. Webb, *Industrial Dublin since 1698* (1913).

INDEX

Abbott, Jack 137
Advertising 50, 110, 114, 117-8, 138-9, 147, 158
Agreements 40-1, 69-70, 113-6, 121-3, 125, 136-7, 159, 175, 176
Agricultural footwear *see* Heavy boots
Airborne Shoes Ltd 128, 137-8, 154
Alexander, Paul 100
Allen, James, & Sons Ltd, Edinburgh 116
Amalgamation 157
An Foras Tionscail (AFT) 145
Anglo-Irish Free Trade Agreement, 1938 71
Anglo-Irish Free Trade Agreement, 1948 121
Anglo-Irish Free Trade Agreement, 1965 144
Anglo-Irish Treaty 17, 46
Anti-British sentiment 36, 47
Arnall, C.C. 116
Australia 152, 160
Autarky *see* Self-sufficiency
Avalon Leatherboard Co. Ltd, Street 81

Backward integration 139, 157
Ballinasloe 32, 57, 173
Birr Shoes Ltd 126, 157, 165
Blackthorn Shoes Ltd, Dundalk 161
Blake sewer, Blake-sewn construction 23
Bone-Dry (brand) 33
Bostock, James F. 114
Boylan family 104, 114
Boylan, James, & Son 158
Boylans (retailers) 103, 172
Branding 50, 66, 70, 117-9, 141, 161
Britain: balance of payments 151
Britain: economic growth 132, 145, 150-1
British footwear industry: competition from 18-9, 20, 26, 28-9, 156
British footwear industry: general 18-9, 21-5, 48-9, 128, 149
British government 26, 31, 76, 121, 168

British-owned companies in Ireland 29, 32-40, 64, 66, 112, 174
British Shoe Corporation 140, 172
British Trade Commission 82
British United Shoe Machinery Co. (BUSMC) 24-5, 45, 57, 66, 68, 80, 111, 116, 117, 135, 136
Britton, G.B., & Sons, Kingswood, Bristol 155, 157, 158, 165, 173
Buenos Aires 81
Burden, J.L. 138

C.I.C. Engineering Ltd, Bath 155
C-Step 174
Canada 134
Carrick-on-Suir 46
Celt Boot Co., Dundalk 27, 33, 39
Cemented process 80, 105, 106-7, 111
Census of Industrial Production 27, 31-2, 43, 48, 55, 60, 62, 65, 106
Chester, George 86
Children's and youths' footwear 30, 31, 33, 36, 41, 42, 44, 52, 68, 105, 116, 126, 135, 136, 141, 152, 153, 155, 175
Clark, C. & J., Ltd, Street 40-1, 68-70, 76, 109-10, 117-8, 121-3, 125-6, 135, 136, 139, 141, 143, 155, 158, 161, 170, 173, 175, 176
Clark, Daniel 159
Clark, Hugh B. 41
Clark, Lance, 159
Clark, W. Bancroft 41, 69, 116, 121, 123
Clark, William Stephens 22
Clarks Fitting Gauge 110, 118
Clarks Ireland Ltd 69-70, 104, 119-20, 138, 140-1, 158, 170, 173, 174
Clarks Overseas Shoes 159
Clonmel 78
Clothing Rationing Scheme 91
Co-operatives 174
Committee on Industrial Organisation 57, 139, 143, 145, 146-7, 157, 168, 176

Committee on Industrial Progress 58, 161, 167, 168, 176
Company Fraud Department, New Scotland Yard 138
Congress of Irish Unions 100
Connolly, Edward J. 90, 104, 158
Connolly, Kenneth 161
Connolly, Matthew 53, 104
Connolly Shoes, Dundalk 32, 78, 90, 116, 123
Connollys (retailers) 103, 149, 172
Control of Imports Act, 1934 31
Control of Manufactures Acts, 1932 and 1934 35, 130-1, 140, 174
Córas Trachtála (CTT) 124, 130, 134, 145, 147
Corfam 163
Cork 46, 51, 53, 61, 173
Cork Shoe Co. 170
Cosgrave, William T. 17, 27, 31
Costello, John 93
Cox, Arthur, & Co., Dublin 69-70
Craftmaster (brand) 138-9
Crick, Thomas 23
Crilly, Hugh 98, 100-1
Crotty, Thomas 138
Cullen, H. 111
Cumann na nGaedheal 26, 29
Cunnington, Leslie, Ltd 32, 65

Daly, Jim 161
Davis, S.J. 34, 41, 128, 137
de Gaulle, General 144
de Valera, Eamon 29, 30, 31, 34, 46, 69
Densons (retailers) 103-4, 156-7
Department of Finance 95
Department of Industry & Commerce 28, 34, 35, 56, 57, 70, 73, 74- 5, 88, 97, 101, 111, 120, 145, 175
Department of Supplies 73, 75, 76, 83, 96
Department stores 53
Direct selling 53, 68, 118-9, 139
Direct vulcanising 105, 108, 162
Dolcis 140, 156
Donaghy, Edward, & Sons, Drogheda 31, 33, 47, 65, 85, 126, 170
Drogheda 33, 57, 76, 82, 103, 113
Dubarry Shoemakers Ltd 32, 57, 76, 82, 83, 111, 113, 158, 165, 171, 173, 174
Dublin 54, 57, 58, 103, 113, 156, 173
Dublin Industrial Development Association 26, 28
Dundalk 51, 57, 58, 70, 78, 81, 103, 122, 135, 136, 141, 153, 170, 173, 174
Dungarvan, Co. Waterford 46
DuPont 163
Duties *see* Tariffs
Dwyer family 18

Eamonn Andrews 139
Earnings *see* Footwear industry: wages and earnings
East Africa 141
Economic War 31, 37, 50, 55, 71
Economies of scale 56, 163
Economies of specialisation 27, 52, 56, 108, 141, 163
Edenderry Distributors Ltd 173
Edenderry Shoe Co., Edenderry 32, 39, 85-6, 126, 136-7, 165, 168, 171, 173
Edwards & Holmes Ltd, Norwich 113-4, 118, 136, 139
Edwards, Messrs, Dublin 65
Eire Prices Commission 71
Emergency Imposition of Duties (No.5) Order 31
Emergency Imposition of Duties Act, 1932 31
Emergency Powers Acts 74
Emigration 17, 30, 84, 93, 94, 98
English & American Machinery Co. 24
Europe 124, 125, 130, 132, 141, 145-6, 159
European Economic Community (EEC) 132, 141, 144, 145-6, 168, 170, 171, 177
European Free Trade Association (EFTA) 132
European Monetary System 171
Exports Promotion Board *see* Córas Trachtála

Fair Trade Commission 120
Fane Shoes Ltd 160-1
Federation of Boot & Shoe Manufacturers 25, 46, 61, 71, 85-6, 161
Federation of Irish Industry 174
Fianna Fáil 29, 30, 32, 34, 35, 56, 59, 93, 98, 174, 175
Finance Acts, 1956-8 131, 134
Financial Times 138
Fiscal Inquiry Committee 26, 28

Index

Fitzgerald, Garret 59, 93, 94
Fitzpatrick & Co., Athlone 27
Footwear Adaptation Association 146-7, 164, 167
Footwear industry: British market 121, 123-4, 134, 150-2, 167
Footwear industry: capacity 51, 56, 56, 72, 102, 109, 111, 133, 175
Footwear industry: capital and investment 32, 38-40, 64-5, 128-8, 136, 153-4, 174, 176
Footwear industry: company organisation 81, 82, 110-11
Footwear industry: costs 58-9, 60-2, 63, 68, 95, 98-9, 150, 159, 167, 175
Footwear industry: credit terms 54
Footwear industry: dependence upon Britain 22, 25, 40-1, 113-6, 125, 137-8, 150-2
Footwear industry: early factories, U.K. 22
Footwear industry: early history 18-20
Footwear industry: exports 50-51, 111, 121-5, 134, 140-1, 147, 150-2, 171-2, 173, 175-6, 176
Footwear industry: factory organisation 54-5, 71, 107, 109, 161
Footwear industry: foreign ownership 170
Footwear industry: hand production methods 21-2
Footwear industry: home market 50-5, 71, 77, 96, 97, 98, 102-4, 111, 112-3, 147-50, 158, 169, 171-2, 175-6
Footwear industry: hours of work 85
Footwear industry: imports 20, 28, 31, 43-4, 44-5, 71, 77, 97, 98, 101, 102-3, 133, 163, 167-8, 171-2, 176
Footwear industry: labour relations 37, 55, 62, 67, 74, 84-6, 99-100, 175
Footwear industry: location of factories 57-8
Footwear industry: marketing and sales 101, 117-21, 128, 134, 138-9, 146-7, 157-8, 160, 161, 176
Footwear industry: number of firms 31, 65, 173, 175
Footwear industry: numbers employed 19-20, 51, 58, 71, 84, 133, 171-2, 173
Footwear industry: output 20, 27, 41-2, 42-3, 44, 48, 50, 51, 60, 71, 77, 95-6, 102, 133-4, 147, 171-2

Footwear industry: per capita consumption 50, 133, 147
Footwear industry: prices 60, 71, 88-9, 95, 96, 101, 133, 150
Footwear industry: productivity 133-4, 163-4
Footwear industry: profits 62-5, 71, 88-9, 96, 127-8, 134, 141-3, 157, 164-7, 168
Footwear industry: size of firms 31-2, 55-6, 66, 125, 165
Footwear industry: technology: general 20, 22-4, 104-8, 161-3, 176
Footwear industry: training 37-8, 58, 146
Footwear industry: wage rates and structure 46-7
Footwear industry: wages and earnings 60-2, 83, 84-5, 99-100, 106-7, 108
Footwear industry: welfare schemes 86-7
Forward integration 139-40, 155
France 152
Free trade 132, 144, 145, 147, 167, 168, 171, 176, 177
Freer & Co., Cork 27

Galway 173
Gannon Bros., Dublin 53
George & Co. 158
Gluv (brand) 155
Goodyear, Charles 23
Goodyear Shoe Machinery Co. 24
Goodyear welt sewing machine 23
Gorey, Co. Waterford 46
Gorey Leather Co., Gorey 33, 46
Gould, Fred 46
Governey, Michael, & Co., Carlow 27, 19, 104, 114, 123
Government regulation 55-60, 71, 74-5, 82-5, 93, 95-6, 96-8, 101, 130-3, 175-6
Grants 94, 130, 145, 150, 153, 171, 174
Grasshopper (brand) 159-60
Green labour 37, 47, 65, 67
Griffith, Arthur 30
Gross, Eric 155

Halliday, Arthur 40, 51, 54, 61, 68-9, 81-2, 87, 89, 113, 121, 123, 137, 140, 156
Halliday, Fred 33, 37, 40
Halliday, John, & Sons, Dundalk: capital and investment 39, 110, 126-8, 153-5

Halliday, John, & Sons, Dundalk: costs 90-1
Halliday, John, & Sons, Dundalk: expansion 109-110, 116, 136, 152-7
Halliday, John, & Sons, Dundalk: general 40, 98, 104, 109, 113, 115, 117, 126, 138, 151, 158, 161, 170, 175, 176
Halliday, John, & Sons, Dundalk: marketing and sales 51, 109-10, 117-8, 121-3, 140-1, 149-50, 158, 161, 170-1
Halliday, John, & Sons, Dundalk: market share 82, 125-6
Halliday, John, & Sons, Dundalk: origins 27, 29, 32-3
Halliday, John, & Sons, Dundalk: output 51-2, 66, 109
Halliday, John, & Sons, Dundalk: prices 96, 101
Halliday, John, & Sons, Dundalk: production methods 115, 135
Halliday, John, & Sons, Dundalk: profits 63-4, 70, 89-91, 127-8, 141-3, 165-6, 166-7, 168
Halliday, John, & Sons, Dundalk: relations with government 35, 87, 96
Halliday, John, & Sons, Dundalk: relations with unions 47-8, 87
Halliday, John, & Sons, Dundalk: retailing 139-40, 155-7
Halliday, John, & Sons, Dundalk: Second World War 75, 76, 78, 80-2
Halliday, John, & Sons, Dundalk: switch to light footwear 68-70, 71
Halliday, John, & Sons, Dundalk: wages and earnings 115
Halliday, John, & Sons, Dundalk: welfare schemes 87
Hannan & Co., Dublin 53
Hanover Shoe Co., Cork 27, 157
Hawe, J.P. 34
Hearne & Cahill, Waterford 19, 27, 115
Heavy boots 20, 23, 27, 28, 32-3, 35, 36, 42, 44, 52, 53, 64-5, 66, 68, 70, 96, 98, 102-3, 113, 115, 121, 136
Hibernian Bank Ltd 138
Hill, James 70
Hilliard & Palmer Ltd, Killarney 157, 165, 173
Hilliard, R., & Sons, Killarney 18, 27, 40, 57

Hoffman, A.E.S. 138
Hong Kong 141
Horizontal integration 153, 155, 157
Hours of work 61

Import Controls (Britain) 150-1, 159, 174
Import Duties Act, 1932 (U.K.) 31
Import quotas 30, 31, 50, 55, 71, 77, 94, 97, 98, 103, 133, 144, 146, 167-8, 174, 175, 176
In-stock system 33, 54, 120
Independent retailers 53-4, 103-4, 137, 147-9
Industrial Credit Co. 145, 147, 174
Industrial Development (Encouragement of External Investment) Act, 1958 131
Industrial Relations Act, 1946 93, 99
Instep Ltd 158
Ireland: balance of payments 93, 94-5, 130, 131, 132, 146, 176
Ireland: cost of living 88, 106
Ireland: economic growth 93-5, 130-3, 144-6
Ireland: exports 73, 94, 131, 144
Ireland: home market 94-5, 146, 170
Ireland: imports 73, 94, 131, 146
Ireland: incomes 147
Ireland: industrial output 75, 93
Ireland: inflation 100, 146, 169, 171, 173, 177
Ireland: investment 94
Ireland: labour market 58, 60-1
Ireland: productivity 145
Ireland: wages 74, 167, 171
Irish Army 78, 96
Irish Assurance Co. Ltd 87
Irish Development Authority 94, 131
Irish Dunlop Co. Ltd 52, 102, 112
Irish Footwear Fashion Council 147
Irish Oil & Cake Mills Ltd, Drogheda 81
Irish Shipping Ltd 73-4, 83
Irish Shoe & Leather Workers' Union 100-1
Irish Tanners Ltd, Portlaw 46, 106
Irish Trade Union Congress 100
Irons, W.H. 38
Italy 124

Joyce Inc., Cincinnati, Ohio 136-7
Jumping Jacks (brand) 137

Index

Juvenile labour 24, 58, 65, 87

K (brand) 123
Keynes, Maynard 55
Kilkenny 34, 35, 41, 51, 76, 128, 137-8, 154, 159, 171, 173
Killarney 57
Korean War 95, 98, 115, 174
Kraft, Seymour 138

Labour Court 93, 99
Ladies' and women's shoes 33, 34, 35, 41, 42, 51, 52, 68, 69, 105, 107, 113-5, 117, 121, 126, 136, 137, 139, 150, 153, 155, 158, 161, 175
Land annuities 30
Leather industry 36, 45-6, 59, 77, 79, 83, 97, 99, 106, 175
Leather: imports 45-6, 59, 83, 99
Leather: prices 60, 76, 99
Leather: production 59
Leather: supplies 76, 78, 79, 81, 83
Leatherboard 81
Lee Boot Manufacturing Co., Cork 18, 27
Leeds 33
Leicester 22, 67, 137
Lemass, Seán 30, 34, 73, 94
Lennards 156
Leydon, John 73
Light footwear 23, 33, 42, 44, 52, 65, 66, 98, 102, 121, 125, 136, 176
Limerick 53, 100, 173
Limerick Shoe & Slipper Co. 31, 44, 157
Lisbon 73, 81
Local Defence Force 78, 96
Local industrial development committees 34, 37
Lotus Shoes, Stafford 114, 118, 123, 136, 139
Lowry, Sidney 41, 69, 70
Lowry, Stephen 161

MacEntee, Seán 73, 74
Machinery 22-4, 45, 56, 76, 107, 162, 163
Machinery manufacturers 24
Mason & Marson Ltd, Stafford 34, 40
Mavitty & Nesbitt, Dublin 53
Mavitty, Thomas 53
McElligott, J. J. 28
McLerie, Ian 139, 154, 161

McLoughlin, Philip 88, 113, 136, 161
Men's shoes 33-4, 40, 42, 44, 51, 109, 114, 116, 123, 125-6, 135, 136, 137, 138, 152, 153, 154-5, 158, 159
Minister for Industry and Commerce 30, 34, 35, 38, 57, 132
Ministry for Industry and Commerce *see* Department of Industry and Commerce
Mixed bag production 54, 56, 64, 66, 160
Moccasin (brand) 123, 155
Moccasin construction 159, 160
Mullen Mills Ltd, Emyvale 27
Multiple retailers 53-4, 103-4, 137, 139, 140, 147-9, 156, 160, 172-3
Munster & Leinster Bank 138
Munster Shoes Ltd 110-11, 136, 141-2, 157
Murphy, Thomas 19

National Agreements (wages) 46-7, 61, 93, 101
National Agricultural and Industrial Development Association 174
National Arbitration Board 46
National Union of Boot & Shoe Operatives 24, 37, 43, 46-8, 51, 61, 67, 71, 85-6, 98, 99-101
Netherlands 134, 152
New Balance Athletic Shoe Co., Boston and Tralee 171
New Manufacture Licence 35-6, 122
New Ross, Co. Waterford 46
New Zealand 141
Non-leather footwear 30, 42-3, 43, 102, 112, 133, 161, 163, 167
Northampton 38, 41, 137
Norvic (Ireland) Ltd 113
Norvic Ltd 113, 171
O'Neill family 104, 156

Oligopoly 65-7
Organisation for European Economic Co-operation (OEEC) 132

Padmore & Barnes (Ireland) Ltd, Kilkenny 31, 32, 33-4, 35, 38, 39, 40-1, 42, 48, 63, 64-5, 66, 69, 75-6, 80, 121, 123, 126-8, 135, 137-8, 142-3, 151, 153-5, 158-60, 165-6, 168, 170-1, 173
Palmers of Leicester 40
Peter Lord 123, 140

Plastics *also see* Non-leather footwear, PVC, Polyurethane 162, 167
Plunder & Pollak Ltd, Carrick-on-Suir 46
Poland 159
Polyurethane 155, 159, 162
Population 17, 50, 147, 172
Portlaw, Co. Waterford 46
Portugal 159
Price controls 74-5, 83, 94
Price cutting 53
Price Standstill Order (1951) 101
Production units 108, 109, 122, 136, 153, 158
Programme for Economic Expansion, 1958 95, 131-2, 145
Protectionism 30, 49, 50-1, 55, 71, 130, 132, 141, 143, 144, 174, 175
Provisional Government 17, 26
PVC 162

Quotas *see* Import quotas

Radio Éireann 139
Rationing 90-2, 96
Rawson, Benjamin 33, 37, 67, 68, 165
Rawson, John, (Ireland) Ltd, Dundalk 31, 33, 35, 38, 40, 42, 52, 53, 65, 66-7, 68, 82, 109, 114, 123, 126-8, 137, 141-3, 165-6, 176
Redundancies *see* Unemployment
Reference Tribunal 74-5
Reliable Shoe Co., Westport 171
Restrictive Practices Act, 1953 120
Retail price maintenance 120
Retailers *also see* Multiple retailers, Independent retailers 28, 39, 53-4, 68, 97, 101, 103-4, 118-20, 138, 139-40, 147-50, 155-7
Rhodesia 141
Riveting 23
Roberts, Paddy 154, 160
Rubber footwear 43, 52, 102, 105-6, 112, 167
Rubber soles 77-9, 80, 82, 99, 105-6, 136, 153, 162

Sandals 42, 118
Saxone (Ireland) Ltd 117
Saxone Shoe Co. 114, 137, 156
Scandinavia 123, 152

Scientific leather measurement (SLM) 133, 135, 137, 162
Scott, F. J. 67, 82, 111, 158
Second Programme for Economic Expansion, 1963-4 144-5
Second World War 72, 73-92
Self-sufficiency 30, 49, 50-1, 59, 130, 174, 175
Serenity (brand) 121-2, 136, 139, 141
Setanta Shoes 174
Sewing machines 22-3
Sexton, Thomas, M.P. 18
Shoe & Allied Trades Research Association (SATRA) 108, 158, 164
Short time working 51, 56, 61, 67, 70, 71, 72, 76, 77, 82, 97, 102, 111, 175
Simpson, M.S. 138
Sioux Schuhfabriken, Walheim, West Germany 159
Skyline (brand) 110
Slip-lasted construction 107, 117, 162
Slippers 42
Smith, Len 46, 85-6
Soling materials 77-9, 80, 105-6, 153, 155, 159, 162
South Africa 141, 152
Spain 159
Specialisation 58
Standard Wage Orders 74, 84
Stedfast Shoes Ltd, Carrickmacross 32, 39, 42, 139, 153-4, 158, 160-1, 161, 165-6, 171
Stekel, Edmund 138
Street, Somerset 22, 109, 122, 123, 135, 159
Strikes 24, 47, 61, 67, 74, 77, 84-6
Supplementary import licences 97
Sweden 121
Swedish Trade Commission 121

Tanners' Federation 28
Tanning *see* Leather industry
Tara Shoes, Kells 113, 158
Tariff Commission 28
Tariffs 26, 27, 28-9, 30-1, 45-6, 50, 55, 76, 94, 132, 144, 167-8, 171, 174, 175
Team system 24, 55
Telefís Éireann 119, 147
Toone & Son Ltd, Kells 31
Trade Union Act, 1941 74, 85

Index 229

Tralee 171
Traly Footwear Ltd, Tralee 32, 65
Treaty of Rome, 1957 132
Tuf (brand) 155
Tuf Shoes, Killarney 172-3
Turnshoe construction 22, 23
Tyler, John, & Sons, Leicester 103, 172-3
Tylers (retailers) 103, 114, 137, 140, 149, 157, 172-3

Ulster 33, 69, 100, 151-2, 167
Unbranded sector 139, 153, 154, 160
Under-developed areas 94, 130
Unemployment 30, 34, 51, 65, 67, 71, 74, 92, 93, 94, 97, 130, 147, 173, 175
United Shoe Machinery Co. 24
United States 73, 75, 96, 98, 123-5, 130, 134, 152, 159, 160, 168, 171
United States Government 73
United States Shoe Corporation 136

Vertical integration 157

Wages *see* Footwear industry: wages and earnings. Ireland: wages. National Agreements (wages)
Wallabees (brand) 160, 171

Ware, Charles 100
Waterford 76, 173
Wellington boots 43
Welted construction 22, 23
West Germany 123, 134, 152, 159
West Indies 152
Weston Evans & Co. 135
Westport 172, 173
Westport Shoe Co-operative Society 174
Whispies Shoes (Ireland) Ltd, Edenderry 157
Wholesaling 39, 53, 55, 68, 118-9, 139, 160
Wiltshire, S.A., Dublin 27, 29, 53, 115
Winstanley, James, Dublin 18, 27, 52, 78, 102, 104, 119, 123, 158, 165, 173
Wooden soles 78
Woodington, J.H. 67, 82, 113
Woodington, J.H., (Drogheda) Ltd 31, 32, 33, 35, 38, 40, 46, 47, 48, 53, 63-5, 66-7, 68, 75, 78, 82, 83, 88, 89-90, 96, 98-9, 111-2, 113-5, 117, 118-9, 121, 126-8, 136, 139, 141-2, 157, 158, 161, 165-6, 168, 172, 173
Woods of Sligo 53

Youngline Shoes Ltd 170